THE PSYCHOLOGY
OF SECRETS

ABOUT THE AUTHOR

Andrew Gold is an investigative journalist, podcaster and film-maker who has made and presented documentaries for the BBC and HBO. He presents the popular podcast *Heretics*, where he has interviewed Richard Dawkins, Jon Ronson, Robbie Williams and David Baddiel among many others. His documentary on exorcism in Argentina won international festival awards, and his research into sexual deviancy in Germany received a prestigious Whicker Award nomination in 2021. *The Psychology of Secrets* is his first book.

THE **PSYCHOLOGY** OF **SECRETS**

MY ADVENTURES WITH MURDERERS, CULTS AND INFLUENCERS

ANDREW GOLD

MACMILLAN

First published 2024 by Macmillan
an imprint of Pan Macmillan
The Smithson, 6 Briset Street, London EC1M 5NR
EU representative: Macmillan Publishers Ireland Ltd, 1st Floor,
The Liffey Trust Centre, 117–126 Sheriff Street Upper,
Dublin 1, D01 YC43
Associated companies throughout the world
www.panmacmillan.com

ISBN 978-1-0350-0259-7 HB
ISBN 978-1-0350-0260-3 TPB

3 5 7 9 8 6 4 2

A CIP catalogue record for this book is available from the British Library.

Typeset in Sabon LT Std by Palimpsest Book Production Limited, Falkirk, Stirlingshire
Printed and bound by CPI Group (UK) Ltd, Croydon, CR0 4YY

Visit **www.panmacmillan.com** to read more about all our books
and to buy them. You will also find features, author interviews and
news of any author events, and you can sign up for e-newsletters
so that you're always first to hear about our new releases.

To Juli:
May we keep each other's secrets, always.

TABLE OF CONTENTS

INTRODUCTION

She doesn't know it, but Melissa will be a murderer in ten minutes. Just twenty years old, and studying at a university somewhere in the UK, she is returning alone from a night out with friends. As she angles down an alleyway on her route home, she is confronted by two men. One of them lurks in the shadows, and the other creeps towards her. He impedes her way, insisting she stay with them. He reeks of beer and cigarettes, and she feels sick. She wants to get to the end of the alley, but he stands between her and freedom.

Her pulse quickening, she brushes past him towards the light at the end of the alleyway. His threats grow louder and more menacing. She is scared, but refuses to run. She won't give him the satisfaction. Melissa is used to being accosted by men, especially when walking alone at night. Yet there's something about this guy that chills her to the core. But there's freedom at the end of the passage. She knows the neighbourhood well. If she can just make it to the adjacent street, there'll be witnesses to intervene if things turn ugly.

Before she reaches safety, she feels a firm tug at her elbow. She can't breathe or speak . . . his words drone and slur, and fear takes hold of her. Now he is grabbing at her clothes, and the sound of ripped fabric is cutting through the darkness. Melissa lashes out with her right arm, and her hand – and this is the only way she can explain it to me later – passes *through* his eyes.

A decade has passed, and what happened that night still weighs on Melissa. Even after years of therapy, it haunts her nightmares, and fills her waking moments with dread. She can't quite piece together what happened, and perhaps she never will. 'I put my hands through his eyes?' she seems to ask me. When I ask if she can explain it in more detail, she gives me a play by play: 'If you put your hands on the side of someone's face like to passionately kiss them . . . but higher up. You put thumbs really far in, until it feels disgusting. A bit like a half-boiled egg in someone's eye, and you push in,' she explains. 'I was surprised by how much liquid and blood came out. And he dropped me. I don't remember much, but I know that when I dropped to the floor, he ran off, screaming. His mate kicked the shit out of me, and I basically passed out.'

Later, she came to in the alley and set about finding her way home, fingers and wrists stained crimson with the blood of her assailant. She recalls her ripped, frayed clothes billowing in the wind as she stumbled backwards. Strangers gave her a wide berth. She doesn't remember how she got home. Falling in and out of consciousness in her bed that night, she felt the phantom grip of the now-dead attacker on her arm. As she sank somewhere between terrifying dreams and the waking nightmare of her new reality as a killer, throbbing sensations told her that her stomach and legs were in a bad state from the beating she had taken.

She spent the next few days in bed, telling friends and university tutors that she was unwell. Eventually mustering the energy to get up, she combed the local paper for anything revelatory about the night in question. In a sidebar, she discovered a story about a man who had been found dead in an alleyway. 'His eyes had been gouged out,' she tells me.

The news, as well as the traumatic incident itself, has had a profound effect on Melissa. She suffers from panic attacks, PTSD and insomnia, as she replays the images from an alleyway through which she has never since passed. She wonders whether the man had children, and whether there might have been another way out.

Melissa is today a prominent blue-tick professional – at least, she was before Elon Musk rid Twitter (now X) of verification for well-known users. It's possible you know her by her real name. Her anecdote is one of the most curious and affecting I've heard, but it leaves me with more questions than answers. Who was this man? Why did his friend leave him in an alleyway to die? And how do you gouge somebody's eyes out like that? The details don't matter so much to Melissa. She has to live with the burden of a soul-destroying secret. In fact, in the intervening decade, she has only told one person: me. But Melissa knows me only a little better than the man who attacked her; the man she killed. She and I had met briefly in a pub through work colleagues, but hadn't spoken again. And yet, a five-minute WhatsApp voice message she sent me – many months later – let me in on something to which not even her friends and relatives were privy.

I can't help but wonder: *why me?*

Snow pats against the window next to my desk in my Berlin home one December evening, when I notice a new message from someone called Kamilla. Sporting long white hair and pushing sixty, she is a keen Instagrammer and a listener to my podcast, *Heretics*. She has liked a few of my posts, but we've never had a conversation. Her message reads: 'I had a thought for a subject (close to my heart) . . . but you may not want my ideas.' It signs off with two emojis of curiosity and shock.

'Oh, go on, do tell! You never know,' I reply.

'Don't feel bad, just an idea . . . for your eyes/ears only!'

'Of course,' I write. I later ask her permission to use this story, and she suggests the alias of Kamilla. It doesn't seem right for a woman of her generation. Maybe that's the point.

'So, I'm going through a rocky patch in my marriage and in the last few months I've made an online friend who has become an unhealthy addiction, can't stop thinking about him although I know it's pointless, not good for my self-esteem,' she writes, before adding, 'And he's only thirty!'

Horrified and flattered in equal measure, I determine she is talking about me. I am attracting groupies. I rack my brain as to how to let her down gently. I'm about to tell Kamilla that I'm not single, nor prone to cheating with married older women, when those three dots appear – she is typing.

'And he's not even my type.'

At this, I'm a little insulted.

She adds: 'He tells me I'm beautiful, sexy, wants more.'

Since I never said anything of the kind, I conclude that she is deranged. Then, she describes not me, but an American musician with whom she's been exchanging nudes. 'The more I listened, the more I loved his music, it's as if his voice has a weird hypnotic effect on my lady bits,' she adds, with a crying-with-laughter emoji.

'Hmm, interesting,' I reply, as relieved as I am slighted about not being the object of her lady bits' desires. I check out the American's page. I can see why she likes him: he is cool, handsome and a rock star to boot. But what is in it for him?

'Has he ever asked you for money?' I ask, crudely.

'No, never.'

I'm disappointed the narrative doesn't fit my expectations. I apologize, explaining that it is unusual to hear of a man close to my age – a super-cool musician no less – sexting sixty-year-old women. At least, without monetary incentive.

'Oh . . .' she writes. I imagine she is a little hurt. The space for new messages stays white as I stare at the snow out of my window for a few quiet minutes. Then, her ellipsis fizzes and pops. 'Well, I did buy his album.'

'How much did it cost?'

'One hundred dollars on Spotify donations.'

I gulp.

The rock star has been convincing Kamilla – and possibly other vulnerable fans – to give up her savings in return for a music main meal with a spicy side of dick pics. I stare at the phone. Kamilla is an adult. If she wants to give up extortionate sums of money for his music, in the hope of getting something salacious, then that is her right. I decide this is none of my business, and I shouldn't get involved.

Then, I get involved. I recommend she withhold money to see if he continues to send photos. 'Deep down I think he partly is doing it to get $ out of me, which is a horrible feeling,' she replies. This time, the emoji is sad. She goes on to reveal intimate details to me about her three-decade-long marriage. 'TBH, I don't know if I can stay with him. We're too different. I'm just terrified of being alone, broke and homeless. And I think so many women my age are out there feeling that. Unhappy but scared.'

Unhappy but scared. I feel sorry for Kamilla. Even if her story is a little extreme, we've all been deceived by people we thought were our friends. But I wonder why she has chosen to transgress a thirty-year bond of trust with her husband to tell *me* about her indiscretions.

'What was your idea for a podcast episode?' I ask, suddenly remembering her reason for getting in touch.

'So, I was thinking about how many lonely people there are out there trying to find connections, attention, validation. And doing dumb shit like me, e.g., candid photos, pretend sex, fanta-sizing etc.' An emoji of a laughing monkey covering its eyes perches at the end of the sentence. It's laughing, as if to say, 'Humans! What are you like?'

Kamilla doesn't really have an idea for a podcast episode. She just wants to tell me her secret.

Kamilla and Melissa are not anomalies. The larger my podcast grows, the more I find myself the unwitting ruler of a rising stack of sinister and sensational secrets. I didn't covet this. My podcast doesn't have a 'secrets' theme. I interview extreme and controver-sial people, and delve into cults – many of which feature in this book. Yet, almost daily, confessions of wrongdoings and secret desires swamp my socials.

I've noticed something else: I do it, too. I reveal secret informa-tion about myself that had no business being divulged. In particular, I reveal secrets to guests who are themselves journalists. For example, it probably wasn't necessary for me to volunteer to jour-nalist Jon Ronson that I'd been seeing a therapist and had suffered with anxiety. But I felt a sudden compulsion upon meeting him, and blurted it out. And why did I tell eighty-two-year-old evolu-tionary scientist Richard Dawkins that I had read his very serious book about the evolution of flight while in the bath with one of my deluxe salt bath bombs? I couldn't help but reveal this embar-rassing information. I have since found that some of this is related to a phenomenon called 'parasocial interaction', where one person invests energy, emotion and time in a relationship with someone who is completely unaware of their existence, like a talk show host or other celebrity. But still: what would have happened had I withheld that secret information? What compelled me to tell?

My inbox is bursting with the declarations, revelations and confessions of others. Many of my colleagues – podcasters, radio presenters and journalists – are also inundated with confessions. So much for my solipsistic world view. The podcaster and the journalist, I suppose, share this curse with the therapist, the hair-dresser and the air steward. What is it then about our relationships with listeners and clients that compels them to confide in us?

When I ask the sixty-year-old rocker-obsessed dick-pic receiver Kamilla why she told me about her affair and struggling marriage, she simply explains, 'I trust your journalistic integrity and you're the only person I've told.'

The answer is flattering. But it doesn't satisfy me.

I launched my podcast during Covid lockdown in the summer of 2020. At first, I pored over the listening figures, checking in every few minutes to spot any hint of growth. 'Twenty listeners today,' I would excitedly tell my partner Julieta. 'That's double last week's!' With time, the figures rose, and soon, I had hundreds of thousands of loyal listeners waiting for each new interview to come out.

One of the best things about releasing a podcast episode is the instant feedback. Rather than checking stats, I was now scrolling through social media platforms to interact with listeners. At a time when we were all feeling rather cut-off from society, it was a saving grace. But I couldn't have known then that my role as a podcast host would soon have me charged as something perhaps far greater: the keeper of an inordinate number of unsolicited secrets.

At first, I was glad for these glimpses into new and hidden worlds, and for the intimacy and trust that escorted these confessions to my inbox from the most covert corners of the internet. But as the secrets spun from such silly indiscretions as dick pics and online affairs to child sexual abuse and murder, I felt a duty to delve into the darkness at the heart of this phenomenon. What *are* secrets, exactly? What happens to us when we keep them? And why are we so keen to share our darkest moments with total strangers?

After hearing Melissa's secret about the man she killed in the alleyway, I play her WhatsApp audio message on repeat, straining to understand her choice of confidant. Most of the message consists of the story of the attack. Then, she tells me she wants to trust me, and for me to trust her. From the background noise, it sounds like she is in a bar or restaurant.

Surprised, I realize she revealed this to me in a public space. I imagine her alone at a table, indulging in a drink after a friend has left, or waiting for them to return from the toilet. In the audio message, the more shocking the information, the more matter-of-fact Melissa's voice sounds. After repeated listens, I find one clue as to why she chose me. At the beginning of the audio message, she tells me she has been enjoying listening to my podcast.

As listeners continued to share their most intimate stories with me, I found I was overwhelmed and unprepared. I was unqualified to handle the unexpected influx of information coming at me from all sides. So, I determined to learn all I could about one of the darkest, most fascinating and most unexplored human phenomena: secrets. I wanted to know how secrets came to be, how they helped shape who we are today and how they can be used for good – and bad – purposes. And I wanted to learn how your own secrets – and the secrets of others – could be used against you.

During my research, I began to see how secrets have been used throughout history to control us, by authoritarian regimes, religions and cults. And the more I found out, the more I felt you needed to know. And that's because knowledge is the perfect antidote to secrecy. Knowledge prevents malignant forces from manipulating you with secrets.

It turns out, too, that secrets are an integral part of our culture and evolutionary psychology, and their role in society is changing rapidly as our technology develops. This book will show how secrets lurk beneath idiosyncrasies in our language, how they can haunt families for generations and scream at us from the grave.

And it is my hope that, by the end, you'll be armed with enough knowledge of cult dynamics, body language myths and social media influencer tricks to repel those trying to extract your secrets. You might even be able to mine secrets from others in your turn.

First, you're probably more deceitful than you'd like to think. A monstrous 97 per cent of us carry a secret at any given moment, while the average person has 13. There is a 47 per cent chance that one of your secrets involves a breach of trust, more than a 60 per cent chance that it relates to financial impropriety, and a 33 per cent chance that you are holding a secret relating to either theft, a hidden relationship or work dissatisfaction.

But, here's the kicker. Overwhelming evidence now shows that holding onto these secrets can have extreme and negative effects on your well-being and physical health. Secrets make us lose confidence and perform worse in tests. Keeping secrets also increases the likelihood of heart disease, cancer and ulcers.

Ironically, the physical and mental anguish resulting from the keeping of a secret often outweighs the negative repercussions of letting it out. Confiding in those around us can relieve the burden, and allow us to better understand our secrets. It allows us to reframe our secrets by seeing them through the eyes of others. Some of us do just that (like some of my podcast listeners), while others keep shtum. Why? And how else might we diminish the discomfort in secret-keeping, without giving up that most precious of gems: the secret itself?

To unravel these mysteries, we'll delve into the history of secrets. We'll look at how the Bible's take on secrets led to millennia of repression, before fast-forwarding to the present day to find secrets are now financially more valuable than ever. They single-handedly hold up the influencer industry in bizarre and unexpected ways, and can even sway elections. They keep magicians in business and politicians in power. Even insinuating that you have a secret (real or imaginary) is enough to give off the impression of real power.

And right now, secrets are endangered. As Prince Harry and his wife Meghan Markle were revealing the darkest secrets of the British Royal Family to Oprah, comedian David Baddiel summed up the modern state of secrets in a tweet: 'What we're seeing is what happens when an institution that has always relied to some extent on silence has to exist in a world that no longer does silence.'

Camilla Long wrote in *The Times*, 'When does royalty stop being royalty? Answer: when everything is dragged through the courts'. The barrier of secrecy around that most elusive of families has been weakened by the release of Prince Harry's tell-all memoir *Spare*, in which he describes in glorious detail King Charles III doing headstands in his boxers. If an organization as seemingly untouchable as the Royal Family can no longer exist in silence, what hope do the rest of us have of keeping something to ourselves?

We have long been used to the seeping of secrets through the press and word of mouth. But technological advances mean that secrecy today is more vulnerable than ever, and the very concept of keeping something sensational to yourself might soon be a thing of the past. Sex robots, AI and mind-reading technology will make the task of keeping one's private life private harder. Even the famously secretive security service MI5 committed to 'being more open' in the 2020s, and launched its own Instagram account in early 2021. Its boss Ken McCallum encouraged users to follow them, adding, 'You can insert your own joke about whether we will be following you.'

If our world no longer does silence, we're going to have to get a better handle on the essence of our secrets. And so that's what I set out to do. I have used what I learned from psychologists, sociologists and historians to track down and embed myself with the people living with the worst secrets imaginable. I investigated spies living double lives, and found out the secrets of the influencer community. I spoke to the Instagrammers and TikTokers stuck on a hamster wheel of manufactured secrets to quench the viewers' thirst for authenticity and revelation.

I met the world's first ever blogger – an over-sharer who introduced the internet to the dick pic and had a physical fight with writer Kurt Vonnegut – and I got into the mind of the Coffin Confessor, who is paid $10,000 a pop to attend funerals and reveal the secrets of the dead. I spoke with Amanda Knox about how her mismatched body language got her locked up for four years for a murder she didn't commit, and found out from detectives how body behaviour can (under a very specific set of circumstances) reveal what a person might be thinking.

I considered our over-reliance on lie detectors, and how a talk-show host got it so wrong that a guest committed suicide after the filming. I delved into the psychology of secrets, and what keeping them can do to us both physically and mentally, as well as how cults and nefarious actors use them against us. And I got to the crux of the conundrums of our time, such as: What do we do with white lies? And how do we protect our children while also being honest with them? And I looked to the future to see how technology is changing the concept of the secret, such as in the capture of murderers through apps and trackers. This might all be irrelevant once mind-reading – potentially a very real prospect – makes secrets obsolete.

I want you to get a grip on what secrets truly are, how keeping them will affect you, and how to extract them from others. It's my belief that only through understanding the psychology of secrets can we really understand who we are – or, at the very least, who we are when nobody's watching.

1

SECRETS AND POWER

As you tread the streets of Monsey, New York, you might feel as though you have been flung backwards through time. The black hats, wigs and modest dress code of the ultra-orthodox Jewish community that live here make Manhattan seem not miles, but centuries away. Men, garbed in black suits and white shirts, the brims of their black hats catching the sunlight, hurry along, their tzitzit – fringes from their prayer shawls – swaying with each step. Their faces bear the markings of devotion – earnest eyes studying the holy words of the Talmud and Torah, and beards shaped by the sacred prohibition against the razor.

Women in modest attire walk with haste, balancing the roles of matriarchs, educators and wives. The air is punctuated with the sounds of Yiddish, the *mamaloshen* (mother tongue), interlacing seamlessly with English. The kosher delis, Judaica stores and humble homes radiate an austere simplicity, far from the flashing lights of downtown Manhattan.

With the Friday night sunset, the sabbath descends on Monsey like a soothing blanket. The streets grow quiet, the rushing cars cease their hurried journeys, and the air fills with the warm aroma of challah bread. The sacred silence is broken only by the soft murmur of blessings carried on the wind.

But behind these walls, a hidden truth lurks – a community shrouded in secrets, casting a chilling shadow over this pious enclave.

As I kicked off my research into secrecy, one thing became apparent incredibly quickly: secrets and power come hand in hand. And among the largest and most powerful institutions are organized religions and cults. From the old-world sects of Hasidic Judaism and Catholicism to the buzzword New Age cults of Scientology and Heaven's Gate, secrecy has long helped religious entities to tighten a vice around their devotees.

'A big drama was the day Rebitzen Solevetchik found out that Tova had a TV in her home.' So begins one of the many Matilda-like passages in the memoir of former Hasidic Jew turned Netflix reality star and fashion mogul, Julia Haart. Unlike many in the Haredi ultra-orthodox community, Julia's family weren't born religious. Back in the Soviet Union, her father was a high-ranking communist and a master of the piano who performed for the Pope. Her mother held PhDs in philosophy and mathematics. Later, in the Haredi community, her qualifications were cause for great shame.

When Julia was three years old, her family upped roots to America, landing in Austin, Texas. Although her parents refused to discuss the past with her, she speculates as to why they chose a life of religious devotion. She tells me she believes it was a straightforward switch from Soviet communism to ultra-orthodox Judaism. The communist Soviet Union may have been secular in name, but demanded the devoutness, servitude and observance of the most extreme religion. Moving from an authoritarian society with a focus on the collective in the USSR to the individualistic priorities of the American Dream in Texas was a culture shock. Worse still, the anti-Semitism they experienced there increased their isolation and rootlessness.

Like her mother, Julia developed into a prodigious talent. Her elementary school grades were among the best in Texas. As she recounts in her memoir, *Brazen*, her score brought her to the attention of a prominent Texas entrepreneur called Jeremy, who had some involvement with one of the most esteemed schools in Austin. He believed it would be easy to get Julia in. It proved anything but. 'After making excuses that they had no room for me, the principal finally had a meeting with Jeremy and told him that they didn't want to take me because I was a Jew. The principal told Jeremy that he had managed to keep all the Jews out, and he wasn't going to make an exception with me, no matter how promising or intelligent I was.'

Seeking familiarity and acceptance, the family soon moved to New York's Monsey community, renowned as a hive of extreme religious orthodoxy. Julia describes it as 'like the eighteenth century'. Women wear wigs to hide their real hair from the gaze of men, lest it distract them from their Torah study. Here, Julia was brought up to be invisible. Her parents grew cold and distant as they fell further into orthodoxy.

Julia had been an only child for ten years, but her parents embarked on a pious passage of procreation, until she found herself one of eight siblings. Her parents left the seven other children in the care of their older sister Julia for days or weeks at a time. They regularly forgot her birthday, stripped her of individuality and privacy (she slept in the laundry room), and made her scrub the floors. Even the tiniest crumb of wheat or bread discovered in the kitchen during Passover would be enough to confine Julia to be 'separated from the rest of the Jewish people for all eternity, even after death.' She'd be excommunicated and confined to eternal damnation, they told her. She spent an entire month each year ensuring the absence of such crumbs.

Listening to her story when we meet, I'm reminded of Cinderella. The extreme parts of the Monsey community sound to me like a cold and hostile world that uses secrecy and misogyny to control its people. I was raised Jewish, and still feel culturally in touch, particularly around the humour and anxiety popularized by Woody Allen, Mel Brooks and Larry David. I attended synagogue a couple of times a year on high-holy days, learned to read Hebrew and had a bar mitzvah at thirteen years old. It's strange to look back on; how nervous I felt, having to stand up in front of a room full of strangers and familiars, and sing from an ancient script.

Those rare escapades into religion aside, I grew up secular. The world Julia inhabited makes up a tiny portion of Jews, and is as far removed from secular Jews as Jehovah's Witnesses are from non-religious Christians. As an atheist with no access to the ultra-orthodox community, I have had to rely on the accounts of Julia and other ex-Haredi defectors I've interviewed. Many ultra-orthodox Jews – particularly those flouting strict Haredi codes to use the internet and comment beneath my videos – refute her accounts, and paint an altogether more flattering picture of their world: one of laughter, culture and community, in which children gather excitedly around storytellers as part of an oral tradition lost to many of us in the West. Women in these communities assure me in the comment section that they are happy. When I bring this up with Julia, she points out that many women were against obtaining the vote during the suffragette movement. It's not about individual happiness, she tells me: it's about fairness, equality and opportunity.

And yet, as a child and young adult, Julia was one of the women who grew to embrace and love her role in the Haredi community. She found herself competing for righteousness and modesty, which they call *tznius*. The community rewards displays of *tznius* with praise, so she paradoxically competed to be the most modest girl at her school.

This competitive humility features in many fundamentalist communities. It's a big part of ensuring that secrecy reigns. Ex-Jehovah's Witness Harrison Cother told me about how Jehovah's

Witnesses compete for modesty and righteousness to earn the term 'slave' (implying you help others despite getting nothing in return). 'You get onto the hamster wheel,' he tells me. 'And you get more privileges. You get given the microphone duty to take round the Kingdom Hall. You get to do the sound system. You then can go on the platform and give talks to the congregation. Every step of the way, you are commended and congratulated. It's this ego boost, it's this false sense of pride and self-esteem. They tell you to be humble. But everyone knows that you're in a higher position of power, and that you have more authority over everyone else beneath you.'

When leaders of a cult or extreme religion have members competing with one another for righteousness and humility, it becomes easier to hide the secrets of the outside world from them. In cults and extreme religions, devotees are indoctrinated to wear their ignorance with pride. They venerate secrets, particularly those kept from them. So, in her ambitious pursuit of modesty, Julia cut her hair short (long hair was deemed immodest). She made sure her skirts were the longest. She prayed, and chastised herself for having bad thoughts about her parents. She was compliant, and stayed away from the outside world.

When her parents forgot her birthday, and neglected to throw her a bat mitzvah (to celebrate becoming a woman at twelve years old), she refused to complain. 'I waited and waited for my parents to remember my bat mitzvah was coming up. Finally, during Passover, on the night of my birthday, my father looked at me, and said, "Hey, isn't it your birthday tonight? How old are you turning?" I tried so hard not to cry, but I know my voice betrayed my hurt as I said, "I'm twelve." My parents looked at each other and laughed about how they had completely forgotten.'

Julia grew strong, and refused to let them see her cry. That strength would later help her break free from the Haredi community, start a new life from scratch, become the CEO of a leading fashion firm, and work with model and media star Kendall Jenner and actress Gwyneth Paltrow. She founded and starred in the Netflix reality show *My Unorthodox Life*, a mix between the Kardashians and a cult defector series. It details how she and her children are transitioning to the outside world, while becoming fashionistas and influencers.

Everything she does appears to be in defiance of her authoritarian upbringing. In escaping the extreme secretive collectivism of the Haredi community, she has embraced the expressive individualism of modern America. Through their reality series, she and her children appear to share their every thought and desire – no matter how personal – with the world. In the first episode, she chastises her youngest daughter Miriam for musing that she might be 'kind of' bisexual.

'Not "kind of",' Julia replies: 'You *are* bisexual. Own it.'

It's a sharp contrast to the Julia of Monsey. She had never given clues about her mounting discontent, so when she left the community, her friends and family were shocked. The secret of wanting to leave weighed on her so heavily that she considered taking her own life, only holding back for fear of what it would do to the rest of her family and their standing in the community.

Now, free on the outside, she is prohibited from speaking to anyone from her old world. For a while, she kept up a relationship with one of her sisters at a distance. But the community put a stop to that, because she is an external influence to be shunned, lest the secrets of the outside world corrupt.

Within the Monsey community, women in particular are shielded from such worldly evils. Julia's elementary school there only taught the basic elements of her religion, amid other lessons about immodesty, and taking care of babies. She tells me that that is the sole role of a woman in the community. 'Their only way into heaven is through a man.' The school had a chemistry lab that was never used. It was just there for appearances in case of government inspections. She and her classmates were not supposed to learn or be taught anything of the modern world.

For this reason, there were few sins more egregious than possessing a television. And rumours began to swirl that a family of one of the pupils had a secret TV in their home.

'The rebbitzen [wife of a rabbi] came into our classroom with fury in her eyes, and we sat there trembling in our seats, wondering who was going to bear the brunt of this wrath – each praying that it wasn't us,' writes Julia.

When she recounts the anecdote to me, she acts out her teacher's grisly piousness with a bellowing voice and wide eyes, like the Giant in *Jack and the Beanstalk*: 'I smell TUMAH (impurity)! I smell TUMAH!' bawled the rebbitzen. The rebbitzen slunk up and down the classroom aisles, as though able to sniff the scent of televisual malevolence, before stopping at the suspect's seat and confirming the stench's source.

This teacher – who berated and humiliated the pupil in front of the class – held sway in the community. A bad word from her could ruin a girl's prospects of attracting a husband, and therefore her standing with God. She ordered that the girl return home and take an axe to the TV, her family's last window to the outside world. The exact method is unknown, but the schoolgirl's family promptly purged themselves of the forbidden television.

As I would come to see, by banishing the TV, they collided with fragments of the first secret ever told, as it bounded down the corridors of time: the secret of the Tree of Knowledge.

'You are free to eat from any tree in the garden; but you must not eat from the tree of knowledge of good and evil, for when you eat from it you will certainly die,' said God to Adam and Eve. If you believe the Bible, those were the first words spoken to man. Buried in that immortal first line is a secret.

To me, the word 'certainly' feels superfluous. God is trying too hard to hide something. If someone tells me they'll *certainly* be on time for a meeting, it fills me with doubt. Perhaps that's just a quirk of modern parlance, a linguistic nuance that hadn't yet developed while Adam and Eve were knocking about. We'll delve later into the ways we hide secrets in language, but it's an inauspicious start for the first recorded attempt at communication.

God's assertion that the Tree of Knowledge causes death is a lie, but it is also a secret, the unravelling of which cost a serpent its legs and mankind its immortality. The Tree of Knowledge – and the wisdom it imbues – is the first secret kept from humanity.

The second secret – and the first kept *by* humanity – turns up soon afterwards. Keeping it is pretty much the first thing that Adam and Eve do. When they eat the fruit from the Forbidden Tree, they do so in secret. We know this because, when God walks through the garden (yes, God *walks* – I'd always imagined him as a big translucent face in the sky), the two humans hide behind a tree. They realize that they have defied God's will. They consciously try to hide their crime.

God calls out: 'Where are you?' It's peculiar behaviour from an omniscient being, but it might be the first attempt by human or deity to *uncover* a secret – albeit one he presumably already knew about. Compared to the work of FBI agents and Guantanamo Bay interrogators, God's detective work is rudimentary. But it works. Adam steps out and admits that he ate the fruit. Actually, in a cowardly move he blames Eve and – indirectly – God: 'The woman you put here with me,' he accuses. 'She gave me some fruit from the tree, and I ate it.'

Being from the Old Testament, this is the creation story of both Judaism and Christianity. Islam begins with the almost identical parable of Adam and Hawa. But whether they're Adam and Eve or Adam and Hawa, they appear to have been intended to live in eternal ignorance. Today, the censorship of TV in Monsey serves the same purpose.

God means to keep a lot of secrets from Adam and Eve/Hawa, including the apparent shamefulness of genitalia. Their nakedness seems to be the main thing that the Tree of Knowledge makes them aware of. As the Qur'an states, 'And when they tasted of the tree, their private parts became apparent to them, and they began to fasten together over themselves from the leaves of Paradise.' As we'll go on to see, *shame* is so often both the reason for – and result of – secrecy.

The Genesis passage also hints at something at the heart of all authoritarian groups, be they religious or secular. Taken as a morality tale, the Genesis creation story proposes that the pursuit of knowledge is immoral – that too much knowledge can kill you.

The Catholic Church ruled over much of the Western world (and, by extension, much of the world) for centuries, and their method of control was secrecy. Secrecy is so ingrained within the Church's ideals of power that even the origin story of Adam and Eve sees humans punished for uncovering one – that the fruit wouldn't kill them, but would imbue them with knowledge. It makes virtues of repentance and supplication, and implies that secrets must be kept for our own protection. This is something we've seen across religions, cults and dictatorships, from Christianity and Judaism to Scientology and the Stasi.

Depending on your beliefs, or how literally you take the Bible, you may consider Christianity's origin story improbable. You might then deem it not written evidence of the first recorded secret, but a work of fiction. Even so, its role as a morality tale has left its mark on how we handle secrecy, spreading shame and fear into the populace and laying down rules that encourage us to keep secret our transgressions, while rulers keep secrets from us.

But maybe, I wondered, rather than *causing* us to use secrecy, Genesis is itself the *result* of humanity's inclination towards secrets as a means of control. It might be that we just naturally keep secrets to control one another, and reflect that in the stories we tell. I wanted to find out if Adam and Eve was just one of many creation stories and myths designed to keep believers subservient, so I got reading.

I found that in Ancient Greek mythology, the first woman wasn't Eve or Hawa but Pandora. And the creation of her story predates that of Adam and Eve by around seven centuries. The Titan fire god Prometheus stole fire from heaven and gave it to mortals. Zeus was annoyed by this for some reason – I suppose he wanted to keep fire secret as a means to control the mortals. So, he went about getting revenge on Prometheus. He commissioned the patron of craftsmen, Hephaestus, to fashion a woman out of earth: Pandora. Thus, the first woman was created from vengeance and bitterness.

It appears that men were already alive and well, and messing about with their new gadget of fire by then. Pandora was imbued by the gods with beauty, wealth . . . and a deceptive heart and lying tongue. For some reason vaguely related to revenge, Zeus gave Pandora a box – or jar, as it appears to be in the original Greek – that she was commanded never to open.

Is this sounding familiar? Eventually, curiosity overcame her, and she opened the jar, just as Adam and Eve ate from the tree, and just as Julia's classmate watched the TV. Pandora's box unleashed all manner of plagues, sorrow, misfortune and evil. The only thing left in the box when Pandora swiftly closed it was hope.

I was amazed to discover how the ancient civilizations understood the relationship between secrets and power. The Ancient Greeks and Abrahamic religions are calling out to us from the past with a stern message: do not be curious; do not seek knowledge; do not rebel. And this suppression of curiosity and respect for secrets has helped rulers to dominate societies for millennia.

*

Once upon a galactic time, some 75 million years ago, a fella named Xenu held the rather imposing title of Galactic Confederacy Overlord. Imagine, if you will, a space-age Mafia boss ruling seventy-six planets, including Earth (or Teegeeack, as it was known in those celestial circles).

As happens in the annals of cosmic governance, Xenu found himself grappling with a bit of a population crisis. His planets were a touch overpopulated, with an average of 178 billion people per planet. To solve this problem, Xenu crafted an audacious plan.

Under the pretense of income tax inspections, he gathered billions of his unsuspecting citizens. Then, they were swiftly paralysed and frozen using a rather unique cocktail of alcohol and glycol. These poor souls were then flown by spacecraft (that looked suspiciously like DC-8 airliners) all the way to the volcanoes of Teegeeack – remember, that's Earth.

These frozen beings were thrown into the volcanoes, and Xenu sealed the deal with a few well-placed hydrogen bombs. For some reason, the spirits, or 'Thetans', of these beings were released, only to be trapped again by Xenu's elaborate 'electronic ribbon' (a type of wave that sucks people into a vacuum) and forced to watch a '3D, super colossal motion picture' for thirty-six days. This 'movie' fed them false information about religions, implanting misleading concepts about God and Satan that persist even today. These confused and traumatized Thetans (spirits) are said to now cling to human beings, causing them spiritual harm.

Thus begins the saga of Scientology, with a creation story that explains away all the other religions as inventions of brainwashed spirits, and controls members by eroding trust in the outside world. Any negative ideas about Scientology from external sources can be packaged as vile rumours spread by negative Body Thetans that survived the volcanoes.

I've met and interviewed many former Scientologists and other cult defectors who speak of having been indoctrinated in their sect with a fear of knowledge. It is the terror of opening Pandora's box or eating from the forbidden Tree of Knowledge. Scientologists are told that they will develop pneumonia and die if they find out (or someone tells them) about the cult's creation story before they are ready.

You might think that a cult would want its members to know as much as possible about its rules, while prohibiting only outside information. But Scientology's tactic is typical in authoritarian sects. In fact, during my research, I found that cults and secrecy were so intertwined that I eventually had to dedicate a whole chapter to them.

It's worth noting that cults are not all that different from organized religions, at least with regards to what they demand of their followers. Cults are more likely than religions to have a sole enigmatic leader, as well as expensive tiers promising secret knowledge. But there is overlap.

Julia Haart writes at length about how certain ultra-orthodox communities – which you might classify as extreme religion rather than cult – prevent women from studying the Torah. She was ignorant of the context behind the strict rules to which she was forced to adhere. And for thousands of years, knowledge of the Bible was restricted to an elite few. Literacy – and therefore class and education – dictated where that knowledge fell, allowing those in the know to control the masses.

Much of the Abrahamic religions' teachings are freely available to most Westerners today. But more extreme sects continue to keep secret their doctrines from their own worshippers. This means that members are not only deprived of knowledge from the outside world (the 'worldly' realm, as Jehovah's Witnesses call it, or the 'wog' world, according to Scientology terminology) but also from their own community. They're kept in darkness, programmed to bend and break to the will of the keepers of the knowledge, whether these be chief rabbis (Haredi Judaism), the Watchtower (Jehovah's Witnesses) or Tom Cruise (Scientology).

Cruise is not the leader of the cult of Scientology, but ranks extremely highly and is best friends with leader David Miscavige. His image is essential to the survival and popularity of the cult, which is why it awarded him its highest honour: the Freedom Medal of Valor. The award was created especially for him, so that no member can ever reach his heights. When asked about the belief system of Scientology, Cruise never gives answers, but instead speaks in riddles, and insists we 'go find out'. That is the line often wheeled out by other public Scientologists, such as the late actress Kirstie Alley.

Beside contributing to the organization's mystique and power, they do this for two reasons. First, members are expected to pay thousands (or hundreds of thousands) of dollars to access each new level of Scientology information. These levels are called Operating Thetans (OTs), with OT VIII the highest (theoretically, there are fifteen levels, but nothing higher than eight has ever been released). Very few members are afforded – or can afford – the opportunity to reach OT VIII. Kirstie Alley is one of the select few who made it. Tom Cruise's status is unknown to us *wogs*, but those who were close to him and have since defected reveal he was already at OT VII in the early 2000s. Others claim he's now at OT VIII.

Second, cults rely on coercive psychology, such as the 'boiling frog' concept and the 'sunk cost' fallacy. The former means members are very slowly 'boiled' with information that at first seems sensible and positive, and which turns wacky (or boils) too slowly for members to notice. If they were hit with the outlandish secret lore of Lord Xenu from the start, they'd jump out like a frog from hot water. If done slowly enough, the cult member is indoctrinated – the frog is dead – before he or she realizes what is happening.

As for sunk cost, the cult relies on members being in so deep (and out of pocket) by the time they hear about the creation story that they feel they have no choice but to keep going. They can't face up to the fact that they have bankrupted their families and shunned their friends for nonsense created by science-fiction writer L. Ron Hubbard.

The introductory Scientology courses teach pseudo-science philosophies that can sometimes help people. Much of it is ridiculous, but there are parts that work for some members. Otherwise, no one would sign up. It's not too dissimilar to psychologist Jordan Peterson's borrowed 'Make Your Bed' concept, which suggests that if you start taking control of the smaller parts of your life, the rest will follow. The central tenet for Peterson and Scientology is that you are in control of your life and need to make sure you have everything in order before looking at those around you. It's a philosophy that works for some people but doesn't for others.

This being a cult, Scientology takes this concept to the extreme, so that *anything* that happens to you is your fault. This was a key part of the 2023 trial of *That '70s Show* actor Danny Masterson, a Scientologist found guilty of raping women he was purported to have drugged. Ex-Scientologists have told me that in these circumstances, the victims take the blame. It's called 'pulling it in', and implies that if someone rapes you, if someone crashes into your car, or you become gravely ill, you must have done something to make it happen.

The idea that you are in control of your destiny is appealing to a lot of people who join Scientology. But even if that could work for you – since you now know about Lord Xenu and the Galactic Federation – you're unlikely to start courses at the lower tiers of Scientology. That's why, for the sake of Scientology, it's best kept secret.

Marc Headley was in Scientology for years, and devoted much of his life to it. He was even audited (coached) in one-on-one sessions by the big cheese himself, Tom Cruise. But Headley only found out about Lord Xenu after leaving. How did he find out? *South Park*!

When *South Park* released their infamous 'Trapped in the Closet' episode in 2005, they ridiculed Tom Cruise and John Travolta. What really hurt the cult weren't the jokes about the Hollywood pair, but the disclosure of the secret folklore at the heart of Scientology. Headley believes that this 'woke up' countless Scientology members, and prevented many more from joining.

The Church of Scientology was pissed off. Headley showed me documents proving that the cult's Office of Special Affairs (OSA) went through the *South Park* creators' rubbish, tracked their cars and tried to infiltrate their catering staff. They wanted to learn their writers' secrets, and use them against them. They tried to put a stop to the episode and take revenge on *South Park*'s team (a tactic unofficially known as 'fair game').

'I knew nothing about what they were talking about in that episode,' Headley tells me. 'Not a single thing.' He explains that you don't learn about Xenu until you reach OT III, which is $100,000–$200,000 up the chart. Headley's wife Claire – who left Scientology with him – was at OT V, so was aware of Lord Xenu – but couldn't share it with Marc, for fear he'd die of pneumonia from learning too much too soon.

Even after leaving cults and extreme religions, many defectors still feel superstitious around their former belief systems. When Headley woke up the morning after watching the *South Park* episode, however, he realized: 'I didn't even have a sniffle – it's bull! That was it. I was deprogrammed overnight.'

Headley believes that fewer than 10 per cent of Scientologists know about its creation story. 'This is all about money,' he adds. It is also about power and control; but those paths also lead to money. By depriving Scientology of its core secrets, *South Park* weakened it immeasurably. Even ex-Scientologist Jenna Miscavige Hill, the niece of Scientology leader David Miscavige, admits she first learned about Lord Xenu and the cult's creation story from *South Park*. That's how tightly extreme authoritarian groups wrap up their secrets.

While Scientology might be making headlines today, the creation stories found in the Abrahamic and Ancient Greek cultures show us that humans have long promoted, engaged in and used secrecy for control and malevolent means. In fact, not only was the Judaeo-Christian creation story in favour of secrecy, but – just like Scientology – the Catholic Church grew by depriving believers of knowledge of its scriptures. Catholics had faith – of that, they were certain – but in what, they often knew not.

After the unified Catholic Church was established in the fourth century AD, explains psychology professor Bernard Starr, 'the Church actually discouraged the populace from reading the Bible on their own.' He explains that this intensified in the Middle Ages, with the prohibition of native translations.

The teachings of the Bible remained in the hands of an elite few, protecting it from scrutiny by the masses. Rather than read, study and dissect, worshippers were only able to hear snippets from the sermons of priests in church, and make out what they could from sculptures and artistic tapestries.

Professor Starr believes this secrecy enabled churches to adorn their naves and aisles with classical artworks that depict Jesus and the saints as 'fair-skinned Northern Europeans living in pala-tial Romanesque settings – images completely alien to their actual Jewish lives in a rural village in Galilee.' He calls this a 'Christianizing process' and an 'ethnic cleansing of Judaism'. Even today, many of us associate the stories from the Bible with ecclesiastical artworks rather than the actual words of the Bible.

Secrecy helped create an image of Christianity that worked for worshippers across Europe, and also kept believers coming back to church to listen to the stories. Devotees kept the community active with their regular attendance, and supported it with donations, while obeying rules that they couldn't even read. They were trained to be pliable.

The donations to the Holy See became known as Peter's Pence in the eleventh century. Today, the Peter's Pence charity fund has been used to buy luxury properties and fund Hollywood movies, to the point that even Pope Francis admitted there was financial corruption within the Vatican.

You no longer have to attend a church or synagogue – or pay a donation or tax – to learn about the Bible or the Torah. Most of the information has become freely available, initially – to an extent – through the printing press, and later via TV and the internet. The PEW Research Center found that, in 1976, 91 per cent of Americans identified as Christians. In 2022, after information had become more freely available through advancements in technology, that figure fell to 64 per cent. PEW predicts that Christians could make up as little as 35 per cent of the American population by 2070. There are likely multiple factors involved in the decline of religious belief but, principally, the Church has lost its ability to retain secrets, and with that, much of its control over its devotees' lives and money. That's why Tom Cruise won't tell you about Lord Xenu.

Many active members of cults and religions deny that they are suppressing knowledge. In his research into the medieval suppression of the Bible, Professor Starr claims that he received a backlash from Catholics claiming it never happened. In response, he points to various decrees, such as this thirteenth-century ruling from the Council of Tarragona: 'No one may possess the books of the Old and New Testaments in the Romance language, and if anyone possesses them he must turn them over to the local bishop within eight days after promulgation of this decree, so that they may be burned.'

Sadly, it wasn't just books that were burned in an effort to keep the Church's teachings secret from its acolytes. William Tyndale graduated from Oxford University in the early 1500s, before teaching at Cambridge University. There, he fell in with a crowd of humanist scholars, and became convinced that all worshippers should have access to the Bible. He went about translating an Ancient Greek version of the New Testament to English in 1523, but was forced to flee England after Church authorities caught wind of his intentions. With patronage from affluent London merchants, he travelled to Germany and completed his translation there. The books were then smuggled into England – where they were denounced and banned.

Tyndale was captured by authorities while working on the Old Testament in Antwerp. Condemned for heresy, he was executed by strangulation, and then burned at the stake. His legacy endured: 18,000 copies of his translated New Testament were printed, and two complete volumes remain today. His work served as a model for the King James Version of the Bible that was published in 1611. By revealing the truth about a belief system to its worshippers, Tyndale was the *South Park* of his time (without the satire, mockery and celebrity caricatures).

Tyndale was a sixteenth-century Christian prevented from making Christian teachings accessible to other Christians. Marc Headley was a Scientologist convinced he would develop pneumonia should he find out anything about Lord Xenu. And Julia Haart was an ultra-orthodox Jew whose teacher claimed she could smell the evil emitted by a television. What binds the three are their places in fundamental belief systems that have sourced power and dominion from secrecy.

But what happens when institutions tighten their iron grip? And how do they use secrecy to sow the seeds of fear in the very soul of a society?

'Secrecy is the freedom tyrants dream of,' said former director of the Council on Foreign Affairs and White House Press Secretary Bill D. Moyers. Since the dawn of recorded history, brutal regimes have used secrets against their citizens. We all know how frustrating it is to be left in uncertainty. Tyrants and authoritarian sects know this too, exploiting secrets and hiding information just as God did with the Tree of Knowledge. If the dark side of history is as cyclical as a slasher movie on repeat, then secrecy is its masked antagonist.

As I continued my research into the history of secrets, I saw another theme emerge. I found countless examples of folks driven to secrecy not only through power but through *fear* – fear of persecution, discrimination and torture. And behind every fearful secret-keeper lay a terrifying institution intent on using secrecy for its own gain.

Our knowledge of ancient history is hazy. But it is thought that one of the earliest known secret-keeping rulers united China in the third century BC. Qin Shi Huangdi reigned with ruthlessness. He was obsessed with secrecy. He conscripted enormous numbers of workers to build a mausoleum packed with more than 6,000 life-size terracotta soldiers, only to murder his builders on completion to preserve the site's secrecy. Looking back through the lens of bloody history, it's astounding how expendable life has been to vicious rulers. Qin also murdered scholars whose views he disliked, burning their books to suppress any challenging information. He wasn't the first or last to engage in this quashing of dissenting knowledge. Qin also constructed the initial version of the Great Wall of China, another symbol of a fixation with keeping the outside world unknown.

Just a few centuries later, Roman Emperor Caligula allegedly forced the parents of dissenters to watch the execution of their children. That, supposedly, was just Caligula's way of crushing opposing points of view. Caligula is also said to have made his horse a priest, slept with his own sisters and sold their services to other men. He was so brutal and irrational that his own guardsmen took it upon themselves to kill him, stabbing him thirty times. (Historians still debate the veracity of the claims, with some now believed to have been concocted by his enemies.)

Fast-forward to the seventh century and we meet a fourteen-year-old concubine who would become one of the cruellest and most successful leaders of China to rule by secrets and fear: Wu Zetian. China's only ever female leader, Wu was originally fifth concubine – ranked beneath a wife and four other mistresses – to Emperor Taizong. The emperor was taken by her spirit and intelligence, according to historian Dr Yuen Ting Lee, and employed Wu as his personal secretary, a role she carried out for ten years.

When Taizong died, Wu and the other concubines were sent to shave their heads, become Buddhist nuns and pray for his soul. They were set to spend the rest of their lives in confinement, as a living tomb for the late emperor. As luck would have it, the next ruler, Emperor Gaozong, visited the temple to offer incense, and spotted Wu. She obviously got the measure of the man, and saw him as her route to freedom and power. 'Even though you are the Son of Heaven,' she teased, 'you can't do anything about [my confinement].'

Gaozong replied: 'Oh, can't I? I can do anything I wish.' It was a moment of reverse psychology that would eventually lead to the excruciating deaths of countless citizens.

Gaozong employed Wu as second concubine – a promotion three tiers above her previously held position – and allowed her to grow her hair again. Wu bore Gaozong four sons, which pleased him. She also went about winning the court attendants over with her friendliness and generosity. In turn, they began slipping Wu secret information about her rivals.

Wu knew that Empress Wang loved children, so she began hatching a grisly plan. Shortly after Wu gave birth to a daughter, she waited for Empress Wang to play with her. Then, she murdered her own baby, and blamed Wang. Emperor Gaozong believed Wu's lie, and dismissed Empress Wang, promoting Wu to empress. She immediately put her love rivals to death and exiled their relatives and supporters.

After Emperor Gaozong's death, her sons became emperors in name, with Wu acting as puppeteer, pulling the strings behind the scenes. She eventually disposed of this patriarchal convention, naming herself Holy and Divine Emperor, and founding the Zhou Dynasty. Ruthless and cunning, Wu went on to wipe out all other claimants to the throne, destroying fifteen family lines in just one year. She was known for summoning enemies to the throne room, before making them commit suicide in front of her.

Wu kept her people in line – and forced them to keep secrets – by executing anybody who dared reveal harmful truths. But she also exploited secrecy to trump up accusations of treason. She set up an anonymous urn as a comment box. It was purportedly there to prevent corruption and serve justice, but in reality, the urn was an excuse for snitching and punishing. She ordered her own spies and secret police to place anonymous accusations in the urn, giving her free rein to execute people at will. Versions of this tactic have been repeated through the centuries, from the Salem Witch Trials to the Stasi.

Because China – like much of the world – has long been run by patriarchal societies, the story of Wu is told by an unreliable narrator. It is possible that she has been demonized by those looking to cast doubt on the integrity and ability of a female ruler. Indeed, many historians now focus on her achievements instead. In recruiting officials, Wu is credited with selecting based not on 'personal integrity' but levels of education and intelligence. She expanded China's imperial sovereignty, conquering new territories through military force and diplomacy. And she implemented agricultural techniques throughout China, ordering the composition of farming textbooks, creating irrigation systems and reducing taxes.

Much of Wu's life remains a mystery, her secrets dying with her; Wu insisted that her gravestone be unmarked by any eulogy.

She expected later periods to better evaluate her legacy; here was someone who knew the value of mystique.

As with the aforementioned religions and cults, I found time and time again that authoritarian political rulers like Wu and Qin have wielded power and spread fear through secrets and uncertainty. These power-hungry leaders have also led inquisitions into the secret inner thoughts of their citizens, and brutally executed and incarcerated individuals. In the fifth century BC, Ancient Greek philosopher Socrates stood accused of corrupting the minds of the youth of Athens, worshipping false gods and not following the state religion. It was claimed that Socrates denied that the gods did bad things, and believed in an inner voice deity called a *daimonion*. Such was their fear around differing viewpoints and potential political uprisings that jurors opted to execute Socrates. He was made to drink poisoned hemlock.

Around 1,500 years later, the Middle Ages brought about investigations into the secret thoughts of others. This was a time of medieval Catholic inquisitions, propped up by Pope Innocent IV's authorization of torture to elicit confessions from heretics. The Pope found a loophole that would allow his inquisitors to employ abhorrent methods and still go to heaven: he granted them absolution for using instruments of torture.

Paranoia prospered among Protestants, who feared the cruelty of these Catholic inquisitions. Divisions were drawn. Then, as disorder reigned through the Black Death, the Little Ice Age and various wars, people looked for scapegoats. That's when the major Western Christian denominations took to persecuting witches. For the most part in England and Scotland, it was the Protestant state that carried out the hangings of women (and some men).

One of the most infamous witch inquisitors, Heinrich Kramer (c. 1420–1505), blamed bad weather on witches, and wrote a book about how to catch and exterminate them. Even though theologians and inquisitors initially rejected Kramer's ideas, he was able to widely disperse his work and, with it, the paranoid idea that society need look out for secret witches. Johannes Gutenberg had invented his printing press in the mid-fourteenth century, while woodblock printing had been practised in China since the ninth century.

The Crucible aside, we've whitewashed witches. We think of *Harry Potter*, *Bewitched*, and other witch-related books and movies that lit up our childhoods. But it must have been terrifying to be a woman living under constant suspicion of harbouring secret thoughts, while in fear of execution and torture. Kramer's reputation grew, and he served as an expert witch detector, helping to convict women for secrets that they didn't have.

It's not only nefarious dictators and inquisitors who employ secrets, but those forced to flee them. Many have had to keep secrets over the years to escape persecution. My surname, Gold, was changed by my dad when he was younger from Goldstein, as a way of hiding our Jewishness from anti-Semites. Others followed suit, so that now Gold is just as good a giveaway, which I'm reminded of most days by viewers of my podcast on YouTube, often not in a nice way (even if the vast majority of my viewers are lovely).

In any case, Goldstein is just a name that was given at random to my great-grandparents when they arrived on British shores from Eastern Europe at the start of the twentieth century. I once asked my late grandpa what our real name had been, and he told me something Russian-sounding. I later told my dad, who shook his head with a smile: 'That word just means "idiot" in Yiddish.' My grandpa had forgotten the name his parents were born with. Now, it's a secret even to us. But I'm pleased to have had that inadvertently funny interaction with my grandpa.

History is filled with examples of Jews having to keep their identity secret to escape persecutors. German-born Jewish girl

Anne Frank hid from Nazi tyranny in a concealed room behind a bookcase in Amsterdam. Most are familiar with her story, but are surprised to realize quite how long she and her family secreted themselves from the world: 761 days.

For her ninth birthday, Anne's grandmother gifted her a fountain pen. She wrote about it: 'When I was nine, my fountain pen (packed in cotton wool) arrived as a "sample of no commercial value" all the way from Aachen, where my grandmother (the kindly donor) used to live. I lay in bed with flu, while the February winds howled around our flat. This splendid fountain pen came in a red leather case, and I showed it to my girlfriends the first chance I got. Me, Anne Frank, the proud owner of a fountain pen.' The words written by that pen have survived almost a century, and stand as a symbol of resistance to tyranny. Their documentation of the tyranny of the Nazis is held up as a contrast to the humanity of Anne's everyday existence. We read how she falls in – and out – of love with a boy called Peter, with whom she hides. She gets her first kiss, and writes of her burgeoning feminism.

It was on her thirteenth birthday, in June 1942, that her parents took her to a bookshop to pick out the diary, something she had long desired. At the beginning of the same year, a high-ranking officer of the German SS called Reinhard Heydrich outlined a plan to murder Europe's Jews. He set it in motion at a conference in Berlin's Wannsee, a picturesque lake district where – eight decades later – I swam many times while living in Germany.

Anne Frank received her diary two months after exterminations of Jews began in Belzec. By the end of the year, 600,000 Jews had been murdered there. Gas chambers were already ending the lives of thousands of Jews in Sobibor. Many Jews fought back, and rebel units were being set up in the forests of Byelorussia and the Baltic right about the time that Anne got her diary.

Anne Frank also fought back. Her famous diary was written over a period of a few months. But she continued to write various other texts, including *The Secret Annex*. This was inspired by an appeal she heard on the radio from Dutch minister Gerrit Bolkestein, who had fled to London. In the transmission, he asked that Dutch citizens hold onto important documents so that the Nazis would find it harder to keep secret what they had done during their occupation of the Netherlands. In just a few months, fifteen-year-old Anne wrote 50,000 words about what had been happening to her family. 'The nicest part is being able to write down all my thoughts and feelings; otherwise, I'd absolutely suffocate,' she writes. We'll go on to consider how revealing secrets – and keeping them – can have very real effects on our mental health.

In the first months of Anne's diary in 1942, Jews were being deported to murder centres from Belgium, Croatia, France, Poland and her own country, the Netherlands. Armed resistance was growing in the ghettos in which Jews were enclosed. By the end of 1942, German, Greek and Norwegian Jews were also forced onto the trains and taken to the camps.

The very idea that the Nazis would be able to murder so many millions of people based on their lineage alone seemed impossible at the time. 'Common sense could not understand that it was possible to exterminate tens and hundreds of thousands of Jews,' said Yitzhak Zuckerman, a Jewish resistance leader from the time in Warsaw. But the propaganda and exploitation of secrecy had been in the works for years, much like Scientology's boiling frog approach.

Hitler's first move was to win over the German public. He did so by playing on age-old myths about Jewish people. The Nazis – and in particular minister of propaganda Joseph Goebbels – were able to print articles and photos, propagate movies and emit radio broadcasts that painted Hitler as supreme, and Jews as *Untermensch* (subhuman).

All external press and radio broadcasts were censored and

controlled, ensuring they too ran slurs about Jews and tightened their grip of fear on the nation. One such smear was recently repeated by the world's biggest podcaster Joe Rogan, who said: 'The idea that Jewish people are not into money is ridiculous. That's like saying Italians aren't into pizza, it's fucking stupid.' Another time, he said of Jews: 'Look at all the puppeteering. Pulling all those strings at CNN, Hollywood . . .'

The reality is that many Jews got into Hollywood decades ago when those jobs were available to the working class. Many of their descendants continue to work in Hollywood. It is also typical for minorities suffering from a history of persecution to pull together and form communities around industries – not that this helped Jews when the Nazis came in and took away their rights, their property, their dignity and ultimately their lives.

Rogan is right that Jews care about money. But he is wrong to suggest they care more than anyone else. The America we know today was formed around the concept of the American Dream; the Great Gatsby aspiration of making a fortune against all odds.

And that's why the myth about Jews and money is so powerful: *because* everyone cares about money. For that reason, telling people that a minority is secretly after your money – be they Jewish, Chinese or Scottish (three of the many groups often wrongly labelled as stingy or money-obsessed) – is effective. I write this fresh from watching a video by Scottish comedian Limmy, in which he criticizes the portrayal of infamously avaricious Disney character Scrooge McDuck. The rest of Scrooge's family, Limmy points out with outrage, simply bear the surname 'Duck'. 'McDuck' suggests that Scrooge alone is of Scottish lineage.

It's the go-to insult to hurl at your neighbours. It suggests that you and your people are above such lowly pursuits as money, while your enemy is finance-obsessed, and therefore not to be trusted. To show how arbitrary this is, I started typing random nationalities and cultures into Google with the word 'stingy'. I was greeted with such articles as *The Daily Telegraph*'s 'The Real Reason Why the Dutch Are So Stingy', *RTÉ Today*'s 'Are Irish People Stingy Tippers?' and *Salon*'s 'Stingy, white and fat: Here's what the rest of the world thinks of Americans'.

The only people who don't care about money are those who have it in spades. I've heard that the etiquette within the circles of the Royal Family demands that money not be discussed. The concept of earning it is beneath them. Yet, within a year of leaving the Royal Family, Prince Harry and Meghan Markle brought in a reported $100 million Netflix deal, a $20 million Spotify deal and a $20 million book deal – on top of various eye-watering inheritances and allowances, which add up to amounts most of us would need a hundred lifetimes to earn – while also publicly squabbling with Harry's father, King Charles III, over funds for his security and living.

We all care about money. But Hitler had malicious and anti-Semitic intentions. He had the will to eliminate a particular minority, and the political sway to make it happen. All he had to do was suggest that the Jews had a secret.

He made it clear that they were at fault for the country's economic downturn, and were conspiring to steal the money of honest, hard-working Germans. This struck a powerful chord with many of the Germans of the time because they were in the midst of a severe economic crisis, in a country still licking its wounds from the First World War; the idea that there is one particular race or nation secretly conspiring to take away your money is central to many conspiracy theories. Even I, a Jew, am ashamed to admit I have found myself wondering whether a secret cabal of fellow Jews really do gather – it'd be just typical that I was the only one not invited.

Within two months of Hitler being appointed Chancellor of Germany, the boycott of Jewish shops and businesses commenced. The message was clear: the Jews are not to be trusted as business partners – to save the German economy, they must be shunned. Within a week of the beginning of the boycott, Jews were banned from holding civil service, university and state positions. One month after that, there were public burnings of books written by Jews. Two months later, Eastern European Jewish immigrants were stripped of their German citizenship.

They lived this way for two years, during which time Hitler took on the role of Führer and Reich Chancellor. Germans were slowly being turned against the Jewish people (even though many also resisted and offered aid to them). Then, in 1935, with Jews relegated to the status of subhumans, the Nuremberg Laws were passed. Jews were no longer considered German. They weren't allowed to marry Aryans. Jewish doctors were banned from practising medicine.

Mussolini's Italy followed suit with many of the laws, which also spread to Austria, Switzerland and beyond. In November 1938, Jewish pupils were finally expelled from German schools, Jewish businesses handed over to Aryans, and then came the Kristallnacht (Night of Broken Glass) pogrom. Two hundred synagogues were destroyed, 7,500 Jewish shops looted and 30,000 male Jews sent to concentration camps. The *Holocaust Encyclopaedia* explains how something so seemingly unimaginable could come to pass: 'Propaganda encouraged passivity and acceptance of the impending measures against Jews, as these appeared to depict the Nazi government as stepping in and "restoring order."' This is part of how the 'banality of evil' can take hold of large groups of humans.

The irony is that Jews were attacked from both sides of the political spectrum. They were portrayed to socialists as affluent capitalists cutting non-Jews out of deals and stealing their money. Yet at the same time, German capitalists were being warned of the 'Judaeo-Bolshevik' threat: Jews were communists conspiring to take down capitalism. At once, they were seen as super rich and powerful – and as subhuman parasites obsessed with sex. Both stereotypes had something in common: they painted Jews as conspiratorial secret-keepers whose only goal was to bring down the German economy.

We've seen how secrets were used by Qin Shi Huangdi to hide his mausoleum of soldiers and the murders of its construction workers from his people. We've seen how Wu Zetian used deception to climb the ranks to empress, and secrets to encourage her courtiers to spy on one another. Hitler used secrecy to similar effect: he hid the murder of the Jews from his people (at least, at first) and, through the Gestapo and the SS, forced the German people to spy on one another and spread mistrust and uncertainty.

He also exploited secrecy by implying that his enemies – the Jews – were the ones keeping secrets. Made chancellor in 1933, he started promulgating anti-Semitic lies about Jewish secrets that were already present in society. He claimed they were racially inferior, were at fault for Germany's financial woes and were planning global domination. He did this relatively slowly, but so effectively that by 1939, he was able to publicly call for the extermination of European Jews.

On the morning of 4 August 1944, the SS stormed the house that was hiding Anne Frank and her family. They were sent to Punishment Barracks for hard labour. Anne Frank died at Bergen-Belsen concentration camp in February or March of 1945. She was aged sixteen.

Anne's father Otto survived. He returned to Amsterdam, and began the search for his family. Over the subsequent weeks, he learned that his wife and two daughters, Anne and Margot, had died. Upon returning to the house in Amsterdam, he discovered that his former secretaries had kept Anne's diary. Otto had lost everything and everyone dear to him. And here was this diary –

the preserved hidden inner reality of his departed daughter. I can't imagine what it must have felt like to hold it in his hands, to sense the scratches of that prized fountain pen and to return her to life through the words she wrote in captivity.

One of history's most brutal and repressive regimes had taken everything from Otto. It did so by controlling information, spreading false anti-Semitic propaganda and silencing dissent. In keeping secrets and spreading fear, they forced their targets into secrecy. Anne Frank – a most expressive girl – was made to hide for years, her diary serving as a one-sided communication to the outside world that would arrive far too late.

Otto decided to fulfil his daughter's greatest wish, to be a writer, by publishing her diaries in 1947. *Anne Frank's Diary* tells the story of just one person among the 6 million European Jews – and millions more prisoners of war, Romany people, Jehovah's Witnesses, homosexual people, disabled people and dissenters – who were brutally murdered during the Holocaust. It stands as a symbol of resistance to Nazi oppression, free of any censorship. Flying in the face of their forced secrecy, the home in which she hid is now open to the public as a museum. As Anne wrote, 'I don't think of all the misery but of the beauty that still remains.'

2

SECRETS, PRIVACY AND LIES

When she was aged thirteen, Madeleine Black stopped talking. Her voice disappeared at school and with friends. At home, her silence haunted the rooms, devastating her parents. The happy, chatty child they knew seemed to vanish. To make matters worse, she stopped eating, too, as though willing herself out of existence.

Her family took her to a psychiatrist, who tried to coax her into speaking. He didn't ask her *why* she wasn't talking. He didn't consider that there might be a secret worth extracting. As with everyone else, she didn't speak to him. Eventually, her parents were left with no option but to commit her to a psychiatric ward. Even there, she stayed mute. 'Nobody ever, ever asked me any of the right questions,' she tells me, decades later. 'They just put me down as a suicidal teenager with anorexia.'

Now, she wants parents to let their kids know that they are open and non-judgemental. That – whatever secrets their children reveal to them – nothing can shock them. 'You'll always be there. You won't judge them.' As a child, Madeleine didn't feel that way. And that's why she kept her secret.

Here's why she stopped talking. One night, she told her parents that she was staying with a friend, but didn't mention that the friend's mum was away. Her friend was 'really cool', and Madeleine looked up to her. 'Her father was American and she was English, but when she was with people she suddenly became very American, so her accent changed. She was, I guess, a lot more mature than me. I didn't wear makeup or snazzy clothes. She was the kind of girl that everybody wanted to be.'

The girls had the flat to themselves that evening. They bought a bottle of vodka. 'I've never been able to smell or drink vodka again,' she tells me. They took the alcohol to a Mexican fast-food cafe in North London, and mixed the spirit with orange juice, before drinking it in secret with two seventeen-year-old males that her friend knew. Madeleine had never drunk before – and she was thirteen – so the alcohol turned her inside out. She threw up all over the cafe, and was kicked out by the owner.

The seventeen-year-olds were sons of diplomats from America. They put her and her friend in a taxi home . . . and got in with them. 'I've always thought about that taxi driver,' she adds. 'He must have seen that I was already being assaulted.' But he said nothing. When they arrived at the flat, she describes herself as 'literally legless'. They carried her up four flights of steps to the top floor, before putting the girls in separate bedrooms. 'It became very obvious that they weren't there just to take me out of the clothes that I'd been sick in. They were there for something else. What ensued was about four or five hours of raping me and torturing me every way that they possibly could.'

In her book, *Unbroken*, Madeleine details every violent act that was carried out on her during that ordeal. The rape was about more than sexual gratification. The boys gloated and tortured her. At the end, one of them dangled her from the edge of a balcony, with the intention of dropping her, before the other intervened. 'I could have easily been another statistic of someone who was raped and then killed.' She adds, 'I was scared to fight back, so I just let them do whatever they wanted.'

They told her that if she told anyone, they'd kill her.

So, she stopped talking.

Psychologist Dr Sissela Bok describes secrecy as 'intentional concealment'. She believes there is something *active* about secret-keeping,
so it precludes unconsciously repressed thoughts. Your unconscious
may hold loads of fears that you don't even know about, but that
doesn't mean you're keeping them secret. There are also things –
like how much money we make – that we may decide not to talk
about, but these are not secrets. It's the difference between simply
not volunteering information and *intentionally* holding it back
from others. The former sits more comfortably in the realm of
privacy, while the latter makes for secrecy.

Social psychologist Dr James Pennebaker calls secrecy an 'active
inhibition of disclosure'. I liked that use of 'active': I was learning
that secrets have to be deliberate and conscious. Just as with
gossip, there is also something *social* about secrets. It isn't just
about you. It's defined by the fact you are hiding the secret from
others.

Often, you don't want *anybody* to know about your secret.
Other times, secrets are kept from specific targets (say, a spouse
or a best friend). In these cases, other people can be invited to
share the burden of the secret. The fact that these secrets need to
be kept in the first place means that secrets are usually social
transgressions. But they can also be positive, such as a surprise
birthday party, or an elaborately planned marriage proposal – at
a sports stadium, for some inexplicable reason – that seems to
have more to do with the ego of the proposer than the happiness
of the prospective spouse.

The type of secret also influences how we experience keeping
it. According to Michael Slepian, an academic who has conducted
extensive research on secrecy, there are three main groups into

which we sort our secrets: immoral, relational and aspirational. Perhaps the most difficult secrets are those that encapsulate all three categories.

'I have grown to love secrecy,' wrote Oscar Wilde in *The Picture of Dorian Gray*, published in 1891. 'It seems to be the one thing that can make modern life mysterious or marvellous to us. The commonest thing is delightful if only one hides it.' This line encapsulates the power of secrecy. Secrets produce the gossip that glues us together and tears us apart. They make dull things seem exciting. A little dose of secrecy – in the right hands – is healthy and fun. Wilde's book is about a man who hides a secret painting that keeps him young, while itself taking on the burden of ageing. Keeping this secret, the real Dorian Gray is able to retain his beauty, but grows uglier on the inside.

Yet, keeping secrets can be harmful in itself. Wilde's line praising secrecy is actually written for the character Basil Hallward. Although Hallward appears to express many views Wilde held about art, beauty and society, the character's view on secrecy is more complex. Wilde may have agreed with the sentiment about mystique, but also felt that keeping his sexuality secret was making him uglier on the inside, just like his fictional character, Dorian Gray.

You could argue that Wilde's homosexuality fits into all three categories of secrets. At the time, it was an immoral secret because homosexuality was very much a moral issue at the end of the nineteenth century. Relational secrets involve keeping an affair secret, which Wilde had to do as part of hiding his sexuality. Aspirational or goal-oriented secrets relate to your profession: say, you've been cheating at school or fudging the accounts at work. And because homosexuality was illegal at the time, his sexuality and affair had to be kept secret for the sake of his career and liberty.

These categories don't always overlap. For example, it is possible to have an aspirational secret that isn't necessarily an immoral secret, such as a secret ambition.

People often end up being forced to keep secrets both for themselves and other people. One way to avoid finding yourself in such a pickle is to stay clear of areas that thrive on secrecy. This could be anything involving drugs, sex and other taboo topics. The point isn't that those things have an innate immoral value. Drugs and sex are not objectively negative – in fact, many people take great joy in their regular consumption – but aspects of those worlds contravene the conventions of courteous conversation. And once you enter those realms, it's likely that secrets will seek you out. 'People who are really open to new experiences,' says Slepian, 'tend to find themselves in the kinds of situations people more often keep secret.'

In a private letter about his own secret, Wilde wrote: 'I feel that if I kept it secret it might grow in my mind (as poisonous things grow in the dark) and take its place with the other terrible thoughts that gnaw me.' As an active homosexual in a time when it was illegal, Wilde carried a secret that would one day contribute to his incarceration. He described keeping a secret as a thorn that he 'must pluck out of [his] flesh'.

A mix of gossip, outrage and vengeance eventually plucked that thorn. In 1895, Wilde was a well-known playwright who had just produced *The Importance of Being Earnest*, when the Marquess of Queensbury denounced him as a homosexual. Queensbury had left a calling card at Wilde's club with the words: 'For Oscar Wilde, posing Somdomite [*sic*]'. Wilde had been in a physical relationship with the marquess's son for four years. Even so, he sued the marquess for criminal libel. Against a backdrop of media hysteria, Queensbury's lawyers presented Wilde as a lecherous older man.

Wilde gave up the libel case once he was informed of a list of male prostitutes who had been called to testify against him. He was arrested and sentenced to two years of hard labour. Here's a thought: on some level, did Wilde sue for libel knowing full well that he would lose but that the truth would come to light? Was hard labour preferable to the aching thorn of the secret in his side?

I was eight years old when I opened the door to my parents' bedroom to find my dad sitting idly in a chair, sideways-on and facing the wall, leaves of foil knotted through his long, brown-blond hair. I remember specks of white goo oozing from the silver. That he was dyeing his hair meant nothing to my childish mind. But I'll never forget the look of terror in the eyes of my father – who was usually a picture of calm – when he saw me peer behind the door. Sunlight from a window at the back of the room silhouetted my father's face, igniting some of the folds in the foil that scaled his crown. 'No, don't look at me!' he bellowed.

Medusa on fire still burns peroxide-white in my retinas today. Although I didn't understand that to which I bore unwitting witness, and although the act itself was trivial, I knew I had walked in on something I wasn't supposed to see: a secret. And that was enough for it to sear into my forever memory.

During my work as an interviewer, I've crossed paths with such dramatic secrets as extramarital affairs, incest, rape, substance abuse, abortion and infertility. But while the darkest and most stigmatizing secrets are the ones that inflict the most psychological damage on their keepers, a measure of the strength of secrecy lies in its ability to elevate the 'commonest thing' to the sublime. Under the spectre of secrecy, even something as humdrum as hair dye can leave a lasting impression.

I imagine some of your first memories relate to secrecy: snippets you weren't supposed to see. You'll have forgotten all sorts of big occasions, but may well remember some equivalent to the time I walked in on my grandma urinating.

As long as I can remember, I've always been stricken with a terrible memory. So many moments I wish I could recall lie just beyond my grasp, lost to time. But this memory stands out from before the hair dye. I was about five when I opened the bathroom door and it thudded against my grandma's leg. She wasn't massive or anything; it was just a small bathroom. I saw little more than a pale and knobbly knee, and its elderly owner's fretted face.

I carry these two childhood memories with me like phantoms. Of course, as far as phantoms go, they're more *Casper the Friendly Ghost* than *Poltergeist*. But I still find it remarkable that such mundane events take pride of place on the mantelpiece of memory.

The two stories differ in their secret intensity. My dad was doing something less routine for a man of his age and time: getting highlights in his hair. This was unbecoming of a man and a father born in the 1950s. Like Dorian Gray, he wanted to stay young.

Although I don't believe it was enough for my father to grow ugly on the inside, his reaction speaks of some degree of inner turmoil. He was transgressing societal expectations, so his hair dyeing was a secret. This was a moral secret because it was unusual for a man to do. It was a relational secret because he hid it from his children. And it was an aspirational secret, because he presumably wanted to present a younger image at work.

Now it's thirty years later, and it's in a book. Hi, Dad. But what of my grandma? How does her situation differ from that of my father? Is urinating not a simple act of privacy, rather than secrecy? Really, it'd be more worthy of secret-hood if someone *never* urinated. That would be strange, and they'd likely want to actively hide it, so as not to invite the attention of the world's press.

Pretty quickly, it became obvious to me that secrets are only one mechanism through which we withhold information. Someone who refuses to share their bathroom habits isn't being secretive; they're being reasonably private.

To really understand secrecy, then, I realized that I'd have to grasp what it is not: *privacy*.

As I took a look through the peephole of privacy, I hoped to find out what we're really like away from prying eyes. But first, what *is* privacy? Professor of Psychology at the University of Notre Dame, Anita E. Kelly, writes that privacy suggests an expectation that your information be 'free from unsanctioned intrusion'. You expect privacy while getting dressed or simply relaxing alone at home, though these are not secret acts.

Tom Frijns, a psychology lecturer at Utrecht University, has written extensively about the line between privacy and secrecy. He explains: 'Privacy protects morally neutral information that is accepted or valued by society, whereas secrecy protects information that is morally negative and condemned by society.' Many psychologists agree that it is the relevance of the information to outsiders – as well as the degree to which it subverts a society's morals – that turns something private into secret.

Privacy entails your family life, your sex life (providing it's societally typical), and how often you brush your teeth. These matters become secret – while also remaining private – when they challenge expectations. For example, it would best be kept secret if you *never* brushed your teeth (although Scientology leader L. Ron Hubbard's yellow, rotten teeth are testament to the difficulty of keeping his disdain for the dentist secret).

I've always been fascinated by the line between the taboo and the conventional. For instance, none of us like to think of our parents having sex. As teenagers, we want to imagine they only did it once for our creation. Any siblings can be explained by secret adoption. As long as that option is on the table (did they do it there, too?), the possibility remains – however slight – that your parents never had sex outside of your conception.

At the beginning of the infamous 'The Contest' episode of *Seinfeld*, Jerry explains it'd be great news to find out he were adopted because 'technically, it's possible that my mother and my father are really just really great friends. I mean, sex is great, but you don't want to think that your whole life began because somebody maybe had a little too much wine with dinner.'

Seinfeld is right that you don't want to think of your parents getting steamy for your procreation. But as you get older, a funny thing happens. The idea that your parents *never* have sex becomes terribly sad. We still don't want to envisage the act itself. It's just that our society decrees that a sexless marriage is *atypical* and the marker of a loveless relationship. This is of course not true – couples vary hugely. But it is why sex for a couple is closer to privacy than secrecy. We *expect* couples to have a sexual relationship, even though we don't talk about it. If a couple *stops* having sex, something that was merely private begins to overlap with secrecy. It becomes gossip-worthy.

Think of a man who makes love every night to a sex doll called Margery. This is irrelevant to the rest of us. It is private, and should be 'free from unsanctioned intrusion'. So why does it feel like a secret? What separates privacy and secrecy is the perceived acceptance or rejection by society. If sex dolls, as some futurists suggest, become more lifelike and universal, they might become less subversive and, therefore, less secret-worthy. For now, keep Margery to yourself.

This is also why the fact a couple *has* sex isn't a secret, but the fact a couple *never* has sex is. We imagine our friends would judge us, however unfairly, if they found out we weren't having sex. This is why we lie about how often we're at it. We think that if we are seen to be having it more often, we'll be deemed a well-matched couple, much like the ones we see on TV. The problem is: if we all lie, and believe each other's lies, we create expectations that can never be met. That spells shame, misery and relational turmoil all around. Go us!

Social media is rife with this kind of deception. One of my podcast listeners recently told me she was deleting Instagram because it was full of happy couples and their babies. She was struggling to conceive. This unhappy fact is private, but also a secret. It's the kind of thing that sparks titillated whispers behind backs. My friend wouldn't post it on Instagram, and neither would many others in her situation, because they fear the judgement, pity or schadenfreude of their picture-perfect public.

The result is that the app gives off the impression that everyone else is swimming in babies. A simple Google search will show you that at least 10 per cent of women struggle getting or staying pregnant. Moreover, if you ever go to the house of a couple with a new baby in real life, you can see they're typically far from the postcard-pretty Insta portrayal. They're miserable and exhausted. In fact, a childhood acquaintance of mine is now a professional Insta mum with 100,000 followers whose account is bursting with smiling photos of her husband and their kids. Turns out the dad was schtupping his male hairdresser. But that wouldn't make for a family-friendly portrait on the socials, would it? What would the brands say?

In any case, the hypothetical sexless couple and my listener who can't have children still have the right to a lack of intrusion. These *are* private matters. It's just that they're – unfairly – also shrouded in secrecy: they're private secrets. These two are often in cahoots. An affair is still private, because each person has the right to a lack of incursion from without. Yet, it is also a secret – a whopper at that – because it is relevant to outsiders: harmed partners, potential offspring and friends. It makes for great gossip, because it runs counter to the morals of the time.

Zack Weiner, twenty-six, had a bright career ahead of him, as he ran for Manhattan City Council. Then, one day in 2021, he woke to find the *New York Post* had broken a story featuring a video of him being whipped by a dominatrix. Why did the newspaper run the article? Was he not entitled to privacy? Around the same time in the UK, politician Matt Hancock was caught cheating on his wife, after the CCTV footage of the act was leaked to the press. Was this too not a private matter? Or was the public interest too great? The fact he was breaking his own Covid lockdown social-distancing laws to engage in the affair didn't help his cause. Newspapers were keen to stress this – as well as the fact that his mistress worked for him, and her salary was paid by taxpayers' money.

This battle between what is private and what is relevant to the public is at the heart of an ongoing war between the press and its protagonists. Things don't get much clearer in media law. Look at Article 8 of the European Convention on Human Rights: everyone has the right to respect 'for his private and family life, his home and his correspondence.' That seems to be pretty clear, but jump down a couple of points to Article 10, the right to one's 'freedom of expression . . . to receive and impart information', and things get murky. Journalists often interpret the latter as a right to publish any private information they find out about someone. The trick is to find a way to justify it 'in the public interest'. They're allowed to print certain 'private secrets', then, but not matters that are purely private.

To get a better grip on privacy and satiate my own curiosity, I wanted to find out what others were like at home. Privacy at home is a modern luxury in the developed world, which resulted from larger houses. Centuries ago, most families shared a solitary room. Often, they lived in that room with other families. Children were accustomed to listening to – even witnessing – their parents having sex. Yep, pretty revolting. Corridors weren't even installed in most homes until the nineteenth century. Many of today's homes provide space for us to be ourselves, and I figured an insight into what we get up to alone might help us to be more forgiving of our own ugly-but-natural traits.

I sent out a survey about secret habits to my friends on social media and my podcast listeners. You'll have to take it with a pinch of salt, because it was taken from a select demographic: my friends and listeners. Still, there's a fair amount of diversity across ethnicity, age groups and beliefs in there, so it is somewhat reflective of society. The survey found that we are not the people we say we are.

This was a relief to me, because it meant I am far from the only one whose private self lives in the shameful shadow of its public persona. The results felt like an earthy antidote to the polished portrayals of social media. And that's important, because a huge amount of shame is caused by the discrepancy between the self that we present to the world and the flatulent, ridiculous identity we leave at home.

For that reason, I tried to look at some of the grosser and more innocuous private secrets that other, more reputable surveys might avoid. From my 400 responses, 67 per cent confessed they were keeping a secret right then. An additional 11 per cent later admitted that they realized during the survey that they did indeed have at least one secret. Frustratingly, 30 per cent of respondents wrote that they were keeping secrets from my secret test. They gave various reasons for this:

'If I admit to them then that makes them true.'

'My other secrets are too dark to share.'

'Trust no one.'

'Because you're too nice and I think you'd rather not read my filth.'

'Too traumatic/difficult to admit even for an anonymous survey.'

My survey found that 90 per cent said they pick their noses at least very occasionally, with one in ten ticking the 'surprisingly excessive' box. When I told a friend about my survey, he opened up about his own shameful story that has plagued him. He was twelve years old and sitting in the back of a car, in the middle of a nose dig. The car was in slow traffic, and when he turned to look out of the window, he noticed a group of girls had been walking alongside the car, laughing at him. It has scarred him for twenty years. But, had he known the 90 per cent figure – if we all knew a little more about what the other does in their private life – he might have been able to laugh it off.

Moving on to less revolting, but perhaps more painful secrets: more than a third of respondents in relationships said they had cheated either emotionally or physically on their current partners. The relatively high figure makes for depressing reading: if you have always been faithful, then it's mathematically plausible your other half has not. As for masturbation, it probably comes as no surprise to men that 40 per cent of you practise the art at least once a day. More than one in ten men do so multiple times per day. In fact, of all the men questioned, just two limit their self-affection to 'once or twice a month', and one man selected 'never'. That respondent admitted in a later question on his form that he had kept secrets from the survey. He also wrote that his 'biggest or darkest secret' was that he 'used to rub his face on page forty-nine of every book he owned, or borrowed'.

This produced something of a moral quandary for me. A family member told me he had filled out the form. Although it was anonymous, I can't avoid knowing that I have unwittingly read about his masturbation habits – just without realizing which specific form was his. But, since 99 per cent of the male respondents confessed that they did so fairly regularly, it's hard to continue suspending my disbelief that said family member lives in some sort of cartoonish 'family man' sphere outside of the ugliness of porn and masturbation. With the right amount of cognitive dissonance, I could force myself to believe he could be the one respondent who never does the deed . . . but that would mean he rubs his face in book pages. I've made a mental note to avoid books and magazines in his house, because in the folds of the forty-ninth pages lie answers I'd rather not know.

To be honest, having this knowledge confirmed wouldn't be the worst thing in the world, because our society tends to put this down to 'boys being boys', even in polite conversation. Male friends of mine might reference their naughty habit in the gaps between words in an explanation for why they're late to meet me, or why they're relieved their partner has left the house for the afternoon. What is talked about less, at least from my naive male perspective, is how often women do it.

The popular women's magazine *Glamour* ran its own survey, finding 91 per cent of women masturbate, while more than one third do so once or twice a week. Interestingly, the author of the article, Marie-Claire Chappet, writes, 'Clearly, a majority of you view masturbating – not [as] a sordid sexual secret – but as a vital part of your mental and physical well-being. Why then, do 53% of you feel uncomfortable discussing it?' Again, we've stumbled along a blurred line between secrecy and privacy. I think these stats might surprise a lot of men (especially the boyfriends), and, according to writer and activist Nimko Ali, women too.

In her book, *What We're Told Not to Talk About* (2019), she writes: 'For centuries, women have known little about or been banned from understanding how this part of their body works. They have either whispered tiny bits of fanny information or, like my relatives, spoken in code. Everything to do with "down there" is spoken of in whispers and shrouded in secrecy and shame.' She writes about how the full anatomy of the clitoris was only properly discovered by Australian urologist Helen O'Connell as recently as 1998. 'Aside from masturbation being natural and healthy,' writes Nimko, 'it teaches girls what they like sexually.'

For women like Nimko, masturbation is even more taboo and complex. She is a survivor of Female Genital Mutilation (FGM). She writes of women's sexuality and genitals inspiring 'fear, terror, shame and pleasure'. This is an example of how a patriarchal or religious society can influence what lies within the boundaries of an acceptable private act . . . and, conversely, what is seen as secret sin. That a man indulges in self-love is privacy with a dash of secrecy. That a woman does so is the reverse. Ali adds, 'I can almost feel the heat from your face as you read this. It's not very British to talk about fannies, it's not very polite; in fact, it's downright rude. But . . . all women have a relationship with their vagina.'

Things do seem to be changing, as more publications and individuals write and talk openly about female masturbation. *Bustle* ran an article about research by sex toy organization TENGA, which found that women masturbate on average about eight times per month, while men do so fifteen times. Another survey by *Quartz India* found that 30 per cent of women in India masturbate daily. Since vibrators are not always readily available there, many use old Nokia phones as capable alternatives.

We rely on surveys about secrets to find out more about societally acceptable behaviour that should simply be private. We should be able to do whatever we want in our own private time – without shame – providing it doesn't affect others. Yet, we feel the burning glow of shame. I don't suggest we start nose-picking and masturbating in public. But perhaps more open and honest dialogue about the naughty and icky things we do at home could relieve some of that burden, and relieve simply private matters from the heavy cloak of secrecy.

My investigation into the sphere of privacy helped me get a better grasp of what secrecy is, and what it is *not*. But I came to realize that secrets have another unkind bedfellow for whom they are often mistaken: lies.

*

It's 1940, and you are harbouring a Jew from the Nazis. You are putting your life at risk for the sake of another. But what's this? A Nazi is at your door, and he is asking if there is a Jew in your attic. For the purposes of this hypothetical scenario, he is not a very insistent Nazi. If you say no, he'll walk off and go about his other Nazi business. Surely, in this situation, it's acceptable to lie?

Not if you're a truth purist. For instance, the neuroscientist Sam Harris believes that it is never OK to lie. As a Jew, I make a note not to turn to Harris (also a Jew) when the Gestapo come calling. 'Lying is the royal road to chaos,' he writes, in a short book called *Lying* (2013). He writes of a professor who had a profound impact on him when he was at university: 'What was so fascinating about this seminar was how difficult it was to find examples of virtuous lies that could withstand Professor Howard's scrutiny. Even with Nazis at the door and Anne Frank in the attic, Howard always seemed to find truths worth telling and paths to even greater catastrophe that could be opened by lying.'

Harris doesn't elaborate on the truths found by his old professor, so we'll need to get into philosophy for the argument as to why lying to the Nazis is wrong. But I don't want to delve too deeply into lies before looking at how they overlap with secrecy. A secret isn't necessarily a lie, but all lies involve secrets in some way. They encompass the concealment of some truth. So where do the two concepts differ? As with privacy-secrecy, it's a question of nuance, intent and subjectivity, rather than an exact science.

Lies are more active than secrets. They involve what psychologists Lane and Wegner call an 'act of commission', as opposed to a secret, which is an act of 'omission'. The psychologist Bella DePaulo writes of deception: 'A truth is secreted away, and an imposter unleashed in its place.' Lies are often falsehoods that are told to protect a secret. They are the public face of a shameful secret; the polished red skin veiling the venom within the apple. Secrecy expert Tom Frijns cites an example: 'An impotent man may conceal his ineptitude and feign sexual prowess by spinning tales of his sexual escapades.' Here, impotence is the secret. But the stories of sexual prowess are the lies that give it credence.

We keep a lot of secrets. And to cover them, we lie a lot. College students lie to 38 per cent of the people in their lives, according to a 1996 study in a paper called 'Lying in Everyday Life'. It makes you think: what's the point in discussing anything? I remember an old friend at university who had us all believe he'd been a heroin addict and pill popper in his teenage years. A year later, a childhood friend of his came to visit, and revealed this was an utter fabrication. Another common lie I heard back then from fellow students (including the aforementioned) was, 'I was accepted by Oxford and Cambridge, but . . .' This was clearly designed to imply that they were smarter than the rest of us, but humble enough to decline the intellectual pomp of Oxbridge.

One survey of 1,000 Americans by Professor Timothy R. Levine found that almost half of all lies are told by just 5 per cent of people. That means that some of us are prolific liars. Still, a *Reader's Digest* poll from 2004 found that 93 per cent of 2,861 readers admitted to one or more acts of dishonesty at school or work. And 96 per cent reported being dishonest with family and friends.

A lie can be necessary: a means of guarding a secret. Had they been asked publicly about their various secrets, the respondents in my survey might have been forced to lie. It might have been in their interest to do so. For example, one in five parents answered that they like or love one of their children more than another. In this case, they should never have to lie to keep that secret, providing nobody asks them directly. But, if asked straight out, you'd imagine they would have to lie.

Ten per cent of my respondents admitted to posting online

about causes they didn't care about because it made them look good. These deceitful posts give off false impressions about users' intelligence, beauty or political leanings (33 per cent admitted to feeling they had to hide their political beliefs). One third of participants admitted keeping secrets from the secret survey. Since many of the questions were multiple choice, the survey didn't allow for a simple 'omission' for secrecy. This means that respondents deliberately clicked a different answer: an act of commission. They lied. This is understandable. But there are many reasons to tell the truth, even if it appears to be the rougher path.

Sam Harris tells a story about a close friend whose mother contracted MS in her late thirties. The doctor lied, informing her she didn't have it, while telling her husband the truth. This may seem absurd, but it was surprisingly common just a few decades ago to leave a woman in the dark about her own medical condition. The mother in Harris's story looked up her own symptoms and realized she did indeed have the disease. She kept that to herself. Husband and wife spent a year without revealing the secret to one another, each bearing the burden alone. Harris's friend writes: 'My brother found out accidentally about a year later, when my mother had breast cancer surgery. The surgeon walked into the room and essentially said, "This won't affect the MS."

'My brother said, "What MS?" I think it was a couple more years before anyone told me or my sister about Mom's MS . . . Rather than feeling grateful and protected, I felt sadness that we hadn't come together as a family to face her illness and support each other.

'My mother never told her mother about the MS, which meant that none of us could tell friends and family, for fear that her mother would find out. She didn't want to hurt her mother. I think she deprived herself of the opportunity to have a closer relationship with her mother.'

This is a common deception: a white lie meant to protect others from hearing about an illness. When somebody in a family or friendship circle becomes ill, the first thought is often: 'OK, how can we prevent so-and-so from finding out.' I wonder if this is really more about feeling like an active protector, rather than a helpless victim. In deciding who should be privy to the bad news, you're able to exert some power over a situation that is otherwise out of your hands. This is very different from the authoritarian religions and regimes of the first chapter, but I'm reminded of that link between secrets and control. In these cases, it seems that telling the truth about an illness and relinquishing your control over your environment – while feeling more painful in the first instance – might well be a better course in the long run. It's ripping the Band-Aid off.

However, there is also an argument for keeping secret the truth about an illness from a patient. The nocebo effect – the opposite of placebo – has shown that patients' health can deteriorate rapidly once given negative news. The mother of my stepmother died recently of a very quick and aggressive cancer. It was a shock, as she was relatively young. My stepmother blames doctors for her rapid decline. She wishes they hadn't revealed to her mother the extent of her illness.

So, what about that Nazi at the door? The Band-Aid might be ripped off by the confession of truth about who you are harbouring, but it means a torturous death, not only for the person you're hiding, but for you and your family too. Surely, in this scenario, it's best to lie?

In the late eighteenth century, a rivalry developed between French philosopher Benjamin Constant and his German adversary Immanuel Kant. It has not escaped my attention that the latter has a funny last name, and even more so when following on from his rival Constant. Kant had been writing about something called a 'categorical imperative'. It stipulates rules that have intrinsic moral value in all situations, and don't depend on external factors.

One of his untouchable rules was that it is never right to lie.

Constant thought this absurd, and to show as much, brought up the example of being asked by a murderer to reveal the secret location of their prey. 'No one has a right to a truth which injures others,' he wrote. Surely, this showed a flaw in Kant's stance on truth? Not one to be deterred, Kant performed impressive mental gymnastics to prove his point:

> After you have honestly answered the murderer's question as to whether this intended victim is at home, it may be that [the intended victim] has slipped out so that he does not come in the way of the murderer, and thus that the murder may not be committed. But if you had lied and said [the intended victim] was not at home when he had really gone out without your knowing it, and if the murderer had then met him as he went away and murdered him, you might justly be accused as the cause of his death.

By Kantian logic, you shouldn't lie to the murderer (or Nazi, in the concept's modern incarnation) because it'll be your fault if the attacker leaves and later happens upon the person you were harbouring, who may have escaped from your house without you realizing. You might say this is a case of the philosopher living up to his surname.

I should add that there is more to Kant's reasoning. He is more interested in what is right, moral and lawful than what would be the best thing to do for you and the intended victim. But it doesn't compute, by our modern standards of morality. In fact, we kind of like liars, if the movie characters we fall in love with are anything to go by. Think of most heist movies, and the deceitful-but-loveable characters played by our Hollywood heroes. Think of Leonardo DiCaprio's *Catch Me If You Can*, based on the real-life story of Frank Abagnale, a con man who falsified at least eight identities, including those of an airline pilot, a physician, and a lawyer. We even enjoy being conned in the movie into falling for the character.

I once asked a psychopath I was interviewing whether she could enjoy movies, given she's unable to empathize with characters the way we do. She laughed: 'You may think that what you're doing watching a movie is empathizing. But actually, you're being manipulated . . . a really great example of this is horror. You can be scared, and there's not a character who is scared. You're not empathizing. You actually are just scared of the situation.' Her favourite film is Alfred Hitchcock's *Vertigo*, 'because the viewer is totally manipulated'. She laughed maniacally. 'You think the movie is about one thing . . . but there's a twist!' She appreciates how the director screws with us, and she believes that on some level, we appreciate it too. It's why we love magicians: we enjoy being deceived.

This doesn't mean that we necessarily want to befriend someone like Abagnale or even Hitchcock in real life. But it might suggest that we champion those who lie and break social conventions for good reasons. You can imagine Kant sulking outside the cinema, just after DiCaprio's slippery character is spared jail for a cushy FBI job, or as *Vertigo* flips on its head.

Even Sam Harris admits, despite earlier praise of his Kant-aligned professor, that 'though it has the obvious virtue of clarity, never tell a lie, in practice this rule can produce behaviour that only a psychopath might endorse.' He concludes, 'I cannot see any reason to take Kant seriously on this point. However, this does not mean that lying is easily justified. Even as a means to ward off violence, lying often closes the door to acts of honest communication that may be more effective.'

With his depictions of families torn apart by lies, Sam Harris makes a compelling case for airing the truth. Equally, my survey taught me about how much we are all hiding, another point in favour of revealing the truth. That said, revealing these things might make our lives worse. I don't follow Kant's logic. I'm ashamed to admit I can't see myself harbouring anyone if it might get me killed. Actually, I'm not ashamed, because I think that's quite a reasonable and common response. And who knows? Perhaps I'd rise to the occasion. If so, I certainly wouldn't admit to a Nazi that I had been harbouring an enemy of the state. I also wouldn't recommend to Melissa, who killed her attacker in an alleyway, that she should tell the truth publicly, nor do I think that the sixty-year-old Instagrammer Kamilla should be frank with her husband about the dick pics, even if I can see how some good might come from honest communication about their marriage. I came into this investigation with the naive belief that secrets and lies were for other people. Now, I'm starting to see how wrapped up in the pair I might be.

One of the most contentious questions around lies is whether or not to use them on your children. I know this is a divisive issue, because philosopher Tim Urban of the 'Wait But Why' blog posted on social media: 'Did you/will you tell your real or hypothetical kids that Santa is real?' More than 11,000 of his followers voted in the first twenty-four hours, with 41 per cent picking 'Yes' and 38 per cent 'No'. The remaining 21 per cent selected, 'I'm torn'. We really don't know how to feel about lying to or withholding information from our kids.

Typical secrets we keep from our children 'for their own sake' include: pretending a certain shop or activity is closed today so that we don't have to explain why we're not taking them to it; that we'll turn the car round right now if they don't start behaving; and that we'll leave them in the playground for ever if they don't leave with us right now. And then there's: 'Father Christmas just called, and said he won't come this year unless you go to bed now!'

A 2014 study found that parents lie to kids for several reasons, such as: to control their emotions; to control their behaviour; to get them to cooperate; to avoid having to explain complicated concepts. Many parents might start off by wanting to bring up their children with scrupulous honesty. However, as the tantrums pile up and begin to wear you down, shrouding truth in secrecy becomes more and more appealing.

Yet, even little slices of dishonesty can have lasting negative effects on your kids. Recent research in Singapore's Nanyang Technological University shows that children who were lied to often were more likely to lie to their parents as adults. It's a cycle. Those who are lied to also find certain psychological and social challenges more difficult. And they are, on average, more selfish, and experience higher levels of guilt and shame. With this in mind, parents are advised to try explaining to their kids the real reasons they have to leave the playground, or whatever it might be. Of course, children are not always receptive to logical explanations.

Parenting blogger Elisa Cinelli believes we should tell the truth, even if that means tantrums. She writes, 'A little protest is not the end of the world. But maybe, a kid who grows up dishonest feels like it is.' Cinelli suggests that 'investing in honesty' will 'pay off when your teenager comes to you with hard truths, and you can guide them with love'. She believes it's worth enduring a tantrum if it means your kids won't turn into manipulative psychopaths. This philosophy, though noble, is basically impossible to carry out. I've been to the houses of friends and family members with small children. Sometimes, it's eat or be eaten. Lie, or be screamed at.

Despite the research, we know anecdotally that most of us were lied to many times as children. And, for the most part, we function OK. The research is also unclear as to cause and correlation. Were participants worse at adjusting to society because of lies by their parents? Or because parents who felt it necessary to engage in more egregious lies were part of households with deeper problems? Or, were those who remembered more of the lies (and noted them down in the experiment) simply a touch more rancorous and ill-adjusted on average as adults than others?

Perhaps it's about moderation. You might have to lie and keep secrets enough to get you through the day when the screaming and hysteria that make up child-rearing just won't stop. There is, of course, a world of difference between lying to suggest you're not afraid of the dark or spiders (to protect your kids from fear), and lying by promising sweets as a reward for doing a chore – with no intention of delivering. The latter might indeed harm the child and their perception of honesty.

Psychology professor Robert Feldman, who has studied lying in depth, is concerned about that second kind of lying. He believes that while Santa is a belief that children grow out of, *real* deception is something they can grow *into*.

There are also unnecessary lies in the presence of your children, in cases where the truth wouldn't provoke a tantrum or bring them harm. Journalist Judi Ketteler writes in *Time* about a moment of deception in a shop with her daughter. 'When I told the cashier that I didn't have an email address when she asked for one, my daughter gave me the side eye. That's when I realized I was teaching her how to swat off annoyances with little lies. (I now simply say, in a pleasant voice, "I don't want to give you an email right now.")' Ketteler cites etiquette expert Lizzie Post: 'We always think we need a story that justifies how we feel.' Perhaps, then, we can still tell the big lies – the ones that really do appear to protect our kids from harm (I can almost hear truth obsessive Immanuel Kant spinning in his grave) – and put honesty ahead of inconsequential concerns about offending people we don't know.

There is a school of thought that lying to our children can have positive effects. Editor of the *Greater Good* magazine Jeremy Adam Smith writes, 'We actually coach [our children] to lie, as when we ask them to express delight at tube socks from Aunt Judy or Uncle Bob's not-so-delicious beef stew.' These kinds of white lies are known by scientists as 'prosocial lies'. They are for the benefit of others, rather than ourselves. Kids learn to lie at about three years old, and, by five, they tend to be at it all the time to avoid chores and get away with misbehaving. It's from age seven to eleven that they begin to tell those prosocial (or selfless) lies for the benefit or protection of others. They are moved to do so by strong feelings of empathy and compassion. It's pleasing to learn this about children, because they can appear a little sociopathic from afar.

So, what of Santa? We tell children the legends of Father Christmas, the Tooth Fairy and the Easter Bunny to fill their world with wonder, and protect them from bleak truths – that magic isn't real. Those of us who were lucky enough to have indulged in such fantasies may have fond memories of that protected early stage. Those memories sit with us as adults like a warm, nostalgic embrace. And we want our children to feel that same way, if only for a little while.

We know on some level that it is wrong to lie, particularly to those we care about. Father Christmas is a strange kind of deception, too, because it's one we know will be uncovered sooner or later. We want our children to believe us wholeheartedly when we speak to them of the magic of Father Christmas. And yet, with each passing year, the ruse becomes a little stranger. If they still believe our lie at ten years old, then we might start to be concerned. If they still believe at fifteen, we might send them to a doctor. It's a lie that we know – and hope – will be found out. But this little white lie has become a societal expectation. It's one we're not – in any direct way – punished for by our offspring.

That said, I remember an argument I had with my half-sister when she was about seven, and I was twenty-five. I asked her if she was excited about Father Christmas, and she broke down in tears. 'I know you made him up! You're a liar! You're *all* lying to me!' she screamed in a frenzy. The funny thing is, just one year later, she was back to apparently believing in Father Christmas, as she presented me with an exhaustive list of gifts for the bearded sleigh rider to procure for her. At first, I wondered if this was about cognitive dissonance; perhaps she got herself into a state of mind where it was too painful to believe he didn't exist. But I soon realized she had simply become old and wise enough to know how to leverage a made-up belief in a made-up Father Christmas to get bigger and better presents. And those were very much real.

Lies all contain traces of secrecy. Father Christmas is a prosocial lie we tell our kids. It masks the secret that he isn't real. My sister aside, children often react well (at least, long-term) to learning that secret. The reactions of the people to whom we confess are essential. We are far less likely to reveal a secret if we feel as if it will spark a negative response. And for good reason, too.

The psychologist Anita E. Kelly cites as an example Michael Jackson's failure to admit – after settling in court – to sexual abuse with a minor. If he admitted what he did, it would compel the confidants (all of us) to make a moral choice when choosing to listen to his music. Years after his death, the general consensus is that Jackson was a child abuser (since initially writing this, I've come to realize there's a large and fiercely passionate subculture of Jackson fans who'll write me angry emails demanding I do my research before writing smears – and to those people, I say: 'Jacko was innocent, please don't send me hate mail'). Yet, because he didn't confess, it's less concrete – we find it a little easier to put it out of our minds when 'Billie Jean' comes on. Another example provided by Kelly is Hillary Clinton's decision not to confess that she knew about her husband Bill's affair, because her lack of intervention to support the young intern Monica Lewinsky might have made her seem complicit, and would have elicited a negative response to her.

We'll go on to look at the health benefits that come from revealing secrets. But they amount to little, if the secret is told to an 'indiscreet, judgemental, or rejecting confidant'. Revealing the truth makes confessors more physiologically relaxed, despite dire consequences that arise from it, such as prison time from admitting to a crime. But even one of the worst serial killers of all time, Edmund Kemper, found it hard to confess to a group of confidants – police officers – who responded negatively: 'I just talk, getting the thing out, and later on it hits me. I spent the whole afternoon in there trying to decide whether I was gonna climb the bars and jump off or hang myself.'

Another problem with revealing intimate information about yourself to others is that most people are terrible secret-keepers. In fact, we're dreadful, particularly when it comes to keeping someone else's secret. Studies by psychologists Christophe and Rime (1997) found that we reveal the secrets of others in up to 78 per cent of cases. This was despite 85 per cent of participants considering themselves 'intimates' of the people whose secrets they gave away. But you can trust your close friends with really important secrets, right? Wrong. The more 'emotionally intense' your secret, the *more* your friends spread them. What's more, they typically tell more than two other people about your secret. If you want to stop your secret from spreading, you'd do well not to share it with anyone.

Even if your confidant is a good listener and will keep your secret until their dying day, you always run the risk that they will respond negatively. Victims of trauma, writes Anita E. Kelly, 'fear that they will burden the listener, and are likely to receive unsatisfactory responses'. There are many reasons why trauma victims receive unsatisfactory answers, including: listeners might not be trained to respond appropriately, they might find it too difficult to hear about trauma, or the situation might even trigger difficult memories of similar occurrences in their own lives.

A fear of burdening others and receiving negative reactions is why Madeleine Black stopped talking.

It wasn't just her words and her intake of food that stopped. Madeleine also stopped thinking. Her mind 'shut off the trauma', and now, she can hardly remember anything else that happened around the time of the rape. The attack had lasting effects. After an adolescence spent in and out of a psychiatric ward where nobody asked her about her secret, she suffered from bulimia, PTSD and depression. With time, she suppressed the symptoms enough to marry and raise a family. But the secret gnawed at her. It caused her to act out in what she describes as obsessive and controlling ways.

Keeping the secret inside, she tells me, was 'like walking through treacle'. She spent years 'pushing it down, pushing it down to keep up with the pretence. It was like wearing a mask. It was exhausting pretending to be this person that you're not.'

Her life didn't really change until she was fifty. That's when she decided to confront things head-on, and talk about her secret. 'What I had to do was to face all of what was done to me.' She told her husband and parents the truth. Her parents called the friend, who denied all knowledge of the rape. Madeleine never saw her again. But Madeleine's family and friends rallied around her. Their reaction made her feel better.

Psychologist James W. Pennebaker advises that 'confronting traumatic experiences through disclosure is physically beneficial'. And Madeleine attained a new lease of life through the lifting of her secret. Now, she regularly gives interviews about her secret, and has even hosted a TED Talk. When she got a book deal for her memoir, she initially wanted to hold back on the details, such was the shame involved in her trauma. Her editor suggested she only partially disclose what happened. After giving it some thought, she replied, 'If I'm going to tell my story, then I'll tell my story. I need to paint a true picture of what violent rape looks like.' There was a survey in the publishing office: 'Should she or shouldn't she publish all the details?' What they decided was: they would put everything on the table – with a warning at the beginning of the chapter. When I interviewed Madeleine, she told me: 'Nothing is off limits.'

It is important to point out that the trauma from the rape itself – as well as the keeping of the secret – is a huge factor in Madeleine's mental and physical ailments. Nevertheless, when Madeleine was finally able to tell her family, all those decades later, she felt better. With a lot of time and talking, she came to be able to stand in the same room as men without feeling uncomfortable, and even to work as a counsellor for men who have been abused. Once she disclosed her traumatic secret to her kids, a weight was lifted, and she no longer felt the need to control every aspect of their world. Talking about her secret was cathartic. 'I'm really, really OK now. It really doesn't impact on my life in any way. If anything, I think I have post-traumatic growth.'

For decades, Madeleine's secret prevented her from recovery. Its revelation was like the release of that thorn in Oscar Wilde's side. But what can the keeping of secrets really do to your body and mind? And how bad can it get?

3

SECRETS, BODY AND MIND

Chris Atkins is a journalist and documentary maker who became known in the 2000s for shining a light on social and financial inequalities. His first feature film, *Taking Liberties* (2007), criticized former prime minister Tony Blair's government for the way it had undermined civil liberties since the war on terror. Such was his fervour to expose wrongdoings that he was even held under anti-terror laws after trying to speak to the home secretary at a Labour Party conference. The resulting documentary was nominated for a BAFTA.

In the years that followed, Chris – who I later came to meet – championed social causes in documentaries that exposed corruption and financial coercion. No one was safe: celebrities selling fake stories to the press, journalists spying on famous people, celebrity publicist Max Clifford, Live Aid charity rock star Bob Geldof, Brexit-supporting political party UKIP, and even the cast of British soap opera *Coronation Street*. He used undercover reporting techniques, with hidden cameras and microphones, to catch moral transgressors red-handed.

Chris's career was blossoming. He was the face of moral virtue and decency, fighting the good fight against corporations, newspapers and celebrities on behalf of the little person. And then, in

2016, it all came crashing down. Chris was sentenced to five years in prison for large-scale tax fraud. It was exactly the kind of double standard that Chris had been exposing in others.

Undeterred by his fall from the ramparts of justice, he saw his spell in Wandsworth Prison as a social experiment. He decided he would document what happens when a self-described middle-class leftie liberal goes to prison. Halfway between hysterical and tragic, his memoir, *A Bit of a Stretch* (2020), documents the Kafka-esque madness of the prison system, and the camaraderie of the prisoners of different classes and backgrounds, who bond over their shared helplessness. Prisoners are able to take up jobs, which get them out of their cell, help to pass the time, and look good on their records, helping them apply to move cells or get out early on good behaviour. By far the most important – and most fearsome – job, Chris found, is that of the Listener.

The Listener Scheme was initially introduced at HMP Swansea in 1991, and is now a common practice in every prison in the UK and the Republic of Ireland. Around 1,500 Listeners attend to more than 50,000 requests from Callers (also prisoners) each year. On completion of training by Samaritans and other prison volunteers, Listeners receive certificates, and offer support around the clock.

Initially, Chris became a Listener because it helped him move into a cushier cell. However, he soon found the process profound and, at times, overwhelming. There was a month of intensive training, when he would go along with other Listeners to see Callers who needed to talk. It was a way for prisoners – many of whom were big and burly – to share their secret innermost thoughts and worries with a kind and willing soul. It was dangerous work. Callers sometimes physically attacked Listeners. Chris tells of arriving to find a 'large, agitated prisoner who announced that he hadn't taken his antipsychotic medication'. Another Listener recounts being stuck alone in a locked cell for hours with a 'big', 'aggressive' Caller, after a riot had broken out outside the Listener Suite.

More concerning was the psychological toll. 'The listening itself was traumatizing,' Chris explains. 'Violence is quite easy to get desensitized to in an odd way. It's all quite clinical and it's just people hitting each other. That sounds ridiculous but . . . hearing someone suffering in a very intimate way – which the listening was – was devastating. You just thought: "You're not going to survive here."'

Listening created a burden for Chris, who became 'increasingly upset at [his] inability to provide significant help' for the 'constant despair and trauma'. He witnessed 'more suffering in a single day than [he] would have previously seen in a whole year.' Another Listener called Les began behaving more and more erratically, and eventually he quit the job, as it was 'tipping him over the edge'. Les said: 'I've been Listening for two years, and it's fucking me up. Sometimes I can't sleep at night.' Few Listeners were able to stay the course, and their dwindling numbers meant that Chris was seeing five contacts a day. He describes the work as 'extremely gruelling'. 'I often feel like I'm hanging round the executioner's steps, simply giving people a friendly smile as they're led off to their fate.'

Chris was delving deeper into the perils of Listening to the secrets of others, and slowly becoming accustomed to the role. And then, disaster struck. An eighteen-year-old prisoner called Osvaldas Pagirys – who had been sentenced for stealing sweets – was found hanging unconscious in his cell. He soon died of his injuries. He had rung his emergency bell for a Listener, but the prison staff took thirty-seven minutes to respond. He had been found with a noose around his neck on five previous occasions, so the delay was negligent. A dark cloud fell over the prison, and the Listeners took it to heart.

Research on keeping the secrets of others suggests that we often take on the burden of the secret. At the same time, 'we tend to like [the confider] more, and disclose more to them in turn, which increases feelings of intimacy.' It makes sense that the Listener Scheme was attempted in prisons – where social networks are everything – in spite of the dark and burdensome side of taking in other people's secrets. Tests show that simply *hearing about* someone's secret doesn't increase the level of burden or intimacy. But when someone reveals their secret to us directly, the sense of burden – and what is known as 'mind-wandering', where we can't help but keep thinking of the secret – rises. The positive aspect is that the more we mind-wander to our confider's secret, the closer we feel to them. On the other side, the closer we feel to that friend or confider, the more we mind-wander . . . and the more intense becomes not only the bond but the burden. This is especially true if the secret pertains to someone else in your social group, meaning you'll have to hide it from them.

In other words, keeping secrets is stressful and painful, even when we keep them on behalf of our friends. When your best friend reveals something deep, dark and personal to you about another friend, expect to feel a flurry of contrasting emotions: burdens and bonds. This created an incredibly toxic environment for Chris and his inmates, trapped inside a sensitive social ecosystem where the need to offload heavy secrets and feel connected was pressing. The sense of burden spread quickly, and was compounded by the suicide of Pagirys. Chris found the listening harder than any part of his thirty months in Wandsworth Prison.

I wondered what we might learn from Chris's experience. It turns out you can actually manipulate people to feel differently about hearing your secret. In tests where participants were primed to think about the closeness of their relationship with a confider before hearing the secret, participants revealed that they felt more intimacy from the confider's revelation. When made to think about the social network overlap (the friends that the secrets were about), listeners felt more shame and burden after hearing the secret.

How can we apply this practically? If you are asking a friend to keep your secret, realize that you are putting a burden on them, even if the sharing of the secret does increase the closeness between the two of you. But know that they'll react more positively if you prime them first to consider the closeness of your friendship (and not the friends you're keeping secrets from). Even if that is a little manipulative.

If you do find that the secret overlaps with your mutual social network, then your best bet is to focus on the problem-solving aspect of the clandestine information. Rather than simply gossiping together about a mutual friend, you could frame it as though you are asking the confidant's help to resolve an issue that might benefit your entire social network. The problem is that this strategy reduces the intimacy that arises from sharing the secret. To enhance the sense of intimacy, you can reframe the secret as 'revisiting past events to savour and enjoy them'. But again, that also increases the feelings of burden – because it feels like you're simply gossiping about a friend.

When guards in Chris's prison responded quickly enough to calls, the Listener Scheme appears to have had a positive effect on Callers. A 2012 report by the Samaritans detailed the 'cathartic effect of talking to Listeners', as well as the 'relief of getting problems off their chest, feeling like a weight had been lifted.' Between 2002 and 2012, the suicide rates in British prisons dropped dramatically from more than 120 to around 60 per 100,000, suggesting that getting prisoners to talk about what they previously would have kept secret could be the difference between life and death. However, despite the continuation of the project, the suicide rate in prisons rose significantly from 2012 to 2018, leaving authorities searching again for ways to help prisoners to talk more openly about their problems.

Interestingly, Listeners are taught not to try to talk prisoners out of suicide. Chris writes that it is 'often counterproductive to try to convince suicidal people that life is worth living.' The most important part of the Listener's job is listening: 'Get the contact verbalizing their darkest fears.' Listeners were trained to 'steer into the pain' and get Callers to 'talk about their distress'.

It's clear that the Listener Scheme impacted Chris more than anything else behind bars. 'Everything else I've encountered in Wandsworth has been banal and inconsequential, but the Listening is suddenly deadly serious,' he tells me. 'I found it deeply upsetting, so I would then need a Listener.' And that is the issue with sharing secrets with a confidant. There is always a danger that the listener becomes the listened-to in a cycle of mind-wandering and shame.

As I continued my journey into the world of secrets, I wondered why it was so important for prisoners to share theirs. I was also intrigued that Chris was directed to 'steer into the pain', rather than talk contacts out of suicide. To me, this suggested that the very act of talking about your clandestine problems might be beneficial. Are secrets bad for us? If keeping the secrets of others makes us feel burdened, then what is it like to carry our *own* secrets? We've all heard clichés about 'getting things off your chest', and 'better out than in', but I was fascinated to investigate whether this had any empirical grounding.

In 2006, psychologists Walid A. Afifi and John P. Caughlin devised a test following 342 individuals who were keeping a secret. They wanted to find out which kinds of people would divulge their secrets, and which pressures made them fess up. Each secret-keeper wrote down a secret they were keeping from a friend, including information about their own identity and the level of 'rumination' – dwelling repetitively on negative thoughts – that the secret was causing. The test found a direct correlation between the level of rumination in the secret-keeper's mind and the likelihood of them revealing it. Afifi and Caughlin call this the 'fever model'.

When you have a fever, your body makes itself uninhabitable for viruses. Unfortunately, you live there too. It becomes pretty hostile for you by means of a high temperature, runny nose and other grisly symptoms. The hope is that you're stronger than the virus – and that once it has perished, normal service can resume. Your temperature will better regulate, the headaches and shakes will dissipate, and you'll soon feel fine.

Secrets are like viruses. Tom Frijns writes: 'Like a self-inflicted disease, secrecy is assumed to compromise mind and body, ultimately causing great harm to the keeper's physical and psychological well-being.' According to the fever model, the more intense and crippling the rumination, the more likely the secret-keeper is to give up the secret.

Psychologist William B. Stiles writes that 'high disclosure is associated both with sickness and with restoration of health'. In other words, the kinds of people who confess a lot are typically those who get psychologically 'sick' from secret-keeping – and quickly recover upon revelation. This fever is particularly difficult for those with 'neurosis, anxiety, and depression'. The secrets become so 'persistent that they overwhelm other thinking'. Think of the character of Raskolnikov in *Crime and Punishment*. He commits murder (not a spoiler, it's early in the book) and a fever takes hold of his body and mind. The fever we experience is amplified when it seems to say something about our own identity. In Dostoyevsky's book, Raskolnikov's identity was changed by his secret to that of 'murderer'. The secret spoke to the essence of who he was, and made the secret unbearable to keep.

Afifi and Caughlin called their participants back two months later to ask how they were handling their secrets. A strange dynamic developed between identity and rumination. The closer a secret was to a participant's identity (hidden sexuality, abortions, cheating), the less likely they were to reveal it. But identity-related secrets also caused more negative thoughts, making their revelation *more* probable as a way of stopping the rumination. In the experiment, it came down to a battle between the interviewees' 'impression management' (for example, not wanting to reveal a secret that might make people see you badly) and the intensity of their fever.

Many of us have experienced that feeling during a physical fever when we think 'to hell with this – just take me now'. Things that once mattered, such as physical appearance, become secondary to the illness. Similarly, if a psychological fever is too high, your reputation management goes out the window, and the secret escapes with it. Still, it was hard to predict which of their participants were more likely to confess.

Another key facet is that, for decades, psychologists had wrongly considered the act of 'concealment of a secret' to be the principal burden involved in causing the fever. They believed that the efforts that go into concocting a deceitful story and hiding clues from others is what makes secret-keepers feel bad. This can contribute to our anxiety around secrecy. But we now know that it's not the hardest part.

Secrets psychologist Michael L. Slepian finds that the anxiety actually comes from the 'mind-wandering' mentioned earlier in this chapter. His 2017 study of 200 participants – almost all of whom were keeping secrets – found that they had to conceal their secret from another person in conversation just 1.77 times per month. They only had to change the subject, think of alibis or deceive the person from whom they were keeping the secret once or twice. But those same people spontaneously *thought about* their shame-inducing secret – while alone – 4.24 times each month.

'Secrecy is something one can do alone in a room', write psychologists Daniel M. Wegner and Julie D. Lane. In other words, it can make you feel bad even if you don't come across the person from whom you're hiding it. This pleased me, because it shows that we don't just feel bad because we're afraid of being caught. We seem to really care about the morality of our secret-keeping. Funnily enough, in Slepian's study, ten people failed an honesty test, and had to be excluded from the responses . . . for keeping secrets from a secrets study.

Michael Slepian is hoping for a 'fundamental redefinition of secrecy'. Not only is mind-wandering more common than conceal-ing secrets, but it is also the only predictor of 'lower well-being' from secret-keeping. The negative experience of keeping a secret doesn't depend on how often you have to hide it from others, but how often your mind wanders to your secret while engaging in unrelated activities. As you run through a park, gaze out of a window or watch TV in the evening, the secret burrows into the space between your ears. We all recognize that pang of shame when we're at work or on the train, and suddenly recall a dark, shameful secret. I write about 'keeping' secrets, but what really matters is 'having' secrets. The keeping (concealing) isn't what causes the anxiety. Simply having a secret – and thinking about it – does.

A lot of good can come from secrets too, though. In addition to the ways in which we use them to our benefit, or to seem mysterious and interesting, secrets are integral to our development as human beings. Studies show that secrecy is a key indication of an individual child's growing sense of self. It shows they are able to imagine the perspective of another, and how their own actions shape that person's perception of them. It is also part of the journey through adolescence: the use of self-regulation and the separation from others. Secrecy is a key part of standing on one's own feet. Research shows that keeping secrets from one's parents contributes to adolescents' feelings of emotional autonomy. Secrets are integral to our growth and social cohesion.

But we're also about to see just how much damage they can do to you.

*

You might be thinking that you don't keep many secrets. You're not a spy, a liar or a sociopath, after all. Well, you might be. But statistically, you're probably not. Some secrets have a way of sneaking up on you. Take those of a sexual nature. These involve not only extramarital affairs and sexual behaviour, but intrusive thoughts and desires. Many of us do have longings of a romantic or lustful nature that we don't share with our partners. And secrets from a significant other involve far more concealing and mind-wandering than other types, because couples spend so much time together. The participants in Slepian's study with romantic secrets had to conceal their secret from their partner almost once a day. But they mind-wandered to their secrets 2.09 times per day. The happiness of the relationship was inversely proportional to the intensity of the mind-wandering.

Secrets about abortion, sexual orientation, drug use, work discontent and planned marriage proposals are usually not kept to oneself. They remain secret from most people – but you're likely to share them with at least one other person. Yet, we tend not to share romantic secrets with anybody. This can cause us to obsessively reflect, and can ruin relationships.

The only time that secrets are not thought to negatively affect us is when they're positive. Like prosocial lies, ethical secrets are those kept for positive purposes, such as surprises for other people. This is because they're exciting, not shameful. For surprises, more energy is expended in hiding them from others than mind-wandering to them, so they don't induce negative rumination and shame.

I must say, though, that I recently had to keep secret from my father that my brother was coming to surprise him on his birthday trip. I found it a strain. My brother's name was constantly on the tip of my tongue, and I had to think and talk slowly while making sure not to give anything away. His eventual arrival came as a huge relief to me. I could finally be myself, and stop overthinking. Still, it didn't cause me any negative rumination.

You might be wondering whether mind-wandering to any negative thought – not just secrets – is bad for your well-being. Slepian split his participants into two groups. The first were told to think of a negative secret they were keeping. He asked the second to think about something awful, but which their partners were aware of. Secrecy was shown to affect well-being far more than negative thoughts about non-secrets. It's because secret-keeping is almost unique in its ability to make you feel inauthentic. Slepian writes of 'the feeling of holding back from one's partner and not upholding relationship standards and values, central aspects of felt authenticity.'

Mind-wandering doesn't cause guilt, but shame. Think of Hamlet's play within a play. Shakespeare's most famous (and emo) protagonist Hamlet suspects that his uncle Claudius killed his father to take his place on the throne. He puts on a play for the new king in which a similar murder takes place. The idea is that Claudius will be so deeply affected by a theatrical version of what he did that he will show visible signs of shame. It works, and Hamlet is certain that Claudius is his father's murderer.

Shame comes from a discrepancy between the perception of the self we want to present to the world, and the reality – the liar, the secret-keeper. This incongruity boils down to a sense of inauthenticity. Whereas guilt can trigger coping behaviours to make you feel better about yourself, shame differs in that it is a negative evaluation of the self. Guilt is therefore more useful – it might push a secret-keeper to seek resolution. Shame keeps you in a rut, which is why having secrets is so devastating to body and mind.

After that early murder, the protagonist in *Crime and Punishment* becomes 'aware of a terrible disorder within himself'. Yet he isn't able to do much about it without coming clean. He is a classic example of a mind-wanderer. He doesn't always have to conceal the secret from others (although the cat-and-mouse game with a police officer does play a pivotal role) – the secret and the shame of it gnaw at him, and he becomes physically ill. For a less literary look at shame, Netflix cartoon *Big Mouth* does a great job with the Shame Wizard, who compels the children to wallow in their inner turmoil.

This difference between guilt and the shame that accompanies secrecy is summed up by a former Jihadi terrorist I spoke to called Jesse Morton: 'Guilt is feeling bad . . . but being merciful to yourself. Shame is punishing yourself for what you once were, and blaming yourself for what you became. There's no way to mobilize an ability to heal, when you're stuck in that trap.'

Jesse was radicalized in prison. He went on to inspire and provide the ingredients for the bomb that went off in the terrorist attack at the Boston Marathon in 2013. The explosion near the finish line killed three people, and injured hundreds. Later, Jesse turned his life around, and began working for the other side. One of the smartest and most empathetic people I've interviewed, Jesse talked many terrorists down and likely prevented countless more casualties.

Still, you got the impression that he couldn't shake off what he'd done. We continued chatting after the interview, and I was pleased to see how he'd made a go at living despite his shame (worsened by a torturous childhood in which he was beaten by his mother). In November 2021, a few months after I last spoke to him, Jesse passed away unexpectedly. His sons found his body. He was forty-three. As a cause of death has not been made public, we can only speculate as to whether he took his own life. Nevertheless, his words on the inability to heal from shame haunt his absence.

As I learned more about the psychological and physical effects of keeping secrets, I started to understand why some of my podcast listeners wanted – or needed – to let their secrets loose on me. I still wasn't all that clear as to why I was their choice of confidant, and determined to find out, but for the time being, I was hopeful that it helped them to quell that raging fever.

One thing was bothering me, though. *Why?* Why should secrets have such a profound effect upon body and mind? What happened to us to make the human mind so hostile to secrecy?

We can't be sure, but secrecy may have been helpful in our evolution. Tribe dynamics would have functioned well when members felt compelled to reveal the truth to one another. Tribes containing a majority of members who found it painful to keep secrets would have formed strong bonds based on intimacy and trust. These groups would have survived longer, passing on their genes more efficiently than individuals in hypothetical rival tribes who found it painless to engage in secrecy without repercussion. I mean, imagine a tribe of individuals who kept secrets from one another without experiencing any burning fever of shame. If secrets don't make you feel bad, then why would you reveal any – like where your secret stash of food is hidden – to others?

Still, it might have been helpful to have one or two members in the tribe who were deceitful – perhaps even psychopathic – as their mendacious strategizing might help their tribe defeat rivals. A tribe full of people like Flanders (Homer Simpson's cheerful and well-meaning neighbour) is a nice idea, but they wouldn't fare well in war. That's possibly why those rare serial liars, narcissists and psychopaths not only exist, but are essential to tribe dynamics and survival.

Yet most of us tend towards honesty. Evolutionary theorists contend that our Palaeolithic relatives wouldn't have been able to survive long enough to pass on their genes without social help and cohesion. 'There is pretty compelling evidence that without cooperation, people are much less likely to survive and thrive,' wrote psychology professor Christian L. Hart in *Psychology Today*. The sick would die and the hungry would starve. By learning to share and help one another, humans devised a very early insurance policy for when they have a bad hunt or fall ill. What might appear better for an individual (such as hiding that secret stash of food) is worse for the tribe as a whole; and what is worse for the tribe might often be worse for its individuals. This is perhaps why our minds are wired to feel pain when holding back information that might help others. It's why we confess and collaborate.

Honesty is thought to have developed out of this cooperation. 'We selectively cooperate with those who are themselves good cooperators.' Humans are adept pattern-seekers, so we're drawn to noting and exposing those around us who have shown they're bad cooperators and deceptive actors: the liars and secret-keepers of the tribe. For that reason, we seek to manage our statuses. We show others that we are good and honest, lest we be expelled. One such example of this is in our virtue signalling. We signal to others around us that we are doing right by whatever morals and values are inherent to a time and culture. If you were able to convince your fellow tribe members that you were a good person – someone who was truthful, kind and generous – then you might be entitled to a greater share of the feasts.

The key here is not necessarily being virtuous, but persuading others that you are. We have also evolved to feel good about doing good, regardless of who finds out. Our brains reward us by making us feel good (or, in my case, smug) when we behave righteously. But from a status and survival perspective, it helps if others notice the good things we do.

Looking good is at least as important to your image as being good. So, we aren't always as good as we seem, and sometimes, those who exhibit their virtues most fervently are hiding some ghastly secret – there are devious people in this world. Look at Jimmy Savile, the British presenter who ostentatiously raised money for charity, and who turned out to be a prolific child sex abuser. This was the polar opposite to George Michael, whose extensive charity work was only widely discovered after his death. Savile was likely a psychopath using virtue against us, while presumably George Michael simply felt good when giving to charity.

As pattern-seekers, we're quite good at spotting those who overtly signal their virtue and hide their secret feelings. We have to be pretty good, then, at keeping secrets and being deceitful if we don't want others to notice. I remember an infamous tweet (or post on Twitter's later incarnation of X) in 2022 from a 'writer and philosopher at Cornell' about Will Smith slapping Chris Rock at the Oscars. I don't want to name her, as she's had a tough enough time of it. She writes: 'You know who you don't need to hear from about the Oscars incident? Me, a white woman.'

The tweet went down badly. By overtly amplifying her apparent selflessness in recognizing her privilege, her public declaration about her decision to retreat into the shadows to let marginalized voices do the talking instead placed *her* firmly front and centre. As many pointed out: if she really felt that way, there was no need to tweet her opinion in the first place to 50k+ followers. The tweet was 'ratioed', which means that far more people replied to it (mostly angrily) than liked it.

Many retweeted it, with comments such as: 'I think this tweet should be framed and hung in a gallery somewhere, it's so perfect.' It appeared that she was using virtue signalling around race to boost her own profile. Other critics pointed out that by seeing an event that had seemingly nothing to do with race – a celebrity slapping another celebrity – as a racial issue, she was reinforcing stereotypes about violence in the black community. This was the opposite of what she wanted her tweet to suggest, but the Twitter (X) consensus was that she was insincere.

It might not surprise you then that there is a correlation between virtue signalling and 'dark triad traits', a fundamental psychological theory covering the malevolent characteristics of Machiavellianism, narcissism and psychopathy. A study at the University of British Columbia found that those who victim signal (competing for victimhood) and virtue signal are more likely to 'engage in and endorse ethically questionable behaviors, such as lying to earn a bonus, intention to purchase counterfeit products and moral judgments of counterfeiters, and making exaggerated claims about being harmed in an organizational context'.

We shouldn't be too harsh on the writer of the Will Smith tweet, because we all virtue signal. It's in our evolutionary biology. I can't even wash a dish without subtly making sure my wife knows. I'm gutted when the server in a cafe turns away just before I leave a tip, and wonder if there's a way to call her attention to the coins I dropped (extremely loudly). Even now, I'm tempted to change 'coins' to 'notes' in the previous sentence to virtue signal to the reader. But would that be too obvious? Or would it imply I'm Billy-Big-Boots, wandering around chucking notes at people? Better leave it as coins – £2 coins.

Anyway, look how tribal we become when we sense virtue signalling: the poster later wrote that the platform had become 'unusable' to her due to the backlash. Her tweet was misguided, but fairly innocuous – yet she received a 'large uptick in hate mail', and an article about her was written in the *Daily Mail*. As the hate continued, she wrote: 'I am happy to admit, by the way, that I should have phrased my tweet about the Oscars more carefully.'

The problem wasn't that she virtue signalled – we all do that. We massage our public personas and work on our impression management. We don't even hide it – it's what Facebook, Instagram and Twitter (X) are *for*. The problem was that she was *blatant* about her secret intentions. And we have a visceral reaction to those in our tribe trying *too obviously* to pull one over on us.

It's like how we fawn over stylish selfies of hipsters at underground parties or on yachts . . . but disparage those who pout or pose too *obviously*, or accidentally leave any hints of artifice in the shot. We don't like to see how the sausage is made – we want the photos to somehow be effortlessly spectacular. Any effort on the part of the influencer seems to imply conceited and self-interested secret motives, as may have been the case with the above Will Smith tweeter. We saw the secret: that she wanted to exploit a public spat to garner clout on social media. We all do it; she just did it *badly*.

Virtue signalling is also often well-meaning and vitally important. It can provoke fence-sitters into action over important human rights causes. It has long played a key role in struggles for equality, such as the civil rights movement, the Suffragettes' struggle and LGBT activism. This is a different kind of behaviour that encourages real, impactful change, rather than a tweet fashioned to feel good about oneself. If we all stayed quiet out of a distaste for virtue signalling, or fear of being perceived as a faker, very little progress could be achieved. So just as we need the psychopaths who use virtue signalling to manipulate us, we need empaths who use it to make real changes.

In our everyday lives, the path to popularity is to let the good that we do show in a subtle manner. It's fair to imagine that our ancestors who were blatant about massaging their public personas to impress the rest of their tribe would not have been looked upon kindly, and would not have received a large share of the food. I imagine a hipster caveman explaining feminism to all the cavewomen, who wait until he falls asleep to bonk him over the head with a wooden club.

Most of us are not very convincing actors. The risk of being found out for our deception and secret intentions is too great. If we don't want to receive backlash – if we want a larger portion of the tribe's food – it's best to keep things honest. Since our impression management is so important to our status and our place in the tribe, our minds help us out by making us feel good when we do things that'll look good to others – like confessing secrets – and making us feel bad for doing things that fall foul of societal expectations (such as being devious or *keeping* secrets).

This is why you feel bad when you deceive others. It is your brain's way of warning you that, if you do this too often, you'll be found out. It is why you feel shame about lying and holding secrets. Concludes Professor Hart: 'Whether these drivers of honesty are hardwired into our brains or whether they are products of cultural evolution is still a matter of debate, but there does seem to be a compelling case that we humans, at least the majority of us, have evolved a tendency toward honesty, not deception.'

I could understand why we were so keen to reveal our secrets, and stay honest about them. But what about the flip side of the coin? My podcast listeners had divulged their information to me unprompted. But I'd be lying if I didn't admit to the slightest frisson of intrigue. Why is it that we are so often desperate to learn the secrets of others?

To fully understand the trajectory of secrets, I realized we must look at two of the reasons that secrecy became so integral to mankind, from God's first words to humanity in the Bible, to the core of every human civilization thereafter. I'm talking about the *curiosity* that drives us to uncover secrets – and the *gossip* that makes them spread. And nowhere are the two better exemplified than in today's celebrity culture.

Before I started writing this book, the Anglophone world was engrossed in two of the most gossip-worthy legal cases of all time. In the US, actor Johnny Depp was suing his ex-wife – actress Amber Heard – for $50 million for defamation, after she accused him of intimate partner violence. She was counter-suing for $100 million. This being in the States, video footage of the hearing was allowed to be broadcast to hundreds of millions of eager oglers, each awaiting the next globule of gossip from this Hollywood power couple. We saw how Heard allegedly left human faeces on Depp's side of the bed, how she allegedly threw a bottle at him that severed his finger, and how Depp allegedly had to lock himself in the bathroom to escape her violent attacks. On the other side, it was said that Depp is a jealous and controlling drug-addicted alcoholic. Neither of them came out of it looking great; their names and faces – already comfortably 'household' – were thrust into the realms of legendary.

Meanwhile, across the pond, we had the Wagatha Christie trial, so-named as a pun on the WAG (Wives And Girlfriends) tag that haunts spouses of football stars in the UK, and the mystery element of a case befitting an Agatha Christie novel. Coleen Rooney, wife of footballer Wayne, accused Rebekah Vardy, wife of footballer Jamie, of selling her private stories to the press. To find out who was leaking her stories, Coleen employed a clever process of elimination, putting out fake stories on Instagram that only certain friends could see. She gradually reduced the number of friends who could see her fake gossip, until only one person was privy to it. Still, the stories made the press. So, she named that person with the immortal line: 'It's..........Rebekah Vardy's account.' (I made sure to get the number of dots right, which was no easy task.) Denying leaking the stories, Rebekah sued Coleen for defamation.

Although we didn't have video access to the trial, since recording devices are prohibited in English and Welsh courts, the inadvertently funny drawings of Wayne Rooney in court along with reported slip-ups and misunderstandings from proceedings made for titillating press snippets. The crucial piece of evidence in the case – Rebekah's phone – was apparently accidentally dropped into the North Sea while she was out on a boat trip off the coast of Scotland. Coleen's lawyer sarcastically noted it was a shame it had been lost to such a 'series of unfortunate events', and was now 'lying at the bottom of the sea in Davy Jones's locker.'

'Who is Davy Jones?' enquired Rebekah.

'It just means the bottom of the sea,' explained the judge.

Other gossipy moments on which we feasted include Rebekah comparing Coleen to a pigeon, in that 'you can tell it that you are right and it is wrong, but it's still going to [poop] in your hair.' We got a sneak peek of their inner lives too, with Wayne looking away as Coleen explained they had separated for some time. Wayne then testified that former England manager Roy Hodgson asked him to speak to Jamie about his wife being a distraction at the Euro 2016 tournament. Jamie denied this.

The secret inner lives of other famous figures were unwittingly brought into these trials through what is called 'collateral intrusion'. Many such incidents occurred in the Depp–Heard case, where actor Paul Bettany's texts to Depp about Heard were read out in court. These included a reference to Heard's 'beaver', and this message from Bettany: 'I'm not sure we should burn Amber. She is delightful company and pleasing on the eye. We could of course do the English course of action and perform a drowning test. Thoughts? You have a swimming pool.'

Depp replied: 'Let's drown her before we burn her!!! I will fuck her burnt corpse afterwards to make sure she's dead.'

This wasn't ideal exposure for Depp (who claims the text was a reference to a Monty Python comedy skit), given he was trying to prove in court that he is non-violent. But it raises an intriguing question about secrets and gossip. One imagines Bettany would have liked to have kept secret the messages he sent to Depp. Once out in the open, the messages were bound to make it into the papers to satisfy our appetite for gossip. 'Can you imagine what it would be like, honestly, to have a bunch of lawyers go through every one of your emails and texts for ten years?' asked Paul Bettany. 'All I can tell you is that it was an unpleasant feeling.'

That these cases were exploding at once is indicative of our tech-heavy time. Of course, secrets will always find a way to exist in some form, but today, anything that you write or say to a friend could be fair game for exposure in the courts or the press. With phones and computers, we've created technology that allows for more open and accessible communication, but this has come at the cost of privacy. Even private messages between close friends or married partners are recorded for ever. And unless you drop your phone in the North Sea, they may one day be used against you in court or the media. This is the state of the modern world. But the reason that nasty text messages and the inner secrets of the relationships of the Depps, Heards, Rooneys and Vardys attract so much attention is down to something more timeless: curiosity.

It makes sense that humans should be inquisitive. Those who were curious in tribes were more likely to survive and pass on their genes. Curiosity took us to new lands. It found us food, delivered us to shelter and rocketed us beyond the stratosphere. It is a form of hunger or lust, science writer David Robson explains in *The Intelligence Trap* (2019). It is also a sign of wisdom and autonomy, and is a better predictor of future success in children than IQ tests. It is associated with better job performance, as evaluated by participants' bosses. The more curious among us even tend to be less aggressive in stressful situations, and less defensive when provoked. It is no surprise then that, on feeling curious, the brain activates dopamine; it feels good to wonder about the secrets of the world, the secrets of others.

We evolved to be curious gossipmongers. Anthropologist Robin Dunbar adds that language evolved through gossip. He found that 65 per cent of our conversations involve talking *about* each other. He maintains that this allows us to maintain social coherence in large groups. Along with language, gossip replaced the previously held social glue of physical grooming. Grooming one another kept us clean, while also serving a cohesive function in tribes. But it becomes difficult to groom your mate while hunting, eating and providing for a large tribe.

Dunbar posits that, as we grew larger, grooming became too time-consuming. Because of how long it takes, and the fact that it can only be carried out by two people at once, he believes it has an upper limit of groups of eighty people, which our tribes exceeded (eventually reaching around 150). Gossiping and talking about social topics became the new glue that held us together.

Those of our ancestors who exhibited curiosity had better success hunting and finding shelter, and those of us who gossiped about others had healthier social cohesion. Uncovering secrets within your tribe had benefits, too. If you were motivated to uncover plots to steal food from you, you had a better chance of surviving long enough to pass on your genes. The downside of this manifests itself in the form of paranoia or, as we see today, extreme conspiracy theory. *Skeptic Magazine* founder Michael Shermer explains to me how, on hearing a rustle in the bushes, an incurious bystander might assume it's just the wind, when it might be a venomous snake. That bystander is less likely to survive to pass on their genes. A more curious, paranoid person might investigate (from a safe distance), conjuring up images in the mind of a poisonous behemoth in the bushes. This helped the curious survive and pass on their genes; but has also led to the labyrinth of harmful and false conspiracy theories that now dominate the internet.

That urge to uncover plots and find the snake in the bush is part of why we're so desperate to peek behind even the most opaque of curtains. When a friend tells you that they know some-thing you don't, think of how impatient you are to get it out of them, even though there is a risk that the secret might end up being a burden to you – a metaphorical snake, if you will. It's the result of hundreds of thousands of years of natural selection for gossip (social cohesion) and curiosity (discovery). But once you possess the secret, the excitement dissipates, and you're left with the strain and responsibility of it. Was it worth it?

It depends. Psychologist Benjamin Hayden explains that we often weigh up what we are willing to pay to quench our curiosity. This is an evolutionary trait, too. Macaques will give up prizes to find out if they selected a winning option in a game of chance. Professor Hayden's team presented a group of macaques with a video game, in which they had to select a box to see if they had won a prize. The macaques learned that finding out the outcome (of whether they had won or not) would not affect the time it took to receive the prize. Yet, they opted to be informed about whether they had won immediately. The higher the stakes, the more impatient were the monkeys to know if they had won. They were even willing to forgo 25 per cent of their potential winnings, if it meant finding out sooner whether they had won.

We see this desperation for certainty in all aspects of life. It's partly why playing hard-to-get works in dating. We're drawn to mystique and allure. Like the macaques, we know that coming on too strong will lower our chances with a prospective match. But it feels worth it, just to stop the pain of the uncertainty. It's also why YouTubers reveal just enough about their topic to keep people enticed. Newer social media platforms such as TikTok and Instagram grew around shorter videos, typically one minute or less. Each video is like a scientific experiment on human curiosity. The first few seconds of a successful short video knock the viewer off-kilter with shock and intrigue; they're then compelled to wait until the end to satiate their curiosity and redress the balance.

When I am waiting for a bus without an updated schedule, I sometimes consider how much additional waiting time I'd accept in return for assurance about its arrival time. Perhaps an extra five minutes of waiting, if it satiated my curiosity and uncertainty. That is, I'd rather wait ten minutes, knowing when the bus will arrive, than five minutes with doubts about whether it will come at all.

And therein lies a symbiotic relationship between secrecy and curiosity. Given that some of us are curious, others would be wise to remain secretive. Given we consume gossip, celebrities would do well to remain vigilant and guarded (although many wilfully exploit and sell secret snippets of their own lives for fame and money). And because cult leaders, authoritarian sects and narcissists aim to drown devotees in a sea of secrecy, we'd be advised to learn from the macaques – and stay curious.

Advertisers, movie directors and celebrities have long used a sense of mystique, curiosity and gossip to garner popularity, just as Chinese Empress Wu Zetian did with the blank space on her grave. It is often said that behaving mysteriously can make you appear more attractive to others, because it takes advantage of their curiosity. *The Shawshank Redemption* (1994) tops IMDb's list of the greatest-ever movies. It is fitting that it revolves around one of cinema's most mysterious and elusive heroes, Andy Dufresne. The enigma of Dufresne makes for a magnet not only to his fellow inmates, but to us, the audience. What is he thinking? You have to wait until the end to find out. It's apt that the answer lies behind a poster of Raquel Welch from *One Million Years B.C.*, because the very reason you're still watching the film so intently dates back to prehistory: curiosity.

We're desperate to possess the parts of others' lives that are hidden from us. Nowhere is this truer than in love and lust. Mystique is vital to sex appeal, and our curiosity can lead us to infidelity. Some evolutionary biologists believe men are inclined to maximize their number of partners, and women should secure good genes by having an affair with another partner, while their primary partner provides stable resources. Others consider this an outdated patriarchal viewpoint to reinforce stereotypes of men as dominant and women as passive.

Either way, jealousy and infidelity are part of an incredibly complex evolutionary dynamic. Just as curiosity took us to food sources and shelter, infidelity is considered by evolutionary scientists to be a 'facultative strategy to obtain new partners or increase reproductive success' (Selterman, 2020).

In various studies by the General Social Survey over the years, 20 to 25 per cent of married men and 10 to 15 per cent of married women reported they had sex with someone other than their spouse while married. Another had 57 per cent of males and 54 per cent of females admitting to being unfaithful in a committed relationship (married or not). Of the married cheats, 49 per cent admitted to cheating more than once, 22 per cent to cheating more than three times and 8 per cent to doing so more than five times. These are all conservative estimates, as not everyone is willing to admit to infidelity, even in an anonymous survey. Milan Kundera wrote in *The Unbearable Lightness of Being* (1984) of a protagonist who cheats on his partner with her friends, even while he is aware that they don't hold a candle to her. The one thing they have that she doesn't? They're not her. It is discovering the part of these women that is kept secret in public that arouses him: 'Only in sexuality does the millionth part dissimilarity become precious, because, not accessible in public, it must be conquered.'

Former football player Ashley Cole is rumoured to have put it a little differently, when explaining why he cheated on Cheryl Cole: 'When you go to the Ivy every day, sometimes you just want a McDonald's instead.'

This is why most secrets involve infidelity. One study found 10 per cent of communication between spouses is deceptive. Those of us keeping a secret from our partner tend to think about concealing it from them 0.92 times a day. This may seem low, but is just a measure of how often we actively think of ways to stop the secret getting out. We also mind-wander to that secret more than twice daily, which means we go into deep rumination about the secret while trying to do other tasks. Mind-wandering is a predictor of lower relationship satisfaction, so secrets can be said to dampen relationships.

While curiosity leads us astray, it is also responsible for helping the cuckolded to uncover the truth. In tribes, men had to be curious about whether their female mating partner had been unfaithful. There was no other way of knowing whether the resulting child was theirs. Rather nauseatingly, the bulbous head of the penis is thought to have evolved to remove the semen of love rivals. Equally, women had reason to develop curiosity about whether their partner was faithful, because a rival mother and child might take him away from his role as a carer for her own child.

It makes sense then that sex and sexuality have long held sway over our curiosity and secrecy. In seventeenth-century England, Samuel Pepys's diary detailed how he perfected the art of masturbating with his mind in church. Eventually, he was able to climax without the use of his hands or even blinking. 'God forgive,' he wrote in his diary, after making use of a church sermon to mentally make love to the teenage daughter of a friend.

Pepys's diary was private; it wasn't intended for circulation. This is part of its allure for readers today, because it was written without filter or impression management in an era that we're hungry to know more about. But when did we start to publicly market and make use of people's curiosity about one another?

In the sixteenth and seventeenth centuries, actors and playwrights began to achieve something resembling the fame we see today. But before the printing press, gossip and news spread in the West via an oral tradition. Town criers (hear ye, hear ye) and heralds announced royal proclamations. With the eleventh century, however, came the troubadours. Their main role was to sing funny and vulgar satirical songs about chivalry, war and courtly love. They didn't all travel, but many moved from town to town, and were the primary transmitters of news and information.

Many historians date the commercialization of our obsession with the secret lives of celebrities to the second half of the eighteenth century. A century after Pepys's death, 'scandal sheets' began to circulate through London. The Reverend Sir Henry Bate Dudley was the editor of *The Morning Post*, established in 1772, a gossip magazine that printed 'paragraphs' about public figures. It took fees from social climbers to publish 'positive mentions', a little like how brands pay influencers today to post something about their products. *The Morning Post* also took suppression fees to keep stories out of its columns. We were managing our public images as commodities centuries before Instagram.

Yet, these 'paragraphs' were subtler than our posts today. *Parker's General Advertiser and Morning Intelligencer* wrote that 'the Duke of Bedford resides in France with Lord and Lady Maynard the following summer months'. History lecturer Dr Natalie Hanley-Smith explains: 'Such an account seems innocent, but for those in the know the paragraph acknowledged the beginning of an affair that most of upper-class society would thoroughly disapprove of.'

Inquisitive punters would pay good money for such enticing gossip. Not only did these columns serve to satiate the public's curiosity, but they also helped elites to keep track of intricate dating dynamics in their social groups. As with our prehistoric ancestors, gossip enhanced social cohesion and facilitated sexual pairings. The gossip gleaned from paragraphs helped socialites to avoid making faux pas, while enabling them to better strategize around their own romantic endeavours.

The paragraphs also served as warnings to rivals. A little more on the nose than the previous extract, *The Morning Post* reported that 'all the unmarried Belles of Britain are preparing for the return of the young Duke of Bedford; but those better acquainted with the world of intrigue, know that the affections of his Grace are already fixed. Lady Maynard, in the Autumn of her charms, has him entirely to herself'. This warned potential suitors to the duke to keep their hands to themselves, lest they invite the scorn of Lady Maynard. It's possible she was behind it.

Despite their eloquent tone, the scandal sheets weren't afraid to venture into sexual innuendo, as in *The World*'s description of the above-mentioned affair between duke and lady. The paper stated that while the duke is 'for the removal of his present erection in Bloomsbury-square – Lady Maynard is for letting it stand!' And *The Times* went with: 'Q. Why is a newspaper like Lady Maynard? A. Because it requires more persons than one to supply its wants.'

Coleen Rooney accused Rebekah Vardy of being behind the Secret Wag, an anonymous column in *The Sun* that reveals the secrets of footballers and their wives. Might Lady Maynard have used the press to similar effect? We haven't changed that much. Yet, the world around us is shifting rapidly in the form of double-sided phone cameras, easy-to-use recording devices, and social media platforms that reward revelation of your own secrets with 'Likes'. Our thirst for gossip in the modern age has led to the rise of reality TV and social media. It's why Kylie Jenner – a person with no obvious skill beyond being remarkably watchable and gossip-worthy – has 336 million Instagram followers; that is 50 million more than the combined population of France, Germany, Italy and the UK. She has nations' worth of people awaiting to hear snippets about her private life.

Social media has allowed us a closer look at the secret inner-lives of not only the rich and famous, but the normies around us. Hundreds of thousands of years have passed since grooming turned to gossiping. We have gone from Roman pamphlets to eighteenth-century scandal sheets, before arriving in an age of technological surveillance and Kylie Jenner. In many respects, these worlds are almost unrecognizable from one another – yet our fascination with gossip, curiosity and secrecy remain constant.

I've travelled from hipster cavemen through to the troubadours via the love lives of eighteenth-century high society and modern-day celebrities to better understand the effect of secrets on body and mind. I see now how we need to reveal secrets to stave off a fever that's been burning since prehistory. And how we also have to keep secrets to resist the curiosity and gossip of others.

Secrets have been around for a long time, and we have to live with them. That means learning to deal with the shame of keeping secrets. The instinct is to simply suppress the thoughts. If mind-wandering is the problem, then engage pure mind power and self-control to stop thinking of your secrets. Alas, efforts at suppressing thoughts frequently result in those thoughts intruding even more. This is known as the 'rebound effect', like saying: 'Don't think of a pink elephant.'

When communication scholar Walid A. Afifi ran a two-month study of 342 individuals keeping a secret, he confirmed that mind-wandering is particularly shame-inducing when the secret relates to our identity. It is also more burdensome for people with low self-esteem, because the secrets confirm their worst anxieties and beliefs about themselves.

Rather than trying to suppress the rumination – which would lead to a rebound effect – readers experiencing any of this shame should attempt to make the secret feel less relevant to their identity. Try to remember that the secret – and the fact that you are withholding it – doesn't define who you are. There are other tips for better dealing with the burden of secrecy, too, such as mindfulness, meditation and exercise. You would also do well to try to improve your self-esteem.

Ideally, you're in a position where you might be able to reveal the secret. Slepian writes that talking to another person 'might make all the difference. We want to confide and get the secret off our chests, but we also want to protect ourselves and our relationships. That conflict is what wears us down.' Confiding is key to feeling better about secrets.

Of course, that comes with its own set of issues. Offloading your secrets on others might make you feel better – but it can be hazardous to the health of the person you tell them to. Just think of the Listener scheme. Since the other person now has to keep a secret on your behalf, they inherit those feelings of shame and inauthenticity. Psychologists, police officers and teachers are among those whose professions lumber them with stacks of secrets.

In my work as a journalist and podcaster, I often have to keep the secrets of others. I recently received an email from one of my listeners, detailing their abuse at the hands of an A-list Hollywood movie star. I have no idea what to do with it. Part of me feels like it's made up. Does that make me complicit, like all those who knew – but didn't speak up – about the Harvey Weinstein scandals? Or the Jimmy Savile ones? I can't just report it, as I'll be sued for libel. I decided to reply to her, suggesting she send her account to the police. She didn't respond.

I've been amazed to learn of the fever that infects the mind of the secret-keeper, as well as the ferocity of the gossip and curiosity that leads not only us – but macaques and presumably other animals – to sacrifice privileges in favour of earlier truths. The physiological effect of secrecy is one of the most fascinating concepts I've come across, and it's so strong that it can create bonds of intimacy – and huge burdens – even when secrets are being kept for someone else.

Slepian writes: 'The bad news is that when people share their secrets with us, we feel like we have to guard them. The more people are preoccupied by that secret, or feel they have to hide it on behalf of the confidant, the more burdensome it is.' Listeners share their secrets with me in order to reduce rumination and forge intimacy. They feel better, but they leave me to pick up the bill.

At times, I feel privileged that my listeners appear to trust me, and this creates an intimate bond and a jolt of dopamine. But I find that the responsibility that comes with the keeping of others' secrets can also be draining. This makes me question my compassion. As this relates to my own identity, it brings about shame and a sense of inauthenticity.

But what if my listeners – or anyone else in my life – were less forthcoming with their secrets, and I needed to find out what they were hiding?

4

SECRETS AND DETECTION

To wear an improper expression on your face . . . was itself a punishable offence. There was even a word for it in Newspeak: facecrime, it was called.

George Orwell, *1984*

'No, no. This is just a conversation with Andrew,' says the exorcist, darkly. He blocks my director David, and thrusts me into a room a little larger than a cupboard. Five of his ecclesiastical cronies loiter within, chests pumped, teeth bared. You wouldn't know it, given we're in a drab setting in the perilous suburbs of Buenos Aires, but we're here for a momentous occasion.

On the other side of the wall, the parish nave throbs with believers, while outside, frenzied followers swarm the streets for one of the padre's grandest masses of the year. A police car cordons off one end of the road, its blue flares igniting and darkening the faces of crumpling disciples, after whom clergy scurry like squeegee merchants with spray bottles of holy water. *Pchit pchit*. Another devil vanquished; another soul saved. The place is amok with demons. The crowds roar. Up and down like a Mexican wave, they sing for their master, Padre Manuel, who is grappling in a cupboard with the greatest demon of all: his secret.

For, while devotees chant to an empty podium, the padre struts backstage, sizing me up with rage, as though I'd waged war on his country. 'He's British, they took the Falkland Islands,' our microphones inadvertently record him warning his assistant. 'We can never trust them.' After weeks of putting up with my impertinent questions, the padre is regretting letting me into the church to film his exploits. He expected me to celebrate his talent for vanquishing imps and sprites in the nether regions, but instead found me prodding at his murkiest secrets in, well, his nether regions.

And that's how I end up in the cupboard. I asked too much. This is the natural endpoint when you expose a longstanding secret. It is the result of the years of stress that attend secret-keeping. Now the priest's secret has seen the light of day, it no longer shackles him. He fixes me with rabid eyes.

'I'm getting a bit scared,' I tell his towering clergy in deliberately bad Spanish, hoping to appeal to their dwindling empathy.

The padre has seen enough gangster movies to play the role. Behind him on the wall hangs a cartoonish drawing of him with the same wicked smile he now wears, like that famous scene in *Airplane*. Suddenly, he lurches towards me across a table, thumping his palms between colourful potions and an embossed sign reading: 'Bishop Manuel Acuña'.

'Oh, a bit scared, are you?'

'Yes. Can I go?'

'Sure, no problem,' he says, feigning reaching for the door. 'But first . . . you've interviewed me. Now, I'm going to interview you.' His cronies creep closer, cutting off the faint yellow of a dirty bulb. 'Tell me,' he seethes. 'Why have you been asking about my relationship with Paula?'

'Oh . . . well, it's interesting, no?' I rack my brains, trying to remember what I asked about his assistant Paula, who is a former patient of the exorcist. She has schizophrenia and is less than half his age. 'I think it's a fair question, given the history. She was young and going through some issues, and you exorcised her and . . .'

'And why have you been asking why I kiss her on the mouth?'

'What? I didn't.' I hear my voice quiver, and take a few breaths to steady myself. 'Look, I can show you the video footage.'

As though reading from a script, two comrades advance from the shadows to falsely declare that I questioned them about mouth kisses. With only my director David outside – wrestling with the door – for back-up, and our whereabouts in this midnight suburb known to no others, I worry we're about to be purged. My legs turn to jelly.

How can you know if someone is keeping a secret? The truth is: you can't. Or, at least, *I* can't. I knew the exorcist was kissing girls on the mouth because he told me, right then and there. Another journalist, jealous I was on his turf, whispered poison about me into the ear of the padre. His paranoia made it difficult for him to imagine that I – having snooped around in his church for months – didn't know the obvious about his relations with his schizophrenic young assistant. His feverish guilt, and the weight of keeping the secret, contributed to his revelation. Eventually, he stormed out, and I was able to escape.

On our way out, a kindly old clergyman confirmed the mouth kisses, and assured us they were 'spiritual'. David and I nodded. As we clambered over bodies frothing at the mouth, the last words we heard booming from the speakers around the church – and repeated by fervent believers – were the exorcist's: 'The Devil is in the house. To all evil forces: GET OUT!'

We ran.

As the exorcist found, it can be particularly difficult to keep a secret when you suspect that others are wise to it. As we'll come to see, much of the detective work involved in finding out a suspect's secrets relies on not letting them know how much – or how little – you know. My exorcist failed that test. He thought I knew more than I did, and so he blabbed.

A famous example of this kind of giveaway can be found with Ana Montes, former American senior analyst at the Defense Intelligence Agency (DIA) in Washington DC. She was keeping a whopper of a secret: she was a spy for the Cubans. If found out, she could have been given the death penalty. When her colleague, Scott W. Carmichael, senior counter-intelligence investigator, asked her a few innocent questions about her whereabouts, she reacted strangely. 'She was scared to fucking death. She thought I knew it and I didn't. I had no idea.'

Unlike the exorcist, Montes got away with it. Her fear gave her away, but Carmichael didn't notice it at the time. Carmichael only realized later, when clues about who she really was were revealed to him by code-breakers at the National Security Agency. 'The game was fucking over, and I mean it was over in a heart-beat . . . I was really stunned – speechless stunned. I could have fallen out of my chair.'

Montes had given herself away, and Carmichael – an expert investigator – had missed it. Had the clues not aligned later on, he'd have been none the wiser that one of the DIA's top agents was playing for the other team. And had the exorcist not told me about the mouth kisses, I'd never have stumbled upon his secret. I can't read people's minds.

Still, despite being aware of the limits to my clairvoyance, I can't help but try (ever in vain) to look into someone's soul for truths. There's a point near the end of the *Amanda Knox* documentary (2016), where Amanda – who spent four years in an Italian prison on false charges of murdering her roommate Meredith Kercher – looks into the camera: 'You're looking at me,' she accuses. 'Why? These are my *eyes*. They're not objective evidence.'

Watching her, I almost blush. It's like she sees me through the screen. I've spent the entire documentary fixed on her electric blue eyes, as if something in them might reveal the truth about the murder. The more I know this to be futile, the closer I search. 'You're trying to find the answer in my eyes when the answer is right over there,' she adds, pointing figuratively to the evidence (or lack thereof) in the case against her.

I was learning that human beings, having evolved with honesty and cooperation as a default setting, don't really have any reliable mechanisms for knowing if someone else is hiding something from us. Secrets can't be found in the irises of Amanda Knox. But you can get close with a Game Boy.

Former Guantanamo Bay interrogator Lena Sisco pretended to hook suspects up to those old Nintendo handheld game consoles in her examinations. She would draw out a plot for potential terrorist attacks on a board, and ask detainees to point to 'yes' or 'no' to indicate what they knew about the information. 'We used the Game Boy,' she tells the Eric Hunley YouTube channel, 'to determine whether or not he was telling the truth.'

A Game Boy can't really tell if you're lying. Sisco's machine wasn't even hooked up to the suspect. She pushed buttons to make the Game Boy light up whenever she suspected a secret was being withheld or a lie being told. 'Oh my gosh!' they would say. 'Take the thing off me, I'll tell you the truth.'

She could have used any old thing to convince the detainee she knew more than she did. As with the exorcist and the double agent Ana Montes, it's a case of a suspect being on unsure footing as to what the other person (or Game Boy) knows. 'And – poof – all the truth came! Just from a Game Boy,' she laughs.

'People are so petrified of the thought that that exam exposes them that they usually just give up everything that they know.'

The approach isn't foolproof, but interrogators often pretend they already know their subject's secret in order to fool the subject into revealing more. A similar ruse is carried out by the detectives in the TV series *The Wire*, using McDonald's instead of the Game Boy. They tell a suspect that his accomplice has spilled the beans (even though he hasn't). If he thinks his accomplice has ratted on him, it makes sense for him to fire back before it's too late. 'We even went to Mickey D's for him because he was so motherfucking helpful,' add the officers. Then, they have the unwitting accomplice – who still won't talk to detectives – walk past the suspect's open door, McDonald's in hand. The suspect sees him and the food, and wrongly presumes his friend has ratted him out. He feels he has no option then but to reveal the truth. He thinks they already know it.

You might have the impression so far, from tales of truth purists and violent fevers, that honesty and confession of our secrets is the best way forward. Keeping secrets is bad for our well-being and physical health. So bad, as previously mentioned, that it often negates the benefits that come from keeping the secret in the first place. As psychologists Lane and Wegner suggested, and para-phrased by Frijns, 'people keep secrets from others out of fear of the consequences of exposure, not realizing that the concealment itself can cause severe detriments.'

But is honesty *always* good for us? Should we reveal *everything* of ourselves to our fellows? Sisco hid the reality about her Game Boy from her prisoners to great effect. It appears that secrecy and deceit are also necessary for a functioning society. To understand why, we need to look at 'game theory', which originated with mathematician John von Neumann in the early 1900s, before becoming popular with a range of academics in the 1950s. The theory studies the way that humans make decisions in groups. Its most famous example is the 'prisoners' dilemma', in which two people are arrested for a crime – a little like that scene from *The Wire*.

The police are unsure which of the prisoners committed it, and which of them only assisted. The prisoners' choices are as follows: they can both remain silent, and be released. Or one can betray the other, and be released – while their counterpart is sentenced to time in prison. If each of the suspects betrays the other, they are both held for a shorter time, because they'll share the burden and sentence.

Regardless of the truth, each prisoner would be advised to betray the other, guarding against the possibility that the other person did the same. The only long sentence comes from remaining silent, while your partner accuses you. Best not to stay silent then – and if it were you who committed the crime, best to keep that secret, and betray the other.

This betrayal is known in game theory as the 'dominant strategy'. A variation of it crops up in the British TV quiz show *Golden Balls*, which aired from 2007 to 2009. At the end of the show, two contestants face each other, with a sum of money to play for. They each have to make a decision: split or steal. If they each choose split, then the cash prize will be divided between them. If they both steal, then they lose it all. If one chooses to steal, and the other splits, then the stealer takes everything.

There are many online clips showing just that: the eventual stealer spends minutes keeping secret their true intention, while convincing their foe of their moral integrity and desire to split . . . only to reveal 'steal', before taking all the money for themselves. We're fascinated by the callousness of the dominant strategist. It's a blatant violation of moral codes . . . on live TV, no less. They each come out of this looking bad: the stealer looks manipulative and deceitful, and the splitter weak and naive, leaving with nothing. So, it makes for great TV. So much so that variations have featured across other game shows, including *Shafted*, *Friend or Foe?* and *The Bank Job*.

And yet, *Golden Balls* only ran for two years, before ratings fell in 2009. It was cancelled. My theory is that the contestants figured out a work-around – which speaks to the ingenuity of human cooperation – and ruined the game. In the most talked-about steal-or-split moment of the programme, a contestant called Nick tells his counterpart Ibrahim that he intends to *steal* the £13,600 jackpot. 'Ibrahim, I want you to, um, trust me. One hundred per cent, I'm going to pick the steal ball.' Speech analysts won't have trusted that 'um'.

'Sorry?' asks Ibrahim, flummoxed. Ibrahim has been expecting Nick to try to convince him that he is going to *split*.

Nick continues: 'I want *you* to do split, and I promise you that I will split the money with you.'

The studio erupts with that kind of electric laughter that follows the flipping of a script. That is, apart from the host, Jasper Carrott, who wears the expression of a man who realizes his show is on borrowed time. Carrott sees that the contestant has found a kink in the system.

'I appreciate that,' says Ibrahim. 'Right, I'll give you another alternative. Why don't we just both pick split?'

'I'm not going to pick split. I'm going to steal, Ibrahim.'

'It's in your nature to steal?' asks Ibrahim.

'No. I'm honest. That's why I'm telling you I'm going to steal,' replied Nick. Nick is *not* being honest. He is hiding a secret.

Nick could be lying about splitting the money after the show. But after making a song and dance on live TV about 'being a decent guy' and promising to the whole world that he will split the money, his reputation outside the studio is at stake. Nick is referring to his intentions outside of the show; it's no longer part of the game. Also,

Ibrahim knows that – given Nick's bold promise to steal – the split after the show is his only hope of getting any money.

Nick's dominant strategy is wearing Ibrahim down. Ibrahim is listening. With a face like ash, the host interrupts: 'There is *no* legal requirement for him to give you the money.'

The two contestants begin to dance around vague patriarchal stereotypes of 'men who keep their word'. With so much at stake, Ibrahim begins to lose his cool, calling Nick 'an idiot' several times, while the audience applauds and Nick smiles coyly. This is Nick's Derren Brown magician moment. Eventually, Ibrahim agrees that he is going to split and allow Nick to steal. The spectators go wild.

'You cannot change your mind!' interrupts the host in one last valiant attempt to . . . change his mind, and prevent the derailing of his show. He knows that it can no longer work if contestants simply shake hands and agree to split after the show. The contestants go ahead, and open the balls containing their answers: split or steal.

As agreed, Ibrahim has chosen to split. And here's the beauty of Nick's gesture; his Shawshank classical music moment, his closing of the curtains on one of the UK's most manipulative shows, and the thing that makes this one of British TV's most classic moments (the clip alone has racked up 12 million views on YouTube).

When Nick opens his ball, it reveals that he too has chosen 'SPLIT'. Ibrahim smiles. The audience erupts. Nick's entire spiel about his commitment to stealing was just a ploy to ensure Ibrahim also chose split. They share the money. This is different to the prisoners' dilemma, where both prisoners were encouraged to choose the selfish option. But it shows how deception and secrecy can work out best for everyone. Nick's choice to keep secret his intentions enables the players to share the prize. Had he been honest about choosing split from the start, he would have risked losing everything to Ibrahim. But this way, both players win – and the only loser is the game show.

So important is game theory – the study of strategy, probability and deception – to society that fifteen Nobel Prizes in economics have gone to scholars of variations of the theory. It's also no coincidence that it grew in popularity alongside the Cold War, as the US and the Soviets engaged in a form of it, each side weighing up the pros and cons of secrets and lies, and employing agents, double agents and sleeper agents in a decades-long prisoners' dilemma.

Even so, we mustn't overestimate the benefits – or the prevalence – of deception and secret-keeping. We can all recall occasions of notoriety when politicians, lovers and co-workers had lies and dirty laundry exposed. But the reason these examples stick in the memory is precisely because they are rare. Professor Dr Christian L. Hart writes in *Psychology Today* that 'dishonesty is far outside the norms of society'.

Game theory aside, we are honest creatures. We tell the truth in game-like lab studies involving dice scores, even when lying would financially benefit the participants. In 'Lies in Disguise – An Experimental Study on Cheating' (2013), participants were asked to roll a dice, with higher scores granting them financial prizes. They were told that cheating cannot be detected. From the final scores, it was estimated that almost 40 per cent were entirely honest. Some participants were dishonest, but even they often lied in ways that deliberately failed to take full advantage of the dice scores. For example, 41 per cent lied a bit about their score, without suggesting they had the top score. Hart writes of honesty being 'baked into human psychology along with sociality, curiosity, and language.' We choose honesty time and time again over Machiavellian qualities – such as deception, exploitation and manipulation – that would work better for our own interests.

And when we do stumble across dangerous liars and secret-keepers, we go to drastic lengths to try to expose them.

*

Mohamedou Ould Slahi is Guantanamo Bay's most tortured prisoner. For fourteen years, Mohamedou was detained in Guantanamo, which has the might of the US military supporting its attempted excavations of secrets. Set up in response to the Twin Tower attacks, the base took in almost 800 detainees in pursuit of terrorist-related secrets. While 731 have been moved elsewhere at the time of writing in 2023, thirty still remain in Guantanamo. Nine detainees died there, at least six of whom were reported as suicides.

If I wanted to get a grip on why and how we extract secrets, then Guantanamo – a prison that allegedly uses torture to get to the truth – was a great place to start. The George W. Bush administration denied the torture, but many former detainees – including Mohamedou – insist that it takes place. In reference to the Soviet labour camps, an Amnesty International report called Guantanamo the 'Gulag of our times'. It is not only a secret extractor, but an institution that is itself shrouded in secrecy. Few know what really goes on inside those walls, and the United States Department of Defense has moved to deny allegations that those reported suicides were cover-ups of deaths resulting from torture.

Its continued existence stokes controversy. Many of its practices are said to violate international law. Some say it is too expensive to run, and spreads anti-American sentiment around the world. Its defenders point to the need to mine vital information about terrorism to prevent future attacks, although concrete examples of its successes are hard to come by.

One way it is said to help, writes former United States Attorney General Edwin Meese for CNN, 'in the war against terrorists' is 'by keeping them off the battlefield.' I search, but cannot find a single reported example of Guantanamo Bay extracting a secret through means of torture that has helped to avert an attack or save lives. I ask my contacts. My YouTube friend Eric Hunley has interviewed all kinds of interrogators, including some who worked at Guantanamo Bay. When I ask him if any good has come from torture, he simply tells me, 'People don't like to talk about that.'

As for Guantanamo, it may conjure images of torture and waterboarding, but these practices are said to be on the wane. The institution apparently prefers to use by-the-book interrogation techniques now. Lena Sisco – the Game Boy interrogator – speaks to Eric about offering tea and blankets to those who 'own up to it'. Her psychological methods – aside from the Game Boy – involve incepting in the minds of detainees the idea of 'owning up' as 'courageous'. Former British Ministry of Defence instructor Gavin Stone tells me that 'it's not about the physical torture; it's about breaking the spirit. If you've done your job properly, it should be a relief for suspects that they've told you.'

'It was the first time I realized that fear has a taste,' Mohamedou Ould Slahi tells me. 'It's very bitter. It's like [mimes gasping for breath] you're choking. I saw death so many times.'

It's almost impossible to really tell if someone is holding a secret. And our over-confidence in our ability to know can have dire consequences. Mohamedou was detained after being suspected of connections to terrorism following the 9/11 attacks. He had been involved in al-Qaeda in the 1990s, when they fought along-side America against the communist government in Afghanistan. His brother-in-law was close to Osama Bin Laden, and, as Mohamedou tells it, once called him using Bin Laden's phone. Mohamedou emphasizes to me that this was before Bin Laden became an 'extremist'. From then on, the CIA were onto Mohamedou, who refutes allegations he had anything to do with the Twin Towers attack.

For fourteen long years in Guantanamo, Mohamedou alleges he was tortured. He says that he endured isolation, sleep deprivation, exposure to extreme temperatures, physical beatings and sexual humiliation. One time, he recalls, officers blindfolded him and took him out on a boat to perform a mock execution. Still, he didn't speak. He assures me he had nothing to say.

During his presidency, Donald Trump claimed, 'Torture works.' To an extent, we *feel* like we know this to be true. I'd like to be brave, but I think I would tell my captors anything under torture. In fact, I may do so at the mere threat of torture. Why take the pain of preliminary rounds of torture, if you know you're going to give up the secret anyway? Pride? Bravado? Dignity and self-respect are integral to one's self-image, but sacrificing them is preferable to many of us compared to the potential alternatives of torture: sexual abuse, waterboarding and mock executions.

Still, intelligence instructor Gavin Stone tells me that giving up all my information at the start is a bad technique, as my interrogators will think I'm lying. British Special Forces, he explains, are trained to feign a tough stance if caught and interrogated, before appearing to crack later down the line, at which point they reveal fountains of useless information. If they give up the information too early, the interrogators will assume they're lying, and continue to torture them.

Some Guantanamo torture techniques, according to Mohamedou, are macabre and little-known. For instance, he claims he was forced to drink gallons of water every hour, so that a full bladder would prevent him from sleeping. He states that he lived in unimaginable despair for a long time, and would have told his captors anything to stop the pain.

It seems self-evident, then, that torture *should* work for revealing secrets. And yet, it is not an efficient way of obtaining information from someone. First, we know that people will say anything to make the torture stop, including making false confessions and providing inaccurate information. But there's a deeper biological issue. Torture can 'compromise memory, mood, and cognitive function'.

This might have been at play when detainee Ibn al-Shaykh al-Libi – reported to have later committed suicide in prison – falsely revealed under torture that there was a secret relationship between Saddam Hussein and al-Qaeda. The consequences were devastating: the information was key to George Bush's decision to invade Iraq. It can be argued that they were looking for a pretext, and took whatever they could get from al-Libi, regardless of whether or not it stood up to scrutiny. Nonetheless, torture helped start a war on false charges that led to half a million deaths.

I want to know whether Mohamedou also revealed false information, so I reach out to him. I find him in feisty spirits. When we meet, he speaks to me in German (he and I both lived there), before insinuating that he and I plot in the language to kill people (the suggestion being that German is the language of murder). I'm stunned. He continues, 'I think all Germans should thank Arabs, because we took the heat off their back.'

Later, his tone turns sober, as he speaks of being taken from his home in Mauritania, never to see his mother again. She died while he was in Guantanamo. 'This is knowing that I was innocent. They put me, in 2003, two times on the lie detector. They knew that I was innocent.' Lie detectors (or polygraph tests) can be pretty effective, but they are ultimately inaccurate. Even so, the myth of their absolute power pervades our culture.

When I interviewed Linda Calvey, the Black Widow who went down for the murder of her husband, she kept telling me she had always been innocent, and had passed recent lie detector tests organized by another podcaster. When I suggested that the accuracy of those is debatable, she shook her head in exasperation. Given her purported crime and the more than eighteen years she spent in prison with murderers Myra Hindley and Rose West, I decided not to push my luck. I'm reminded of Morgan Freeman's character, Red, in *Shawshank Redemption*: 'You're gonna fit right in. Everyone in here is innocent.'

Still, Mohamedou insists: 'I absolutely wanted to tell them everything. There is *nothing* I won't tell them. But they wanted something that I don't have. They wanted me to tell them how 9/11 happened! I don't fucking know! There is no fucking way they'll get that out of me, because – if they take *your* ass into prison this very moment, and ask *you* about – I don't know what attack . . . in Nairobi? – there is no way you can tell me anything.'

'Were you tempted to make stuff up?' I ask, thinking about the false confessions of fellow detainee Ibn al-Shaykh al-Libi.

'Later. When I was really tortured, really bad. They threatened my mother. I said, "I'm guilty, I'm sorry, I'm guilty. I need your forgiveness." They told me to write it down.'

So it goes. If we are to believe Mohamedou's story, then somewhere off the coast of Cuba, a man from Mauritania – who once received a call from the phone of Osama bin Laden – signed a false declaration under torture that then contributed to the decision to start a war. You couldn't make it up. But Mohamedou says he did. He had no choice.

If Mohamedou Ould Slahi and Amanda Knox were hiding secrets, the world's pre-eminent interrogators weren't able to extract them. This had me wondering whether those old movie tropes about detectives with a knack for reading people have any grounding in reality. Communication professor Timothy R. Levine also wanted to find out. He carries out countless iterations of the same experiment, in which he sets students a trivia test with a cash prize. He assigns them a 'partner', who is secretly working with Tim. Halfway through the test, the instructor leaves the room, and the 'partner' – scripted – suggests they cheat to get the cash prize. In about 30 per cent of cases, the subject cheats.

After the test, Levine interviews the subject to see if they'll admit to cheating. Journalist Malcolm Gladwell reported spending an afternoon watching these interviews, before admitting: 'I had no idea what to make of anyone.' Levine showed the videos to others, who guessed the liars correctly 56 per cent of the time. Other psychologists have tried similar tests, which average scores of 54 per cent. Perhaps it's to be expected that most of us are not very good at detecting lies and hidden secrets. But here's what surprised me: that number doesn't improve among experts. Gladwell writes in *Talking to Strangers* (2020): 'Just about everyone is terrible: police officers, judges, therapists – even CIA officers running big spy networks overseas. *Everyone.*'

Interrogator Lena Sisco would dispute this. She speaks of 'regular' liars and 'powerful' liars, and believes she can detect both. Regular liars have their stress response system activated by trying to keep up with the lie, she maintains. This makes them easier to detect through manipulation games, like her Game Boy tactic. But powerful liars 'can schmooze'. 'They're so focused on the reward of the lie, that all the stress that comes along with lying isn't there.' She believes that powerful liars are difficult to spot, whereas the lies and secrets of regular liars should be picked up by experts.

Mohamedou spent fourteen years being grilled and tortured by the best interrogators in America. They were none the wiser as to what was happening in his head. As for Amanda Knox, eight years passed between her wrongful conviction and her acquittal. Prosecutors in Italy were looking at her eyes, rather than the evidence.

They're not alone in sentencing an innocent person. The National Registry of Exonerations estimates that between 2 and 10 per cent of individuals in US prisons are innocent. This means that, at any given moment, there are between 46,000 and 230,000 innocent people serving prison terms. It must feel like being buried alive. If detectives and judges really could read people's faces for secrets, then no innocent person would see the inside of a prison cell.

*

Grainy footage captures a handsome Italian man with glasses, a Harry Potter haircut and a preppy scarf, as he softly kisses his girlfriend. It's more like three pecks on the lips than a passionate embrace, but it is nothing out of the ordinary. Yet, these five seconds of footage would be played and repeated around the world for decades. The people in the video are Raffaele Sollecito and Amanda Knox. They are kissing just minutes after discovering that her roommate Meredith Kercher has been brutally murdered.

Is this a sign that they were hiding something? What do our behaviour and looks give away?

Historically, the study of physiognomy led people to believe you could tell personality characteristics from facial features. This made for great gothic literature. 'The idea of Dracula as an exotic animal helps us to understand the nature of the Otherness of the monster,' writes academic Shumpei Fukuhara. He explains how Dracula's animalistic physique suggests shiftiness.

Popular culture remembers the antagonist as a vampire who turns into a bat, but Stoker's original used all sorts of animalistic imagery, transforming him into a dog and a wolf, while his human servant Renfield is 'more like a wild beast than a man.' Across literature, animalistic comparisons are often used to convey negative characteristics, such as in Daniel Keyes's *Flowers for Algernon* (2002). The main character, Charlie, has an operation to make him smarter. But his baser instincts are often compared to those of a laboratory mouse called Algernon.

Over the years, these animalistic comparisons have been used to attack minorities. The Nazis referred to the Jews as rats, pigs, and all manner of other animals. They drew caricatures of tall, blond German Übermenschen, built like superheroes, next to Jews with disproportionally Semitic or Ashkenazi Jewish features. They were made to resemble anything from poisonous fungi to the Three Little Pigs. Anything went, so long as it was distasteful, and gave the impression to the German people that they needn't feel sorry for the Jews because they were inhuman.

The Hutu militias who perpetrated the genocide in Rwanda spoke of the Tutsi as cockroaches. The anti-Tutsi magazine *Kangura* published the Hutu Ten Commandments, which effectively relegated the Tutsi to the status of subhuman. The early markers in the Hutu process for instigating genocide against the Tutsi are shockingly similar to those the Nazis used. The Hutu forbade their own people from marrying, doing business with or having mercy on the Tutsi.

In both cases, the genocide began with animalistic comparisons and physical mockery of the 'other'. It was based on this debunked idea that you can tell secret intentions from looks alone. With this history in mind, many people are concerned today by the language used to describe immigrants. For example, in 2015, then-British prime minister David Cameron referred to prospective immigrants as 'swarms', which brings to mind images of flies and locusts. The American Constitution states that any slave counted as three-fifths of a free individual. The number helped to increase the political power of slaveholders, who totted up the fractions of their slaves. It's much harder to empathize with fractions of people or insects that ruin crops and destroy mythical pharaohs than human beings. It's easier for us to shut off our minds to the sorrow of swarms.

Those who practise geomancy – an art of deciphering physiognomic features – believe that there is a link between people's face shapes and their personalities. It is still popular in some parts today. Chinese face-reading, for example, is a type of geomancy that deems that certain 'lucky' faces will yield good fortune. A smooth forehead is an indicator of prosperity, while lines, spots and moles are dark omens.

Physiognomy has been discredited by the scientific community. Still, a belief prevails in the general public that you can tell a liar or secret-keeper from faces. While many Westerners might pour scorn on such traditional concepts as geomancy, we are still quick to judge by appearance. Just ask Amanda Knox.

Psychologist Jon Freeman asked participants to judge trust-worthiness in photos of male faces across ethnicities. Results show we trust those with upturned eyebrows, pronounced cheekbones, big, baby-like eyes and upward-curving mouths, even if they are not smiling. We also trust people associated with brands and institutions, which is often how scams are run.

All of this just means that we *trust* people based on appearance. But is there is any evidence that looks *actually* say anything about trustworthiness? Apparently not. Which might be why we're so bad at guessing who is keeping a secret. In fact, not only are judges and police officers poor at detecting liars, they are significantly worse than a computer, which doesn't take looks into account.

Sendhil Mullainathan, Professor of Computation and Behavioral Science at the University of Chicago, led an experiment where a computer looked at more than half a million cases in the NYC courts between 2008 and 2013. The computer then made a list of the 400,000 least likely to offend while on bail. Those that the computer picked were 25 per cent less likely to offend again while on bail than those the judges actually let out on bail.

This is likely because judges are prone to human error. They are influenced by the looks and gestures of the defendants. By that same token, Italian judges condemned Amanda Knox because they were looking too intently at *her*. The computer would have looked at the *evidence*. The judges might have done a better job had they gone into the court blindfolded.

I was intrigued about what it is exactly that we're seeing in people that makes us think they're hiding something. With a better understanding of the kinds of things that seem to give us away, might we hide our secrets better?

*

'When Phoebe is surprised, her jaw drops, her eyes go wide, and her eyebrows go up,' notes writer Malcolm Gladwell about an episode of the sitcom *Friends*. He writes of 'matched' and 'mismatched' people, based on the work of the above-mentioned Professor Levine and the psychologist Jennifer Fugate, an expert in Facial Action Coding System. Matched means that one's outward gestures fit what is being felt. Gladwell considers *Friends* an unrealistically well-matched group of characters. He asks Fugate to watch *Friends*, and she lists complex numbers and letters for each facial expression, before concluding that, like silent stars Charlie Chaplin and Buster Keaton before them, they are indeed 'transparent'. You could watch many episodes on mute, and still get a good sense of the plot.

This is typical in films, as a way of communicating to the viewer what is going on in the most transparent way possible. We don't need to go back to the silent era or look at 'broad' humour to find it. The Coen Brothers are renowned for their highbrow work. Yet, they – and other esteemed directors, including Edgar Wright and Wes Anderson – rely heavily on overt physical displays in their movies.

There is a scene in *Burn After Reading* (2008) by the Coen Brothers, when Brad Pitt's character Chad is waiting in a car while staking out the neighbourhood of a house he wants to break into. Not the brightest spark, Chad dances and sings with headphones on in the driver's seat. His expression is vacant and a little daft, to show there is little in his head beside the beeps and bops of his headphones. He drinks a jumbo juice through a thick straw.

Then, a car pulls up, and the homeowner's wife enters the house with another man. Meanwhile, a couple of cars in front of Chad sits another shady character, apparently waiting, just like him. Chad blinks, open-mouthed, at both, as if desperately trying to conjure up a thought and put the dots together. Then, just as you think the thought might have manifested itself, the lights go off, and he continues slurping on his jumbo drink. The viewer is made aware by Brad Pitt's facial expressions alone that, after almost putting things together, the character is unaware of the troubles awaiting him.

Real life isn't as transparent as TV, which is why judges are so much worse than computers at predicting reoffending. Interestingly, although law enforcement agents were no better than you or me at spotting liars among mismatched subjects in Levine's student video tapes, they did score higher with interviewees whose expressions matched their feelings. With matched people, they scored 100 per cent, while a typical person might get around 70 per cent.

I was beginning to realize that while we mustn't rely on gestures and behaviours as evidence, they can *sometimes* be helpful in uncovering secrets – or at least knowing that something is awry – in simple cases.

With mismatched subjects, however, these agents scored just 20 per cent. As for those who Levine categorized as 'sincere-acting liars', the experts spotted their deception just 14 per cent of the time. This is frustrating and useless, because we don't need experts to tell us about matched people. We need them to separate the liars from the truth-tellers among the mismatched.

To flip that round, if you *are* lying, and want to be believed, make sure your external appearance doesn't match your internal state of anxiety. While hiding your secret, speak purposefully and confidently, and give a firm handshake. As you might imagine, anxious, shifty-looking people are less likely to be believed.

Gladwell wrote a chapter in his book *Talking to Strangers* called 'A Short Explanation of the Amanda Knox Case'. He maintains what is a commonly held theory about the Knox–Kercher murder case: that she was convicted for *looking* guilty. 'The Amanda Knox case makes no sense,' he writes, after describing how bizarre it was that she was linked to the murder at all (a lack of evidence, and the fact that the real murderer fled the country and had no real alibi for being in the house at the time of the murder). The kissing scene is one of many mismatched acts that convinced the world she was guilty.

'She's the innocent person who acts guilty,' he writes. Another tip-off about her apparent guilt was that she was seen purchasing red underwear at a lingerie shop with her boyfriend the day after the discovery of the murder. This added to the theory that she was a heartless sex fiend. The benign truth was that she was buying underwear because her house was a closed-off crime scene, and she needed clean clothes.

After the acquittal, news anchor Diane Sawyer interviewed Amanda, and criticized her demeanour in the aftermath of the murder. 'You can see that this does not look like grief. Does not read as grief.' In her introduction to the interview, she explained that Amanda's 'pleas for innocence seemed to many people more cold and calculating than remorseful.'

Gladwell retorts: 'Why would we expect Knox to be remorseful? We expect remorse from the guilty. Knox didn't do anything.' He believes that Amanda was suspected because her actions didn't match her feelings. Gladwell even appeared on her podcast to tell her as much.

I arrange a video call with Amanda to find out how she feels about Gladwell's theory. Does she believe her mismatched facial expressions and gestures condemned her to four years in prison? As our interview beckons, I find I'm increasingly nervous. I don't know why, exactly.

Amanda joins. Just as I had imagined while watching the Netflix documentary; now, those electric blues really *are* staring through the screen at me. My stomach clenches. Then, I hear her refer to her off-screen husband as 'Boo'. We laugh, and the tension dissipates. She's fun and emotionally switched on. She tells me that, for some time, she went along with Gladwell's theory – that her mismatched behaviour at the time of the murder got her locked up. She chastised herself for acting inappropriately or naively at twenty years old. Now, she's believes there are many other factors.

'There's been a lot of speculation about why I was convicted when there's no evidence,' she says. 'Much has been made about how I was reacting differently than, say, Meredith's English friends, or my other roommates even. I've had people say to me that it's also a cultural thing, like: "You're from a Germanic family, you tend to be very stoic people, so you react to crises and drama in a very different way than someone who's from a romantic culture like Italy, where it's very outwardly expressive." That's part of it. I do have the tendency in moments of crisis and shock to get very "deer in headlights".'

But she points to an additional reason that her behaviour differed from expectations – one that was little reported. What many don't realize – and I certainly didn't – is that Amanda didn't see the crime scene. Speaking of her Italian roommate Philomena, Amanda tells me: 'She *saw* inside Meredith's room. And she *saw* the bloody crime scene. She *saw* Meredith's foot coming out from underneath the bedroom comforter. She *saw* the smeared blood on the walls. She *saw*, in the very immediacy, everything that had happened, and understood what we were dealing with.'

That is how Amanda talks – with dramatic flair – in real-time conversations. The way she repeats 'she saw' in a succession of clauses is known as 'anaphora', something that is heavily employed in Martin Luther King's 'I have a dream' and Winston Churchill's 'We shall fight on the beaches' speeches. It is a popular tactic for persuading an audience and emphasizing a point.

If you want to really analyse her words, it is interesting that three of the repeated clauses have exactly eight syllables, once more increasing the impact of the repetition. 'She saw the smeared blood' is also great use of sibilance (repetition of the 's'), its musicality adding to the weight of her argument.

What am I getting at? Some might say she sounds rehearsed. Since interviewing her, I've been bombarded with emails and comments berating me for 'letting her off the hook'. They insist that there is something 'not right' about Amanda; that she is a psychopath. My own theory as to why she sounds rehearsed is that she's well-spoken, and has had to explain her mismatched gestures so many times that she now speaks about it with precision and flair. Even if this were rehearsed and false – even if she were a psychopath – it wouldn't be evidence that she murdered anyone.

The roommate Philomena reacted in line with expectations. She was matched. Amanda says, '[She was] from the very get-go very loud, very hysterical. But meanwhile, I did *not* see into Meredith's room. And I was standing in the kitchen when they broke down the bedroom door. And so, I never saw with my own eyes the crime scene; the gruesome reality of the situation. In those very early days, I didn't have the same kind of visceral reaction to this news that my roommate is dead that Philomena did.'

On Gladwell, she tells me, 'He was like "Amanda just acts like a guilty person and that's why people assumed she was guilty." And it's like, "Honey, people were going out of their way to depict me as guilty." The picking and choosing of those three seconds of my life where Rafaelle is giving me a hug and pecking me on the lips to give me some comfort. The fact that those images have been zoomed in, and in slow motion and on loop. They turn what is a very casual, not passionate moment as pornographic, just to again confirm that feeling of: "Oh she was behaving inappropriately." Those are the three seconds of my life that are the most viewed, most studied, under the microscope, seen to be the definitive moment of my life; people observing my behaviour – and it's me getting a kiss from my boyfriend when I'm just standing there, dazed and confused.'

I remember hearing about Amanda in 2007. The story resonated with me, because I was studying at the same university – Leeds – as the victim, Meredith Kercher, who was murdered in the night by a burglar called Rudy Guede. I was also going on an Erasmus study abroad programme (in France), just like hers in Italy. I took a keen interest, and I recall believing wholly in Amanda's guilt. I was conditioned by the microscopic attentions of the media – as well as my own pursuit of titillation, and expectations of how Amanda should look and act – to feel that her kiss with her boyfriend was salacious; boastful, even. I'm not alone. The lead prosecutor Edgardo Giobbi said, 'We were able to establish guilt by closely observing the suspect's psychological and behavioural reaction during the interrogation. We don't need to rely on other kinds of investigation.'

Now, with more information, less media bias and having spoken with Amanda, I look back at the footage of the infamous kiss, and am surprised to see nothing unusual. She looks not boastful nor cold, but sad, confused and very young. It goes to show that, while Gladwell is right that we mistakenly judge people on their looks, we should also take into account the surrounding context.

In this case, the Italian prosecution and the world's media *wanted* to believe she was guilty and was keeping a terrible secret. Much like any conspiracy theory, we looked for the most salacious story. And she spent four years in prison for it. Her boyfriend Rafaelle even spent six months of his four years in solitary confinement, an unimaginably cruel punishment. We are pattern-seekers with confirmation biases, so when we want to believe something, we're adept at putting the pieces together – even when they don't fit together.

Press intrusion and trauma continue to haunt Amanda, and even in 2021, movies based on her life, such as Matt Damon's *Stillwater* (2021), were exploiting her name and story. While in prison, her diary was leaked to the press, who made public everything that was once precious to her. Her private life and her secrets – including how many men she'd slept with – became diversion for us. It all emanated from our desire for a spicy story and our belief that we can tell people's secrets by looking at them. At the end of her Netflix documentary, Amanda concludes: 'I think people love monsters. So, when they get the chance, they want to see them. It's people projecting their fears. They want the re-assurance that they know who the bad people are . . . and it's not them'.

Frustratingly, I was learning just how hard it was to know if someone was keeping a secret. Much of the world was convinced that Amanda was keeping one – and they . . . we . . . were wrong. I suppose I had been clinging to the idea that our society works in such a way that some people are simply 'experts' and are able to detect dishonesty a mile away. Now I was having to face facts: nobody really knows what they're doing. This concept can be liberating; akin to imagining your audience in their underwear if you have to deliver a speech. But it's also scary to consider that nobody is in control.

Even if we can't *know* what someone is hiding, I wondered if there were techniques that might give us clues. What tips and giveaways might investigators be looking for in a deceptive person? What might you notice about a friend who is keeping something from you? And how might psychopaths, master liars and . . . *you* . . . get away with it?

5

SECRETS AND DECEPTION

From matched and mismatched personalities, to deceptive Game Boy ploys, I'd looked into the kinds of signifiers that prosecutors, interrogators and judges use to spot liars. But what about the flip side? What can you do to hide the fact that you are carrying a secret? In the face of ever-encroaching technology, you might have good reason to try to evade capture. Could you beat a lie detector?

Danish flight attendant Helle Crafts lived with her husband Richard in Connecticut. They made for an attractive, high-status couple. She worked for Pan Am in an era when the role was associated with glamour and beauty, while he piloted planes for Eastern Airlines. By 1986, the couple had three children. From the outside, the postcard-perfect family appeared to be living the American Dream.

Internally, however, things were awry. The marriage was troubled. Helle even began to suspect her husband – who had a troubling temper – of having an affair. She hired a private investigator called Keith Mayo to find out if her suspicions were true, and to record evidence of his adultery. The PI did as asked. He captured photos of Richard kissing another flight attendant. Helle approached a divorce attorney, as she looked to a life without Richard.

After friends dropped her off at the couple's residence following a long flight from Frankfurt, Helle was never seen again. A snowstorm blustered through the area that evening. The following day, Richard had planned to take Helle and the kids to his sister's house. They arrived without her. Over the next few weeks, Richard explained her absence with a series of excuses. She was visiting Denmark. She was touring the Canary Islands. He didn't know where she was.

'If something happens to me,' Helle had warned friends, who were aware of Richard's temper, 'don't assume it was an accident.' It took two weeks for Helle's PI to report her missing. The cops dismissed his concerns. In addition to his work as a pilot, Richard was a voluntary police officer in the town, his status serving as a symbol of trust. Still, they had him take a polygraph test to see if he had anything to do with his wife's disappearance.

It is estimated that around two thirds of women killed by men are murdered by their current or former partners. Although lie-detector tests are inadmissible as evidence in courts, they can be useful to investigators in deciding whether to pursue a case. They're not accurate enough to convict someone, but can be effective. Richard passed the test. An investigator reported: 'Based on the polygraph examination and my numerous conversations with Mr Crafts, he does not know where his wife is.'

The case was a mystery. What had really happened to Helle? Where was she? And who was responsible for her absence? The PI kept pointing the finger at Richard, and took his concerns to the county prosecutor, who got state troopers to search the family home while he was away. Here, things started to look bad for Richard, as did any hope of recovering Helle alive.

They found missing pieces of carpet in places where the family nanny recalled a dark grapefruit-sized stain had briefly appeared. Traces of blood were spotted on the side of the mattress. Further investigations uncovered unusual purchases on Richard's credit card, including a freezer not found on the property, and the rental of a woodchipper. There was a receipt for a chainsaw, later found in Lake Zoar, wrapped in hair and blood that matched Helle's. As reproduced by the Coen Brothers in *Fargo*, it appeared that Richard may have fed Helle's remains through the woodchipper. If true, this would be the State of Connecticut's first ever murder conviction without a body. And yet, he had passed the lie detector with flying colours.

How can you hide a secret in the face of a machine such as a lie detector that is specifically designed to uncover one? The fever model – that theory that your body makes itself uninhabitable for secrets as it would a virus – is what sparks your body into a reaction, and what ultimately can give you away. We already know we can quell the negative effects of the fever by distancing our own identity from the secret or lie in question. As established, many of us perform mental gymnastics to square lies and immoral activity with our conscience and identity. I wondered: if you could control your reactions and rid yourself of the shame of a secret, could you pass a polygraph test?

M. E. Thomas is a self-confessed psychopath. A lawyer (insert joke about lawyers being psychopaths here, reader), she has managed to hide her condition from most people around her. Unlike the psychopaths of film and TV, she holds little ill-will towards others. She's not out to hurt you; it's just that she wouldn't be bothered if someone else did. She did drown an opossum in her swimming pool, but only because it was simpler to nudge it down with her pool net and then remove it, rather than save the live animal struggling in the water. Indifferent to such concepts as empathy and conscience, she'll always choose the path of least resistance and fewest consequences for her. You're fine with her, as long as you're not in her way.

M. E. is her pseudonym, and tells us a lot about the psychopath's solipsistic world view. She explains to me that psychopaths don't feel as though they *have* a 'self'. This is her theory as to why secrets, burdens, shame and guilt don't affect them. 'The thing that's missing is self-expression,' she explains. M. E. claims psychopaths have an 'issue' with the 'sense of self'. She adds, 'That's why they're called personality disorders.'

She compares psychopathy to narcissism, both of which are part of the 'dark triad' of personality disorders, along with Machiavellianism. The three tend to overlap. M. E. explains: 'A narcissist has a *false* sense of self that he presents to the world of, "I'm perfect, everything that I do is great." And an inner sense of self of shame: "I'm worthless, and nobody loves me." Borderline personalities [similar to psychopaths] are like chameleons. You put them in a particular situation, and they will start imitating and picking up on the personality characteristics of the people around them. The psychopath just doesn't have a sense of self.'

There are psychopaths with narcissistic tendencies, and vice versa. Each will have a slightly different personality and experience of self, because – as much as we like to put people in boxes – these disorders exist on a spectrum. But M. E. Thomas explains how, while it is easy to hurt the feelings of a pure narcissist, a pure psychopath is immune. To test that, I tell her that her book is badly written, and that it is shit. 'It doesn't bother me,' she says, blithely. 'It truly doesn't bother me.' I scan her face for any hint of hidden pain.

Then, I spend the rest of the interview worrying about whether she might track me down and kill me. Months later, I'm at a wedding, when I receive a late-night message from her angrily demanding I change the thumbnail of our YouTube interview because, in her opinion, it gives away too much about her real identity. I was out in the middle of nowhere, and knew I wouldn't have enough Wi-Fi to do it for a couple of days. Suffice to say, I had a miserable time expecting my impending murder at the hands of M. E. at any moment.

When I told her that her book was shit, she looked unmoved. And that's the thing. Electrodermal Activity tests – where changes in electrolyte levels in the skin are measured along with fear and other emotional responses – find that psychopaths *are* more stable. The behavioural geneticist David T. Lykken found that non-psychopaths showed a greater difference than psychopaths in skin tension when being truthful and lying.

Since psychopathy crops up on a spectrum, we are all a little psychopathic. We all engage in antisocial behaviour. The Hare Checklist is the go-to list for deciding whether someone is a psychopath. It comprises twenty questions that are scored out of two, such as 'do you have excess glibness or superficial charm?', and 'are you a pathological liar?'. Most of us would score around five out of forty, where anywhere above thirty signifies a true psychopath. I wondered whether extreme psychopaths could lie with no ill-effects. Are they immune to the burden of the fever model?

In Brett A. Stern and Donald J. Krapohl's *The Efficacy of Detecting Deception in Psychopaths Using a Polygraph* (2004), the writers also ask: 'If the psychopath lies with effortless skill, is supposedly indifferent to having his lies detected, is purportedly electrodermally hyporeactive, is regarded as a master manipulator of people, internalizes no guilt about his or her acts no matter how heinous we might view them, how then could their body betray their tongue during the course of a polygraph examination?'

I wonder, too, whether a psychopath would lose sleep ruminating and mind-wandering. I asked M. E. Thomas if she felt lying came more easily to her. 'Psychopaths have a couple advantages in being deceitful,' she said. 'They can compartmentalize very well. They already use that skill to come up with a different persona for the various people they interact with or situations they find themselves in. It's like role-playing, but constantly. So, they are pretty brilliant at pretending to be something they're not. They also don't feel guilt, so there's less of an internal barrier to choosing deceit.'

A lot of viewers on my YouTube channel posted comments accusing her of faking being a psychopath for attention – but I think that would be a somewhat psychopathic thing to do. I suppose she could be exaggerating, but I believe she's likely on the spectrum.

In the 1970s, psychologists David C. Raskin and R. D. Hare assembled a test for forty-eight inmates in British Columbia who had been diagnosed as psychopathic. They were told to enter a room where they wouldn't be monitored, and steal $20 from an envelope that had been left there. Then, they were taken to a polygraph test, and told that if they could fool the system, they'd be rewarded with $20 (which was equivalent to twenty-seven days of pay for prison labour). The polygraph proved correct in 88 per cent of cases. This is high. A further 8 per cent were inconclusive, and just 4 per cent of psychopathic prisoners managed to cheat the test. I was stunned: psychopaths are no better than the rest of us at tricking polygraph tests.

One of the reasons for this is the 'comparison question'. Polygraphs measure fluctuations in blood pressure, pulse, respiration and skin conductivity when answering questions. But to find the participant's base rate, participants are first asked neutral questions that have little to do with the case. This can last hours, as practitioners get an accurate reading of their participant. A psychopath might be significantly calmer than non-psychopaths while answering this comparison question. So, even the slightest of changes while being deceptive would be picked up by the polygraph.

This made me wonder: if psychopaths have no fear, why does the polygraph detect *any* change when lying? It is thought that the polygraph might be their Achilles heel. The examiners explain: 'The psychopath is essentially in competition with an inanimate object and is, therefore, perhaps more challenged than when placed in a face-to-face encounter with a person or people who they have made a habit of duping.' Despite lacking a sense of self, they still have a lot invested in keeping their secret and profiting in the immediate moment. Being highly motivated and faced with an unusual environment might just keep them on their toes enough to register tiny incongruities in a polygraph test.

It is, however, unlikely that, during a test to win $20, the psychopaths felt much fear or anxiety. Another reason that psychopaths' deceit might show up on polygraphs is what we call 'duping delight'. When asked whether they'd been deceptive, they may feel excitement at the prospect of winning the money and duping the testers. They're getting off on it, and this flurry of emotion shows on the test. There is also the joy that accompanies relief, and what psychologist Paul Ekman calls 'smug contempt toward the target'. The psychologist David Lykken explains: 'No psychopath of my acquaintance is deficient in his interest in games, in opportunities to "show off", or in winning money prizes.' We must also remember that, since psychopaths do appear on a spectrum, even the most hardened may retain a sliver of fear. We are dealing with humans, not absolutes.

Incredibly, psychopaths are considered as likely to fail a polygraph test as empaths. In general, polygraph testing is only 70–90 per cent accurate. This is still astoundingly high, when you consider what we're asking of these machines: to look inside the human mind. But it is not high enough to be used to prosecute criminals. It would mean that, for every 100 people tried with a crime, 10–30 would be falsely imprisoned on the information of the machine.

This brings us to 'Blackstone's ratio', imagined by eighteenth-century jurist William Blackstone. He wrote: 'Better that ten guilty persons escape, than that one innocent life suffers.' Benjamin

Franklin went further: 'It is better a hundred guilty persons should escape than one innocent person should suffer.'

It's an argument that I return to when dealing with angry commenters on my podcast's YouTube page, who berate me for believing in Amanda Knox's innocence. Aside from one or two people, none of us can truly know what happened on the night of Meredith Kercher's murder. If Amanda Knox *is* innocent, and having spent four years in an Italian prison, the last thing she deserves is the incessant trolling and bullying she receives online. Best to err on the side of innocent. You'd have to be certain that she did it to feel vindicated in adding to her misery.

It's for this reason, too, that polygraph testing is not permissible in UK or US criminal courts, although it can be used in civil cases at the discretion of the judge in the UK, where it is also being trialled for the management of sex offenders. But the idea that polygraph tests are accurate continues to erroneously pervade in popular culture, misleading the public.

Polygraph tests don't really spot lying; they measure the indirect physical effects that typically come from deceit and secrecy. Forensic psychologist Dr Sophie van der Zee explains, 'There's no human equivalent of Pinocchio's nose. But lying can increase stress . . . and with lie detection techniques you can measure the behavioural and physiological changes that occur when you feel stress.' I always worry that I'll have to answer a polygraph test about a crime I didn't commit. I feel my anxiety will skew the test and make me look guilty, in the same way that I blush red as a tomato when accused of things I didn't do. But lie-detector tests involve an hour of practise beforehand, and no surprise questions are allowed, as they might trigger a response regardless of the participant's honesty.

Can you cheat the test? After a lengthy and high-profile trial for the Woodchipper Murder, Richard Crafts was found guilty of murdering his wife, air stewardess Helle, in 1987. He was sentenced to fifty years in prison. Nobody knows how he passed the lie-detector test as he was quizzed about the whereabouts of his wife. But it appears that you can train yourself through practice and desensitization to fare better on lie detectors.

I wrote earlier of Ana Montes, the Defense Intelligence Agency spy who secretly worked for the Cubans. To join the intelligence service, she managed to fool a polygraph test. DIA counter-intelligence investigator Scott W. Carmichael wrote that she passed 'with flying colours'. *The Washington Post* reported that Montes received special training in Cuba to pass the lie-detector tests. If you answer the questions in similar circumstances enough times, you can apparently trick your mind and body into not reacting. Polygraph trainer Professor Don Grubin suggests you could try putting a drawing pin in your shoe – or finding another way to provoke pain and cause the sweating response that the polygraph measures – so that in the questions when you are being honest, your base line is already heightened and there is no evident further change when being deceitful.

As for the prosecution of criminals, other methods have been tried and tested to extract their secrets. In the 1920s, American neurologist William Bleckwenn developed what he called a narco-analysis or narcosynthesis: his discovery became known as a 'truth serum'. He had been researching drugs to treat catatonic mutism, a type of schizophrenia. He found that sodium amytal helped create a 'lucid interval' in which patients were able to speak and respond to questions. He created silent films showing patients going from rigid and closed – some had survived on feeding tubes for years – to open and conversational with the use of the drug.

In 1931, Bleckwenn injected his truth serum into suspected murderer John Whalen, and his resulting testimony cleared him of wrongdoing and led to his release from custody. With his colleague William Lorenz, Bleckwenn administered it several more times to suspected criminals. The military began using barbiturates to interrogate enemies in the Second World War. They were also used to spot those trying to shirk military duty. On the other side, US prisoners of war were forced to take similar drugs as part of brainwashing attempts by the enemy during the Korean War.

Like polygraph tests, truth serums as absolute detectors of deceit have permeated popular culture. Veritaserum is a potion in the *Harry Potter* book series that forces its drinker to answer questions truthfully.

And take this scene from *Kill Bill*:

Bill: 'I'm going to ask you some questions, and I want you to tell me the truth. However, therein lies a dilemma, because when it comes to the subject of me, I believe you are truly and utterly incapable of telling the truth . . . and I am truly and utterly incapable of believing anything you say.'

The Bride: 'How do you suppose we solve this dilemma?'

Bill: 'Well, it just so happens I have a solution.'

He shoots her with a dart filled with truth serum that he calls his 'greatest invention'.

Unfortunately, or fortunately (depending on whether you're Bill or Uma Thurman's nameless protagonist), not only have truth serums proved ineffective, but their use is considered a violation of international humanitarian law and the Fifth Amendment of the US Constitution (the right to remain silent), and some have labelled it as torture. Bleckwenn's barbiturates – much like alcohol – slow parts of the brain and work as depressants on the central nervous system. They serve as sedatives and anticonvulsants, and can battle insomnia. They are also addictive and potentially lethal. Among the most famous people to die from barbiturate overdoses are Jimi Hendrix, Judy Garland and Marilyn Monroe. Still, so-called truth serums are still in use today. After the Colorado movie-theatre shooting in 2013, the judge ruled that a truth serum could be administered to defendant James Holmes, should he plead not guilty on grounds of insanity.

The evidence that the drugs make you tell the truth is lacking. In a 1932 article, Lorenz admitted that 'in the case of guilty persons, we have not always been successful in obtaining a confession.' Writer and historian Erika Janika states that 'a central issue is the degree of reliability of the memories of the patients and the capricious observations of these memories by witnesses'. And while the drugs make people more *willing* to talk, it doesn't follow that what they say is any more trustworthy.

Participants who have taken the drugs become suggestible, and are more likely to say what they think the questioner wants to hear than the truth. A CIA study on the validity of sodium amytal as a truth serum found that many participants conjured up entirely false memories. I suppose this is a little like being drunk. I've often heard that people say what they *really* think when they are drunk. This is true to an extent, because alcohol stifles reasoning skills. It means we're less likely to hold things back out of a concern for the long-term consequences. But you wouldn't trust a drunk person's testimony enough to convict someone.

How else might you hide your secret? Despite the fact it seems virtually impossible for experts to know if someone is lying from their behaviour, there are certain body movements that some agents look out for. Body behaviour analysis has become a huge money-spinner for YouTubers, who dissect the looks and subtle movements of celebrities, such as those of Alec Baldwin in the aftermath of his fatal shooting of his cinematographer Halyna Hutchins on the set of his film *Rust*.

These influencers contend that, because the celebrity in question looked a certain way, it meant they were showing disdain or disagreement with what was being said. Viewers often comment on my own podcast videos to say they didn't believe what my guest was saying because they looked to the right. The reality is that you can't even tell which way the video is mirrored. On TV and YouTube, what seems like right might just as easily be left. We also don't know how many times a particular scene in a documentary was recorded, so a look of disdain or apparent show of disinterest might simply be down to repeated filming in a boring, hot and smelly production studio.

Veteran FBI Agent Mark Bouton – author of *How to Spot Lies Like the FBI* (2010) – looks out for many signs of deception in the suspects he interrogates. He emphasizes the importance of checking for signs beforehand, while you make small talk, to see what their base reactions are like. As with the lie detector, it's not about the body language, but the difference between their behaviour when lying and when answering routine questions.

If you want to keep your secrets from an FBI agent, just make sure to remain consistent and watch out for Bouton's tells. One is eyes darting back and forward, when a suspect feels uncomfortable. This sounds a little cartoonish, but is apparently an indicator that the suspect is looking for ways to avoid answering the question in a way that'll get him in trouble. Rapid blinking is another, so Bouton says to watch out for people blinking five or six times in succession, though this is not foolproof, because people with Parkinson's disease blink more slowly, while those with schizophrenia blink faster.

Otherwise, it's about getting your story straight. Agents and detectives are trained to spot inconsistencies. FBI agent Joe Navarro once caught a foreign double agent after viewing video footage of the spy carrying flowers. He carried them not upwards from the stalks, as a Westerner might do, but with the stalks held higher, and the flowers facing down towards the street. Navarro says this is typical of Eastern Europeans. It gave the spy away, just as a double agent in the Tarantino movie *Inglourious Basterds* (2009) was found out by the way he held up his fingers to show the number three.

Navarro also checks for eyes to see if they are red, which indicates a lack of sleep. He believes that hands on the waist is a sign someone is feeling territorial, perhaps defending a burdensome secret.

Agents look out for these signs, but they aren't enough to prosecute someone. For now, the best that prosecutors can do is look out for inconsistencies in the suspect's story and employ strategies to catch them in a lie. Human behaviour expert Dr David Lieberman suggests introducing a piece of evidence to the suspect that *could* be true, but might not be. For example, if a suspect claims they were in a particular place at a particular time, Dr Lieberman might say, 'There was a water mains break, and traffic was backed up for hours – it must have taken you a while to get out'. This places the suspect in a pickle. If they weren't where they said they were, they won't know how to respond. They'll hesitate. In this case, if you're keeping a secret, you'd do best to give very little away.

Often, it's not about someone's body or looks, but their choice of words. Dr Lieberman notes how suspects use personal pronouns, such as 'I', 'me' and 'my', when taking ownership of something with integrity. He believes we distance ourselves from those pronouns when we feel on less steady ground. As a linguist myself, I'm fascinated by how language can communicate, manipulate and confuse. Can certain words keep our secrets safe? As we're about to see, a wrong choice of words can ruin a relationship, give away a drug cheat and help to kickstart genocide.

'Art thou Montezuma?' asked the sixteenth-century Spanish conquistador Hernán Cortés.

'Yes, I am he,' replied the Aztec king.

A chain of translators ensured that the words were accurately deciphered in this historic conversation between Cortés – among the first Europeans the Aztecs had ever encountered – and Montezuma. And, according to one interpretation of events, the nuances of language and culture led to one of the bloodiest misunderstandings of all time.

Things started off well, and the Spanish and Aztecs banqueted together. After dinner, Montezuma's people made a speech that appeared to suggest they believed Cortés was a god. As such, they intended to surrender to the Spanish. This was a remarkable turn of events for Cortés, and very much welcomed. But we now know that the Aztec culture of the time was steeped in a kind of false humility. Their language used words of modesty and humility to hide true meaning. Historian Matthew Restall explains how the word for 'noble' is the same as the word for 'child'.

He writes:

The speaker was often obliged to say the opposite of what was really meant. True meaning was embedded in the use of reverential language. Stripped of these nuances in translation, and distorted through the use of multiple interpreters . . . not only was it unlikely that a speech such as Montezuma's would be accurately understood, but it was probable that its meaning would be turned upside down. In that case, Montezuma's speech was not his surrender; it was his acceptance of a Spanish surrender.

In other words, Montezuma was used to operating in a language that hid true meaning. Such were the complexities of translating, that the Spanish took his words to mean he was surrendering, when really, he was expecting them to surrender. Cortés took Montezuma hostage, and then killed him. The Spanish – combined with the smallpox they brought – soon decimated the Aztecs. Much of Latin America's current existence can be said to owe itself to that misunderstanding, although it's probable the Spanish would have invaded regardless of the hidden meanings of after-dinner speeches. Still, the encounter goes down as one of history's greatest misunderstandings, and it is an example of the gulf between cultures that are 'high context' and 'low context'.

So, it's not just languages, but also cultures that hide (or reveal) secrets. The late anthropologist Edward T. Hall wrote of low-context cultures, such as that of the UK or the US. Here, people talk more, and say what they mean – as Cortés's Spanish colonialists might have done. There is less space for secret meanings. Japan, however – just like the Aztecs – has a high-context culture. Concepts are understood without words, through subtle head gestures, hand movements and a deeply engrained historical culture. Authoritative figures aren't expected to explain themselves. You'll find a great variation of low context and high context, not only across countries, but also within companies, professions and social circles.

It has been found that websites with low-context designs (better articulated, and easier to understand without context) do better online. As we move further into a digital world, we can expect our communication to become even more explicit – with universally understood emojis helping provide a refined version of our facial gestures in real life. In an online future, our digital selves might be less likely to fall into the trap of misjudging people with mismatched facial gestures. In a virtual world, Amanda Knox could have just flashed a sad emoji, and got on with her life.

Nevertheless, there is a lot we can learn from looking at a person's choice of words. Take this speech by cyclist Lance Armstrong in 2005, upon winning the Tour de France for the seventh time in a row: 'For the people who don't *believe* in cycling; the *cynics* and the *sceptics*, *I'm sorry* for you, *I'm sorry* you can't dream big, and *I'm sorry* you don't *believe*. There are *no secrets*.'

As far as victory speeches go, it's a little strange. I've emphasized some of the words that stand out as negative and inappropriate for a victory speech. It is laced with bitterness and defensiveness. And a lot of it doesn't make sense. I mean, *who* doesn't 'believe' in cycling? Who are these cynics for whom he feels so sorry? And the ending speaks of a man who – as we now know – was hiding many secrets; namely, his cheating through illicit, performance-enhancing drugs.

We've considered the ways that you can *look* like you're keeping a secret (even if you are not). But secrets also haunt our words and the gaps between them. The wrong choice of words might make it seem like you're hiding something. We must be careful not to make assumptions based on this inexact science. But Armstrong was indeed keeping a whopper, and his victory speech smacks of the unspoken. Professor Levine writes, 'The best available scientific evidence now suggests that accurate human lie detection involves communication content (what is said), rather than demeanour (how it is said) or cues.'

So, let's put aside Armstrong's gestures and mannerisms, and examine the words. Contrary to Armstrong's statement, everybody 'believes in cycling'. But many of us don't believe that all of its best performers win races without cheating with drugs. That is what goes unsaid in Armstrong's speech. The ears of devotees to French psychoanalyst Jacques Lacan will have pricked up.

Psychoanalyst Owen Hewitson devotes a website to the teachings of Lacan, who was a firm believer that our words unconsciously reveal our secrets. Hewitson notes that Lance Armstrong apologizes three times during his victory speech. In picking apart the words, Hewitson asks: 'Why, we might ask, did Armstrong choose to express himself by referring to secrets? Why state that there are no secrets when he could have said there are no shortcuts, no easy answers.'

This is a fundamental and much-debated tenet of Lacanian psychology: the concept that our unconscious reveals itself in our choice of words. If you are looking to hide secrets, you'd do well to consider your words, and ensure there are no Lacanian give-aways. Had Armstrong's advisors read over his speech, they might have warned him about using words like 'secret', and apologizing so many times.

In order to sound innocent, prepare your words in advance. This might seem a little artificial or calculating, but it is what language is for. When I ask Lera Boroditsky, linguist and Professor of Cognitive Science at University of California San Diego, what language *is*, she surprises me: 'What we're always doing when we're speaking is trying to invite another human to look at the world in a particular way. We're trying to create some difference in their brain, and think something that they aren't already thinking.'

'We're like a bunch of manipulators?' I reply.

'That's it. There's no other reason to use language with another human, right? To get them to do something that they aren't already doing!' she laughs.

Language is a tool we use to make others do things for us, and think what we want them to think. On a more positive note, it is also used in collaboration, such as, 'Get out of the way of that truck.' Its main benefit to humanity is enabling more sophisticated coordination and teamwork, which is mutually beneficial. It allows us to hunt and build. Still, in its essence, it is manipulation. Much like deception, language is an act of commission; it is deliberate. But between the words lies that act of omission; something that is being hidden: the secret.

We must be wary of giving our secrets away through this kind of subliminal messaging. To find out what kind of word patterns to avoid, I meet with Associate Professor of Linguistics at Columbia University, John McWhorter. He emphasizes the importance of clarity and specificity to sound trustworthy. As an example of a term to avoid, he suggests: 'and shit'. The Urban Dictionary describes 'and shit' as listing 'things that usually happen such as watching tv, or masturbating.'

As you can see, 'and shit' is quite vague and all-encompassing; a term that is able to jump from TV to self-love in a flash. When somebody uses 'and shit', we ask ourselves: what other secrets might lie behind those words? After speaking to McWhorter, I decide to try to cut down on my use of 'etc', and watch out for any overuse of ellipses in messages to friends. These come across as inauthentic and fake. Another example McWhorter gives is the 'studious display of disgust' at hearing swear words. He believes this is a show (although some people are genuinely perturbed by swearing). The advice seems to be: be you, be direct, own what you are saying and be specific.

As an interviewer I'm fascinated by how different we are. Those at the extreme ends of the spectrum of specificity of words are difficult for different reasons. Take David Baddiel. He's a comedian, and so he answers questions in roundabout and funny ways. It makes his interviews a little harder to edit, and also more difficult to write a title for. How can I sum it up in fifty characters or less in a way that both reflects what we discussed and entices potential viewers to click?

On the other end of the spectrum is evolutionary biologist Richard Dawkins. It's terrifying to interview Dawkins because he is so to-the-point in his answers. If you have an hour with him, you have to prepare for the possibility that he will give extremely short responses to some of your questions. I've interviewed him twice for my podcast, and found he often replies with 'no' or 'I don't know', leaving me running low on questions and conversation topics. The second time, I prepped with extra questions, but still came up short, sitting in a studio I'd hired across from Richard, who was smiling politely at me, while perhaps unaware I'd drawn a total blank. Out of panic, I ended the interview prematurely. That episode is forty-eight minutes long rather than the full hour. I don't think he noticed or minded.

I learned from these encounters that Dawkins's economic use

of language – as with Ernest Hemingway and George Orwell – adds believability and authority to his statements. That's not to denigrate people who talk in a roundabout fashion. Those are very much my people. We need comedians – like Larry David and David Baddiel – to be funny and full of self-doubt. I certainly consider myself closer to the second category, and am quite happy here . . . and shit.

'You lied!' bawls Luli, drunk, as she throws a high heel at Tom's face, before falling backwards into a puddle on the dark cobbled streets of Buenos Aires. She appeals to passing revellers, submitting that Tom pushed her. Unperturbed, these party-goers walk into the night, heels clacking on wet stone. It's a sad end to a relationship that burned brightly for a year, before drowning in a puddle of misunderstanding.

They had met shortly after Tom, who is British, arrived in Argentina to learn Spanish. Soon, it was clear that Luli, a local, was prone to bouts of jealousy. This became the source of many arguments between them, and, as Tom's friend, it was frustrating for me. Dinners alone with him were insufferable, as she interrupted with messages to ask where he was, and why her 'Find My Friends' app appeared to show him in a slightly different location to where he said he was going to be.

Here's what led to the puddle incident. The day before, he told her in English: 'I am with Andrew and his friend'. Later, Luli saw photos on Facebook of Tom and me . . . with my friend. The problem: my friend was female.

This came as a shock to Luli, who mistakenly interpreted the 'his' of 'his friend' to mean my friend was male. It was a linguistic misunderstanding. The problem wasn't only that a woman had been in our company. It was that he had lied to her (or so she thought). What was difficult for such a jealous person to understand in that moment was that English – unlike her native Spanish – is a pretty good secret-keeper, particularly when it comes to gender. In Spanish – and most other languages – speakers are forced to reveal gender. He would have had to specify that the friend was '*una amiga*' (a female friend). A failure to do so would have amounted to a lie; one large enough to put an end to an already doomed relationship.

I speak five languages, and am amazed by the idiosyncrasies in each of them. I find that I become a different person in each language, from the suave Frenchman and brooding Portuguese to the serious German and the relaxed Spaniard. To an extent, these are cultural clichés my subconscious is attaching to the languages. I'm performing. But I wonder whether the difference in languages affects the experiences of the people who speak them.

This, I find, is called Sapir–Whorf theory, and was recently popularized in the film *Arrival*. Octopus-like aliens land on Earth, and one of the top linguists in the US sets out to learn their inky language. Spoiler: she realizes that mastery of the alien language enables one to experience the past, future and present at once. It allows the linguist to experience time differently, and affect moments in the past to shape the future. It means she can travel through time. All just by learning a language.

It's a science-fiction take on Sapir–Whorf. But what about in real life? I wanted to know if languages endow their users with special attributes. I found that the Guugu Yimithirr people in Australia see the geographical world through compass points (and have no use for 'left' and 'right'). Their language (combined with culture) is thought to enhance their spatial awareness. They appear to have a GPS system in their heads. It's like a superpower.

Incredibly, they speak not of the left side of a painting, but the west of it. But if you turn the painting around, and look from the other side, what we'd still refer to as the left would become east to them. When they speak of, say, a shark attack, they describe the shark coming from the west and trying to gobble the human's eastern hand. It is unclear how this superpower would work if they were removed from their familiar surroundings, but they certainly have a greater awareness of cardinal points than the rest of us.

Linguists also marvel over the differences in our perception of colour across different languages. In general, native English speakers see navy and turquoise as a spectrum of blue. As such, we see turquoise as light blue, and very close to navy, or dark blue. In Russian, light blue and dark blue are entirely different colours. Tests have shown that Russians are just as likely to choose green as the closest colour to light blue as they are dark blue.

It's also fascinating to see how gendered language shapes associations to objects. Spanish people are more likely to describe a bridge with typically masculine adjectives, such as sturdy and bold, because the noun, 'el puente' is masculine. The same goes for the French 'le pont'. However, the German 'die Brücke' is feminine, and so poets tend to describe it with stereotypically feminine adjectives, such as elegant and graceful.

Another place where language alters experience is in its ability to keep secrets, as my friend Tom found out the hard way. Had he wanted to, he wouldn't have been able to keep secret the gender of our friend in Spanish, but was able to do so in English. This begs the question whether he deliberately chose to speak in English to obscure that the friend was a woman.

It's surprisingly difficult in many languages to keep someone's gender secret. As English-speaking teenagers, when our parents asked us who we were out with, we could reply: 'A friend!' End of discussion; run up to one's bedroom, shut the door. Spare a thought for a poor French person who would have to divulge such a salacious secret. 'Je sors avec un ami/une amie,' (I'm going out with a male/female friend). English, then, is the language of preference for secret-keeping about boyfriends and girlfriends.

This isn't just abstract theory. Professor Boroditsky explained that her bilingual students tell her that they 'strategically switch into English so that they don't have to press the question' from their parents. 'You want to be able to make the choice whether you're including extra information or not,' she explains.

Languages are becoming better secret-keepers. In many English-speaking countries, gendered words such as actress are losing ground to the male or neutral versions (actor, in this case). Some in progressive circles are choosing the gender-neutral they/them over gender-specific pronouns.

A move towards less revelatory language – said to be more inclusive – is happening around the world. In French, '*il*' (he) and '*elle*' (she) are contending with the gender-neutral '*iel*'. French education minister Jean-Michel Blanquer was affronted, tweeting: 'Inclusive writing is not the future of the French language.' In Latino communities, there is a push in social justice movements to abolish the gender system in their language. No longer will you have an *amigo* (male friend) or *amiga* (female friend), but rather *amigues* (friends). *Chicos* (boys) and *chicas* (girls) becomes *chiques*. I hear it all the time now in Argentina, even among apolitical people and older generations. All adjectives will take on the 'x' form if this push to align the Spanish language with tenets of progressive postmodernism pervade the culture. The merits and disadvantages thereof are worthy of a book in itself. Suffice to say, soon Spanish speakers might be able to keep secrets like we do in English.

Still, ours is not the most secretive of languages. While we in English don't have to reveal the gender of 'a friend' or 'a teacher', we do have pronouns ('he/him' and 'she/her'), which are a source of contention around trans rights because they force speakers to choose one of a binary to which they don't relate. There are many languages in which you can hide gender altogether. In Indonesian, you can choose whether or not to use gender pronouns, in a way that would currently feel awkward for English speakers. Gender is, however, just the tip of the iceberg in terms of potential secrets that are better hidden or revealed in other languages.

For instance, the word for 'no' in Indonesian changes depending on context. One such 'no' is '*belum*', which means 'not yet'. If someone asks you an invasive personal question, such as whether you have children, then you are forced in Indonesian not only to answer, but to stipulate whether you intend to have them in the future. *Belum* would imply you do, just not yet. Another 'no' (*tidak*) means you don't intend to have kids at all. The language doesn't appear to equip speakers with a subtle way out. Here, English is the better secret-keeper, as a simple 'no' will suffice in keeping your intentions secret.

If you want to keep secrets – and be deceptive – you'd do well to choose a language that allows you to hide behind it. Another tip is to learn it fluently. Sports journalist Martin Samuel writes of former England football manager Fabio Capello, who is Italian: 'For a reporter, [he] was a great England coach. He didn't have enough English to dissemble, to cloud words, to deploy nuance, to work the room. Straight questions therefore got straight answers. After one game, Capello was asked rather excitedly about player Theo Walcott. "He played very well, didn't he, Fabio?" "No," said the manager and left it at that.'

I was learning that there is a lot to keeping secrets. To appear honest and avoid arousing suspicions, you have to make sure you look and sound confident, and make sure that remains consistent throughout an interview with a suspicious cop, prosecutor, friend or lover. You have to be direct, avoiding superfluous and vague language. And you might even be able to pass a lie detector, if you practise enough to stop your fever model kicking in after the base questions. But technology is only becoming more advanced and more invasive.

For now, I have found it's still possible to keep things hidden. But I wondered how the technology of the future might make keeping secrets impossible. It might sound dystopian, but could new technology spell the death of secrets?

6

SECRETS AND TECHNOLOGY

Greek helicopter pilot Babis Anagnostopoulos appeared outside his house to speak to the press. Married just two years earlier in Portugal, he and his British wife Caroline Crouch seemed the perfect couple. When she was eight, Caroline's family had moved to the island of Alonnisos, a stunning slice of paradise on the Aegean Sea. She had grown up on the island, and met Babis when she was fifteen. He was twenty-eight at the time. Three years later – before bringing their daughter Lydia into the world – they were married in a ceremony in Portugal. They weren't to know it, but photos from the wedding – beach, cliffs, flowers and toothy smiles – would soon drape the columns of newspapers around the world.

One day, after settling into parenthood, the pair and their crying toddler were found by police tied up and duct-taped on the floor of their home. Once officers removed the tape from Babis's mouth, he explained how Albanian gangsters had targeted them. The story seemed to check out – the house was a tip; a window had been smashed and, amid a jumble of toys, a Monopoly set lay scattered on the ground. Babis later explained that the gang had stolen £13,000 that had been hidden in the game. As soon as police untied him, he ran to his wife's side, trying to nudge her awake. 'Honey, are you okay?' he asked.

She didn't reply.

She was dead.

Greece had just been hit by a string of femicides, which elevated the story to the top of the news cycle. It spread to the UK and beyond due to Caroline's British connections. Few could but sympathize with Babis, who appeared distraught in his appeals for information. He began to fall apart. He was seen clutching his toddler by the side of Caroline's grave, where he mourned for four hours.

As the weeks passed, no news came of the capture of a gang of thieving murderers. A palpably distressed civil protection minister launched a €300,000 bounty to convince people to come forward with leads. Thieves were pulled out of police line-ups, as Babis confirmed that the criminals were Georgian or Albanian. Who were these masked foreign bandits?

Something was off about the whole story, and you get the sense that the press was beginning to suspect as much. It's partly why they focused so much on this story at the time, as though ready to flip the script the moment the evidence presented itself. Still, Babis positioned himself as the great avenger of his wife's murder. Little did we know that the true murderer would soon be betrayed by the very technology that was supposed to help them.

Later, body language expert Judi James noted that Babis 'performs more eye cut-offs . . . rather than straight ahead' in his pleas for information about his wife's murderers. She believes this is a typical tactic of concealment. Other such tip-offs include how Babis blinked 'rapidly and intensely'. She notes how he 'shrugged his shoulders' when asked about the moment he knew his wife was dead, and spoke at speed without a change in tone. These are all apparently indicators that he was guilty of the murder of his wife.

I don't buy it. All this suggests to me is that Babis wasn't a good actor. Many innocent people fail to 'act innocent', too. The above clues about Babis's behaviour are exactly how we might expect a guilty character to act in a film. But real life isn't like the movies. People don't always match their emotions, or react how we might expect. People are unpredictable. A lot of body language analysis – so popular on YouTube – is bunk. In normal circumstances, body language is not enough to get a conviction – the Amanda Knox case aside.

Murder has long fascinated us. Think of how popular true crime is across movies, documentaries or podcasts. I asked psychologist Professor Paul Bloom why that might be, and he explained that we see horror films as a kind of practice for real-life events. The dopamine thrill that makes a zombie apocalypse or a murderous *Scream*-like film so enjoyable is your brain telling you to pay attention: you might learn something that'll save your life.

Horror films are fantasy, but true crime gets us even closer to that training for real-life horrors awaiting us out there. Research finds that women are particularly fond of true crime, which makes sense, as they are so often the victims. There are other reasons why we obsess over true crime. Most of us believe we'd never murder someone. But we can still empathize with a murderer; we can wonder what it is like to end a life; to have to keep it secret; to evade the authorities. That is what makes *Crime and Punishment* such a fascinating read. The protagonist, Raskolnikov, decides to murder to see what it is like. Then ensues a cat-and-mouse game between him and the main police officer.

But the story of *Crime and Punishment* wouldn't work today. Things are no longer quite so antiquated and quaint; we have the technology. Raskolnikov's prints would have been found all over the flat of the old lady he killed. Specks of his DNA might have been discovered, too. That's not to say that murderers can't get away with it today, but it's becoming more difficult to hide their crimes. As I started looking into technology, I was alarmed to find how quickly our chance of keeping anything secret is diminishing. And it'll get harder as we continue to merge our lives with technology.

CCTV is one such technology. There are more than 7 million CCTV cameras installed in the UK alone. You are likely to be caught on camera up to seventy times a day. This figure is only expected to increase, which is a scary thought. But we accept it, because we hope it will serve as a deterrent to murderers and criminals; or at least catch them after the fact. There is resistance to the installation by Mayor of London Sadiq Khan of ULEZ cameras that register vehicle number plates for low emission zones. A spate of vandalism has seen many of the cameras covered up, in one case by a box with the words 'stop electing idiots'. Yet, it seems there's no stemming the tide of encroaching monitoring of our every move. Sometimes it seems you just have to *think* something, and a product related to it will start popping up on your screen. To borrow a friend's laptop is to take a wild ride into the depths of their secret world through the ads that crop up in their browser. Nothing is sacred.

Babis had his own CCTV camera watching his home, but claimed that the masked gangsters disabled it and smashed it up. Later, it was found that Babis did so himself. He took care to cover his tracks, but overlooked one vital component in the modern monitors that had taken over his life: the fitness apps on his and Caroline's smartphones.

So engrained is this technology in our world that we forget about its existence. We go about our lives and wander the streets, as though nobody is watching, and forget about the apps that measure our heart rates, fitness and movement. When combined with the dozens of video recordings from CCTV, we get an accurate picture of most people's movements. Just a few decades ago, this would have seemed like a frightening, dystopian nightmare. Today, it's a proud social media post documenting how many steps you completed on the dog walk.

Smart devices showed that, while Babis was supposed to be tied up, he had in fact been moving around the house, from the attic to the basement, for hours. Babis had claimed to the police that the tape tied around his neck made him pass out for thirty minutes. But the smart devices showed he'd been up and about. There was also online evidence in Caroline's browsing history – yet another tracker – that she had tried to book a hotel to flee, after arguing with Babis. We can confirm this by looking at another technological file: their text message history. Just before he killed her, she had called him 'stupid' in a message.

Yet another clue could be found in Caroline's biometric watch, which measured her pulse. It showed that her heart had stopped beating hours before the time that Babis claimed the masked gangster had murdered her. Police used this technology to trap Babis in a web of lies. The family dog had also been found killed, which was clearly Babis's own work. He was sentenced to life imprisonment for the murder of Caroline, with an additional ten years for the execution of the dog. For misleading the authorities, another eleven years and six months were added.

Had Babis committed his crime in the nineteenth century, there's no telling whether his secret would have come to light. Imagine a historical murderer like Jack the Ripper being caught today by his Wi-Fi-enabled washing machine. For Babis, a pile of technological evidence made his evasion of the law impossible. Caroline's biometric wristwatch, Babis's fitness tracker, the couple's shared text messages, her browsing history and the broken CCTV (found to have been disabled far earlier than Babis claimed) combined to rid the crime scene of secrecy and shine a light on the murderer.

When combined with DNA profiling, we really do appear to live in a futuristic landscape. Through technology, police were able to ascertain that Babis had smothered his wife to death, before setting up an elaborate crime scene, tying himself up and even calling a neighbour and speaking to them as though gagged. Every attempt he made to cover his tracks was, itself, tracked.

In this case, the tech helped serve justice. Our embrace of technology helped to catch a murderer. Perhaps it will even deter others in future, as the possibility of getting away with serious crime dwindles. But the jury is out for the net result of encroaching tech in our lives.

Looking into the potential death of secrets, I was astounded at how technology had already turned the concept of secrecy upside down. We have signed away our privacy and secrecy without even realizing it. Babis remembered the CCTV, but forgot the measurements and recordings of other smart devices. Yet, I soon came to realize that biometric wristwatches and fitness trackers aren't the half of it.

Here's what I found really scary: recordings of your innermost secrets and private moments might soon be tracked and leaked directly from source: your brain.

A list of seemingly unconnected words adorns a screen in front of an audience. 'Book' is most prominent, followed by the words 'character', 'computer screen' and 'building'. Smaller words include 'female', 'male' and 'car'. Beside the words plays a scrambled video of grey scribbles, morphing into indecipherable symbols. The words grow and shrink. New words begin to compete for pride of place, such as 'street' and 'mercantile-establishment'. And then, abruptly, every word falls away, except for the one that now fills the screen: FEMALE. The audience laughs. We are inside the dream of a male participant, and we've just reached the raunchy part.

Presenting the data on stage is cognitive neuroscientist and Dean of Yale, Dr Marvin Chun. His work focuses on deciphering our thoughts and dreams through Functional Magnetic Resonance Imaging (fMRI). It measures the blood flow and activation of neurons in our brains to predict and guess what we're thinking. With this technology, it certainly wouldn't have taken nearly forty days to catch Babis. They could have just popped him in an fMRI machine and read his mind. Even writing that last line, I feel self-conscious of how dated it will sound to anyone reading this in a few decades. It's like someone in the 1960s explaining that – one day – you'll be able to talk to your personal computer machine, which will be small enough to fit in one room. With that in *mind*, I'm imagining you wouldn't pop Babis in an fMRI machine, but just point at him with your phone to download all his secrets. One day soon, we might be unable to keep secrets at all.

This is a difficult concept for us to accept. Many of us like to believe that humans are somehow apart from the rest of the natural world, whether that be through belief in a soul, or simply the vague idea that the brain operates in a more unpredictable way to other matter. But scientists like Dr Chun see the brain as a system made up of atoms that behave like any other elements and chemical compounds in the universe. 'It's basically a massive learning device,' he tells me, of the brain. 'It's like a computer.' To him, the mind is therefore decipherable, even if advances in science aren't quite there yet.

Many scientists disagree that the brain is like a computer. It's a debate at the centre of free will versus determinism. Do we have the ability to decide? Or is that just an illusion? Evidence that our brain appears to commit to a decision – such as moving an arm – before we even become aware of it suggests the brain might be at least a little like a computer. I think one reason that we're so reluctant to grasp this theory is that we want to believe we have free will; but if the brain simply functions like a computer, with neurons interacting with one another in ways scientists can predict, it might suggest a more deterministic reality: we do what our brains are 'wired' to tell us to do. We – whoever 'we' is – are simply playing the sheet music of the organ in the attic. And scientists can already read vague approximations of the secret data you store up there: the chords, if not quite the individual notes.

I think back to Melissa, who shared with me her story about killing a man in a dark alleyway. Imagine a world in which the authorities, the press and all her friends and professors instantly knew what had happened. It's a frightening proposition. I gained a sense of intimacy from her decision to tell me about that night; that's the kind of thing that'll be lost if secrets ever die out.

This is not the only philosophical issue around the concept of mind-reading. Right after showing the audience the man's erotic dream, Dr Chun flicks to a slide that reads '*Minority Report*', in reference to the 2002 Steven Spielberg movie based on Philip K. Dick's short story of the same name. In the film, authorities in 2054 are able to predict crimes before they are committed, and are therefore able to intercede, prevent the crime and lock up the would-be criminal. A concept like this would eradicate crime, but many would feel uneasy about it. We'd be locking people up for something similar to thought crime.

In the movie, the prediction mechanism is quasi-paranormal, provided by three psychics – called 'Precogs'. It's a far cry from the more scientific use of brain scans to read minds. Aside from that, the movie's vision of the future has proven remarkably prescient, from driverless cars and personalized ads to voice-controlled homes and facial recognition. That's not to mention robotic insects and gesture-controlled computers that are in development today. All of this tech has been implemented decades earlier than the 2050s setting of the film. Our police forces have even started using predictive policing through data and artificial intelligence, although it is yet to prove efficient.

But what happens once scientists are able to accurately extract intent from our minds? At the time of writing, computers and scanners are able to tell from the firing of neurons in your brain if you're looking at, say, a cat, or a shoe. We can communicate with people unable to speak by asking 'yes' or 'no' questions, then mining their responses directly from the mind. And we can measure how much pain somebody is in from their brain scan alone.

We are even able to capture grainy, undefined images from brains that resemble their innermost thoughts and dreams. On stage, Dr Chun didn't just show growing and shrinking words from a man's dream. He also wowed the audience with hazy portrayals of American comedian Steve Martin, direct from a mind whose owner was looking at a photo of him while their brain was being scanned.

This raises so many moral dilemmas that it is worthy of an entire book. For example, can our brains be hacked? Our minds have long been compromised by advertising and psychological warfare. Forget nuclear and biological wars; imagine an enemy that can physically infect a nation's minds with new images, thoughts and desires. When I spoke with Jacob Helberg of the Center for a New American Security, he said: 'If countries have the ability to know the deepest darkest secrets of [another country's] judges and politicians . . . is that country then independent? Or is it a satellite state?' Mind-reading adds an extra layer to the complexities of cyber warfare in the future.

Consider the opportunity for blackmail, once you can hack into a wealthy or powerful person's mind, and pluck out their most prized and controversial secrets, like in the movie *Inception*. And what of a *Minority Report* world, wherein authorities uncover all the brains with malignant intent? Might authorities be entitled to take psychopaths or paedophiles, for example, away from society? On the one hand, this would go against our concepts of free will, individual liberty and freedom of thought. (And it might be that we need a smattering of psychopaths in our tribes for societal cohesion and growth.) On the other, are we not responsible – if we know about potential criminals – for any crime they go on to commit?

These are all ethical and existential issues we're going to have to address if mind-reading becomes accurate, affordable and practical. But how far away are we? Dr Chun tells me they are 'basically trying to guess what people are seeing. So you can show people pictures while they're in the scanner and then you can measure your brain activity while you're looking at those images. The goal here is to try to guess and re-draw what people were looking at in the scanner – it's a form of mind-reading, because we're not asking people what they're seeing. We're literally just reading it out from their brain activity.'

Here's a simple look at how it works. Professor Jack Gallant of the University of California, Berkeley is credited as the pioneer of much of this work. His team recorded the neurons that light up under brain imaging while the participants watched all sorts of videos. They painstakingly made notes of which neurons flashed up due to increased blood flow to those areas, while the participants looked at a variety of images.

This enabled them to see exactly which parts of the brain buzzed while a person viewed, say, a plant, a dog or another human. One flash of a group of neurons might suggest a tall woman is being looked at, while another would signify a short man. Gradually, scientists have been building up a model of the neurons expected to light up for each real-world object. 'Based on reading out brain activity while people were looking at videos, you can pull from a dictionary the videos that would most closely match that brain activity.'

This is why Dr Chun refers to it as 'guessing' – the brain is far too complex for us to currently understand the precise relationships between the neurons that fire, and the thoughts and pictures they represent. His team built on Gallant's work in an effort to make the guessing more accurate. They were able to draw accurate portrayals of faces they thought the patients were viewing. The drawings are able to 'reliably' match up with the faces looked at in the scanner, suggesting that this technology could one day be used to uncover memories, view secrets and find out who committed a crime. Other academics are constantly refining the work. Scientists are now able to simply get participants to *imagine* a face, which the machine can draw with accuracy using artificial intelligence algorithms. Forensic sketch artists might soon be out of a job.

It's fascinating to me that our brains are seen to react in ways that are unique to every individual thought and sight. Dr Chun explains: 'We measure all these unique patterns, and we learn their relationship. Basically, we're learning the association. When you see Face A, this is how the brain responds, when you see Face D, this is how the brain responds.' They keep records of all the faces seen – so when a new face appears, they can choose a face from the records that best resembles the pattern of fired-up neurons in your brain.

This 'dictionary' works just as well when participants are asleep, allowing us for the first time in history to have a window into the dreams of others. Dr Chun has spent a long time considering the far-reaching ramifications of such a technology. 'I think one of the most fundamental ethical questions is mental privacy,' Dr Chun tells me. 'If you now have the ability to read out how smart someone is, or how attentive they are, or whether they, for example, may have some kind of clinical disorder, then you better well be very transparent about what you're doing when you have someone in the scanner.' He jokes that he no longer allows his own graduates to analyse his brain activity. When testing the technology on participants, scientists have to make sure to get detailed consent and to inform them of exactly what is being looked at. They also anonymize all the data to ensure privacy.

'But one day, when this becomes more commonplace so that industry or companies may have access to this technology, I think the laws will need to offer important protections for being transparent.' One of Dr Chun's goals is to enhance the hiring process for companies. Rather than relying on questionnaires and CVs – which could be full of false, misleading and subjective information – they'll be able to use brain imaging to get to the truth. These will provide 'more quantitative measures that may be less subject to bias'.

'Imagine using brain imaging to select students to a particular university. The goal there would be not to screen out defective brains. We don't want to ever diminish the value of hard work and determination and motivation. But the goal could be [to help] the students from disadvantaged backgrounds, who did not have the benefits of an education to sharpen their test-taking skills, or get the kinds of grades that you need to get into a selective university. But maybe their brains are very special; maybe they're just geniuses in waiting.'

This does sound promising – particularly if you're a genius in waiting – and it is clearly beneficial to universities and companies who would like to hire these geniuses. But in this futuristic system, I can't help but think of the not-so-smart people who get through on luck and deception by keeping secret their true smarts (or lack thereof). At the moment, there is just enough ambiguity and opaqueness around intelligence that the system can be rigged; it means that with a bit of luck, hard work and bolshiness, anyone might just climb above their potential, no matter how unlikely. But with a rigid brain-reading system that categorizes people based on nothing but their brain scans, a world might arise that is even more rigid and hierarchical than now. Perhaps we need some secrecy and mystique to keep things fluid, and allow for the occasional success of plucky but talentless underdogs.

Personality traits and images (whether imagined, dreamed or viewed) are now being read by scientists with some level of accuracy. But we're not quite at *Minority Report* level with prediction of crime. 'We're still very far away from being able to decode some kind of intent or very specific thoughts; something that is more semantic-based is going to be harder to read,' he explains. 'I get inspiration from the science-fiction movies. *Minority Report* is one of the most fascinating movies I've seen because of the premise that you can predict behaviour, which is I think an ultimate goal for a psychologist and neuroscientist.

'All the technologies we have are really about *present* mind-reading. We can barely read out what people are seeing and thinking in the present. And then using that to predict future behaviours is really far.' He adds, 'Even if you knew every single factor, just because of the essential randomness of physics, you know, quantum mechanics and all that, it's just intrinsically unpredictable, even at the basic atomic level.' He concedes that you could use this kind of machine learning to predict behaviour better 'than a pundit may', and to do 'predictions in much more circumscribed settings. Maybe not *Minority Report*, but can we predict the onset of dementia? Can we scan a baby's brain, and predict whether this child will develop autism?'

While *Minority Report* might be some time away, scientists are getting better at predicting the rate of reoffending of prisoners. Machine learning grants parole judges information to make more accurate decisions. And while we may not be able to predict future behaviour accurately, we can see into the minds of others, whether awake or asleep. This could spell the end of secrets of the mind.

Perhaps some good will come from that. For example, could couples hack one another's minds to better understand each other? As it stands, couples are worse at reading each other's minds the longer they stay together. This is because we create a fixed picture of people in the first few years. We each change dramatically over the years (with some core traits staying consistent). It is said that couples who have more explosive fights actually fare better in long-term relationships. A fiery argument is the best way to hammer home the changes we go through. Those who don't argue can find ten years later that they suddenly don't recognize the person they're with. Might a mind-reading device help us see each other better? Or might it just create further problems? Some thoughts and secrets might be better unsaid.

Should we be concerned about hackers using gadgets to get into our minds? Dr Chun explains, 'I think it won't be possible with MRI because the signals we get are too crude. We're not looking at individual neurons, we're looking at very large populations – tens of millions of neurons at a time. If there emerges a technology that allows us to measure every single neuron's activity and their interactions with other neurons, then it's theoretically possible.'

Dr Chun is speaking speculatively about what he believes will be a distant future. But in the year that passes after my conversation with him, dramatic progress is made with artificial intelligence. Dr Alexander Huth of the University of Texas has participants listen to sixteen hours of podcasts while in an fMRI scanner. His team knows exactly when each word from the podcast was said, and which neurons fired in each person's brain at that time. He puts the data learned from the fMRI scans into AI systems, which are able to learn from our firing neurons at a far greater speed, creating models that better read our minds. 'This is just outrageously effective. Like, shockingly effective. It works so much better than any method that we had before.'

He warns ominously about the privacy implications: 'We thought about this a lot because . . . this whole thing, it's kind of creepy. We're kind of reading thoughts out of someone's head, which I feel like is crossing a line a lot of people would be unnerved by.' For this reason, he had subjects attempt to make it not work to see if they might resist having their minds read. Perhaps it'll come as a relief to know that participants were able to distract the machine from their innermost thoughts by doing mental exercises at the same time, such as naming animals and telling stories in their heads. Who knows whether our minds will be able to escape the more advanced brain invaders of the future.

We are moving towards a future where cyborg technology – inserting artificial intelligence into our own brains – is a potential reality. That might be a way in for hackers. I imagine a future world in which we have to train our brains – like in *Harry Potter* – to prevent our thoughts and secrets being compromised and used as collateral. Might we sense the presence of hackers in our minds? What might that *feel* like? If technology is able to isolate individual neurons in the brain, we'll enter into the age of mind-reading, blowing down the doors of the last refuge of secrecy.

We can only speculate about the future. But I was beginning to see how technology is encroaching on our secret and private lives in scary and unpredictable ways. As a result – in a world of CCTV and wearable technology – we are learning to be more careful. In the early days of Facebook, for example, it was normal to write publicly on friends' pages as though speaking just to them. Yes, we were aware that others could see the posts, but we weren't yet media savvy. We needed to get our fingers burned.

Gradually, we watched in horror and intrigue as social media users got themselves into professional trouble because of their online interactions. The most infamous case is that of Justine Sacco, a name now synonymous with public shaming, and a protagonist in journalist Jon Ronson's 2015 book *So You've Been Publicly Shamed*. In 2013, just as many of us were trying to get to grips with the relationship between the private and the public on social media, Sacco tweeted to her 170 followers: 'Going to Africa. Hope I don't get AIDS. Just kidding. I'm white!' It was meant as an ironic joke about the public's misperception of AIDS and Africa. She told Ronson: 'To me it was so insane of a comment for anyone to make, I thought there was no way that anyone could possibly think it was literal.'

Regardless of intent, the tweet and the ire it attracted flooded the internet, and Justine didn't have a chance to delete the post, because she was on an eleven-hour flight to Cape Town when it went viral. Users tracked her flight, created mocking hashtags about her, and pressured her employers to fire her – which they did. The whole world seemed to be watching and rejoicing in the public shaming and destruction of one woman.

Not only did she lose her job (and friends and family members), but her name and story were hoisted to the front pages of search engines, preventing her from finding new jobs (and new friends and . . . family members). As Ronson's book shows, Sacco was one of many who have found their lives turned upside down by a thoughtless private thought made public in the early days of social media. This has taught us to be vigilant, although people still fall through the cracks every day.

If there is one place where we really should have room for privacy, secrecy and everything in between – a lone refuge where we can relax and be our primal, animalistic selves – it's the bedroom. But I've come to realize that we're not even safe there. I'm not talking about tell-all hit pieces about celebrities by disgruntled lovers. Just as in the murder by the Greek pilot, it's technology that shines a light on secrets.

In 2017, sex toy manufacturer We-Vibe settled a class action suit for almost $4 million. The case was around a Bluetooth-enabled vibrator device called the We-Vibe 4 Plus, which the company marketed as the 'No. 1 Couples Vibrator'. It connects to an app on your phone, which allows couples to 'play together' when they are apart. It's a practical workaround for long-distance couples. It was revealed, however, that the manufacturer had been collecting information about couples' intimate sessions, including the patterns and intensity of vibration they chose. The makers also collected data on the device's temperature when in use, and how often and for how long it was on – along with the email addresses customers used to register.

It's easy to see how such a breach in privacy could be used against the toy's users by discontented employees and hackers. The company claims it used the data to improve its device, but it had no consent to collect the information.

In an even more disturbing case, sex toy maker Lovense was found to have recorded and stored audio of masturbation sessions. This was discovered by users on an online Reddit forum. One user explained how they stumbled upon a six-minute clip titled 'tempSoundPlay.3gp' in the app's folder, and were startled to recognize their own voice and sounds in the file. The company claimed the recording was 'accidental', but it is worrying, and leaves even our sex lives open to hacking, revelation and extortion.

Although discussions around consent in sex are becoming more prominent, consent from sex toy companies is often overlooked, perhaps due to the salacious nature of the devices: people don't want to talk about it, lest they inadvertently admit that they use the toys (which is another sad gauge of the way our society handles privacy and secrecy).

If a hacker is able to extract information – anything from audio and video files to temperature and vibration patterns – of someone's most intimate sexual moments, does that constitute a form of sexual assault? And along with the hacker, is the sex toy company also guilty of it? Hackers could even take control of the functions of the devices. Security researchers were able to do exactly that with Lovense's butt plug, which can be controlled by anyone within Bluetooth range. This would surely be classified as sexual assault from afar if carried out on an unwilling victim.

In her book, *Sex Robots & Vegan Meat*, journalist Jenny Kleeman also references the Siime Eye vibrator, whose built-in camera and movements can be hijacked by strangers. This could mean not only the release of videos of people in their most intimate moments, but the potential for the vibrator to be controlled by others against their wishes.

As technology advances, and we move into the realm of full-body sex robots, the stakes rise due to the physical nature of the robot and its abilities to record and coerce its users. When Kleeman meets the makers of the sex robots of the future, one particularly advanced and lifelike sex robot is, according to its manufacturer, being programmed to 'systematically find out more about you, until she knows all the things that make you you, until all those empty spots are filled.' Hacked sex robots, Kleeman writes, can be 'even more nightmarish than butt plugs gone rogue.'

But even now, the potential data breaches are insidious, with wide-ranging ramifications. Kleeman continues: 'My mind reels when I think about how lucrative it could be to sell the data sex robots collect from their owners to advertisers. Forget Cambridge Analytica and Facebook – the being you love and trust the most might be used as the most powerful marketing tool ever known to convince you to buy stuff. Or vote for stuff. Sex robots could entertain you, satisfy you, but also humiliate, hurt and exploit you.'

This is without even mentioning the non-sexual recording robot devices, such as Siri and Alexa, that we have to worry about. For example, Elon Musk's Tesla assures the millions who buy their electric cars that their privacy 'is and will always be enormously important to us'. But staff at the firm allegedly shared and laughed about recordings made of drivers in their cars. News agency Reuters reported that the shared clips included one of a naked man, and another of 'sexual wellness items'. Memes were allegedly made of the clips, with the funniest ones helping to progress the careers of the staff members who created them. The recordings appear to have been made by the cars' external cameras, showing owners approaching their cars, and giving away their locations.

When you can't get into your car without being recorded; when you can't discuss the daily news over breakfast with your family away from the listening cogs of Alexa; and when even your masturbatory experiences aren't safe from the cruel light of exposure, it's a sign we're flying legs-first into La Petite Mort of secrets.

Whether it be the fMRIs reading your mind, the biometric watches and apps monitoring your every move or the Siri-like sex robots recording your raunchy rhythms, technology is leaving us in a moral quandary. As I considered the future of secrecy, I wondered how we might legislate against further encroachments. Some say that such invasions are necessary. 'If you have something that you don't want anyone to know, maybe you shouldn't be doing it in the first place.' These were the Orwellian words of former Google Chief Executive Eric Schmidt in an interview aired in late 2009. Not long after, media company CNET used Google to reveal personal information about Schmidt. He was incensed, and banned CNET from press events. It's fine for others to be spied on, but not us. We feel safer in a world where others are tracked; but less safe when our own secrets are fair game.

Google's CEO Sundar Pichai admits that chatbots and the advance of AI keep him up at night. AI could change how wars take place, it could make our jobs redundant, and it could even spell the end of humanity (should we be unable to align its interests with ours). In the first draft of this book, I wrote the line: 'I'm all too aware that a book like this could – in not too long a time – be written by AI.' We're already well past that point.

I asked AI bot ChatGPT 4 whether it had the capability to write a non-fiction book like this, and fool the public into believing a human had written it. It responded in the affirmative, with a couple of provisos: it would have to fabricate any personal anecdotes, and it wouldn't be able to 'evolve' and explain how writing the book had changed its mind.

Many believe that one of the most pressing concerns about AI and technology in general is the spread of disinformation, clouding what is true and what isn't. One way we can already see this is through the advance of deepfakes, which most users can now easily create online. We'll never know what to believe and whom to trust. There's no telling how technology might impinge upon our liberties, from politicians being made to look as though they said things they didn't, to deepfake pornographic images of individuals, the sharing of which has just been made illegal in the UK.

This is all a bit scary. But I found there are positive sides to the way technology is interfering with our privacy and secrecy. It is helping us to reveal and share in the human experience. Church confession has long been an integral cog in our society, but has fallen away with dwindling numbers of worshippers. The internet has ensured that confession remains a huge part of our society, whether it be in the form of live streamers on YouTube or Twitch, or photo and video obsessives sharing every waking moment on Facebook, TikTok or Instagram. Some of this confession is for clout, but some of it is to get secrets off chests.

Big-name celebrities broadcast their innermost thoughts live from their bedrooms, while news and gossip channels run 24/7 to inform us about the hidden pieces of others' lives. Let's not kid ourselves: even the driest political commentary is essentially gossip. The Web is a digital recreation of our tribal habitat, enabling us to reveal secrets, resist the fever model and enhance our sense of social cohesion with other humans across the globe through curiosity and gossip.

When I think back to my podcast listeners and their desire to reveal their secrets to me, I see now how advances in technology have helped us to reach out to one another in previously inconceivable ways. As we did traditionally in our churches, we continue to reveal our secrets via the anonymous proxy of confession . . . but to podcasters and bloggers rather than priests.

Writer Sherry Turkle spent six months on confessional blogs. 'One afternoon of reading brings me to "The only reason I haven't killed myself yet is because my mother would kill herself . . . I'm in love with a boy I've never met but we IM each other every day and talk about where we'll live when we're married . . . My bulimia has made me better at giving blowjobs."'

Turkle continues, 'A confession that once might have been made within the bounds of friendship, family, or church now takes place with no bounds or bonds at all. It goes out to whoever is on the site,' writes Turkle.

Later, I'll investigate why exactly we reveal secrets to anonymous users and bots, but it seems it does wonders for our social cohesion and communal intimacy, providing we don't go too far, as MI5 did when it committed to being more open. I imagine most of us would prefer an agency fighting domestic terrorism to keep things tight-lidded.

But how far should power extend in terms of extracting information from *others*? MI5 has in the early 2020s been embroiled in a dispute with Facebook, which they accuse of giving terrorists a free pass by keeping messages on its platform and its messaging service WhatsApp encrypted.

Authorities want access to the messages to fight terrorism and child exploitation, but Facebook and other social media companies have been scrambling messages to ward off hackers and criminals. It's a fascinating debate: do we prioritize individual liberty and privacy? Or do we crack down on blackmailers and child sex offenders? Despite the encryption, many users have left WhatsApp because its security isn't as reputable as other platforms marketed on privacy, such as Signal or Threema.

Why does the average user need an encrypted social media app or messaging service, if – as former Google Chief Executive Eric Schmidt suggested – they weren't doing anything wrong in the first place? Maybe, given the influx of aforementioned tech, we simply need a space that is ours, and ours alone. Or maybe we simply don't trust governments and big tech companies not to read and sell our data behind our backs. We've become so accustomed to batting away annoying pop-ups without reading them, that we often click 'accept' without being aware of what we're agreeing to. These are usually cookies, although it occurs to me they really should be called crumbs. When you click accept, you're agreeing to the website tracking and storing data to be sent back to the website owner. When the cookies are summoned by the website itself, your data is collected by its owner.

Cookies are being replaced by more subtle ways of gathering your data. This is often harmless, and helps brands understand your demographics. It is also a time saver for you, because these baked-in tools help your browser to remember your log-in details and other steps previously completed so that you don't have to keep repeating them. But a nefarious website owner could theoretically identify you and use your data against you. Cookies and other identifying tools that are replacing cookies can include your browsing habits, history, unique user ID, links that you have clicked, your username and password, online identifiers such as your IP address and even personal data like your phone number and address. This kind of data can be used against you. For example, health insurance companies can find out about potential health issues, and raise your insurance costs.

It's not just advertisers you have to be wary of; experts are now warning users not to charge their laptops in USB ports in airports and other public places. The USB ports could be compromised by hackers. You're better off bringing your own charger, and plugging it in the mains.

This is just one type of concern about the technological invasion of your privacy. Many people don't care. I confess to thinking, with regards to my data (my bank account log-in codes aside): 'Whatever, just take it all.' It's easier. The same goes for the government: 'I'm not hiding anything. Build another CCTV camera, see if I care.'

But we know from history that where you find an invasive government, you often find authoritarianism. In spite of – or because of – the good intentions of weeding out immoral behaviour, a slippery slope ensues, as leaders begin wielding increasing power. This is why, for example, there are American survivalists or 'preppers' who take up arms and keep bunkers full of food and other supplies. Whatever the rest of the world thinks of Americans and their guns – and their unparalleled mass shooting statistics – distrust in government is not only understandable, but integral.

For three years, I lived in Berlin, a city once torn in two by an oppressive left-wing regime that employed a secret police. For decades, the Ministry for State Security – a secret force known as the Stasi – ruled over East Germany, terrifying its civilians into obedience. Like Russia's KGB and Nazi Germany's Gestapo, the Stasi operated outside the law to spy on and repress its people. It was efficient and successful too, preventing civilians from travelling, purchasing international products and receiving news from the outside world. It even coerced its own people into spying and reporting on one another. At its peak, it had 173,081 secret informants who were out working for the government by spying on their unsuspecting neighbours.

What surprised me, living there, was the number of Berliners who look back fondly – or at least, without condemnation – on a time when they had little autonomy or agency to make decisions about their lives, and could keep no secrets. To me, this speaks to the curiosity and judgement within each of us that makes us want to know about the lives of others (also the name of a brilliant German film about the Stasi), even if it means giving up our own. This is not unlike the impulse expressed by Google's Eric Schmidt, who was fine with the exposure of the secrets of others, but not his own.

That's not to minimize the abuse and torture suffered by East German citizens during the Stasi's terrifying rule. More than thirty years after the Fall of the Berlin Wall, many former East Germans still experience trauma as a result of it. But many others feel nostalgia for the oppression. There's even a name for the fondness many retain for the East German authoritarian state: *Ostalgie* (a portmanteau of '*Ost*', which is German for 'East', and nostalgia). Across other countries and states, this is known as Communist nostalgia.

In 2009, when German newspaper *Der Spiegel* asked former East German inhabitants if the GDR 'had more good sides than bad sides', 57 per cent answered in the affirmative. There are complex reasons for *Ostalgie*, notably the rise in unemployment (which *officially* didn't exist under the regime) after Germany's reunification. There is a tendency among foreigners and West Germans visiting the East to patronize and offend the locals by wrongly assuming that most of them are relieved to be part of the West.

When Easterners are reminded that they couldn't travel before, many respond that the low wages they're on don't permit them to do so now. They point to the social benefits of the former GDR. They have a point, too: working women had better healthcare and job security, as well as pay equal to their male counterparts. After the wall fell, 70 per cent of East German women lost their jobs because West Germany had more old-fashioned views of gender roles. This affected not only hiring preferences but maternity and childcare laws.

Nostalgia is also felt for local East German brands, which – when the Wall came down – were quickly replaced by impersonal global international equivalents. Others feel that they lost the sense of community – spying on one another notwithstanding – that they enjoyed under Communism.

These are all valid arguments, and speak of a different way of living that focuses on the collective rather than the individual. It makes me think of the interviews I've done with nostalgic defectors of Hasidic Judaism. OK, they weren't permitted to own a television, but that meant that the art of storytelling thrived. While many of our Western, 'free' children sit like zombies (like us, the parents) in front of screens, Hasidic Jewish children spend days anticipating the next story from an animated older member. They learn to tell their own stories, often developing their communication skills, imaginations and personalities. It's the kind of thing many of us would want for our own children. Collective cohesion – enforced with an iron fist – is valued by the community over individual freedoms.

It's very much the *Brave New World* that Aldous Huxley wrote about. In his 1932 book – and in authoritarian sects – many members are surprisingly happy, which – since it differs so drastically from Western individualistic values – is hard for us to understand. Many other members, however, find a Brave New World – or a Hasidic existence – torturous. They have nowhere to turn.

The same applies to those living under the Stasi. It wasn't necessarily so bad if you bought into the philosophy and had a lot of luck (enough to be left alone, to make a living and to not have to hide anything from a terrifying government). But it was horrifying for citizens who desired individual freedom. The nostalgic and romantic portrayals of the GDR are also exactly what the Stasi were employed to evoke at all costs.

On the surface, there was a sense of communal togetherness and universal happiness, but that is only because you'd be reported to the Stasi if you uttered a word of discontent in front of friends and family. You'd never know which of them was working for the secret police. Like a cult, the Stasi collected medical, school and police records on its citizens, as well as interviews with neighbours and relatives, to customize an attack on the mental health of activists and enemies of the regime. This is akin to Scientology's 'fair game' harassment tactics they employ against those who leave or criticize the cult.

In both the GDR and Scientology, blackmail, social shame and physical torture have been used to put off and delegitimize critics. The Stasi even had an official Department of Pornography, which not only framed so-called enemies of the state as avid porn addicts (the symbol of the moral depravity of the West), but filmed its own porn, and forced its members to attend the premieres. Their attendance would later be used against them as blackmail and collateral.

More than one in three civilians at the time were under suspicion. More pages of printed text were produced by the Stasi than by all German authors put together from the Middle Ages to the Second World War. Rumours about activists were spread, and pornographic magazines were stuffed into their mailboxes for their neighbours to see.

Other objectors were simply taken off the streets and committed to asylums. The most frightening place to end up was the Hohenschönhausen, a prison which didn't officially exist, and couldn't be found on maps. With its beige-and-brown fittings, pallid floral wallpaper and clunky television boxes and machines, it made for a soulless 1970s lair. It was where much of the torture took place.

Nowadays, Germans can apply to see their Stasi records. Decades on, these papers continue to break up families and friendships, as people come to realize who was spying on them. The Stasi had so many records about each individual in the state that it could use secrets as collateral to force them to betray others. It's a history lesson that teaches us to be wary of a government or technology that is too easily able to know our secrets.

Orwell was writing about this in the early 1900s, but governments have been aggressively seeking out our secrets for centuries, from present-day China to the Spanish Inquisition. The latter – made even more memorable by the 'Nobody expects the Spanish Inquisition' Monty Python sketch – came from an attempt to maintain Catholic orthodoxy. It was one of a host of brutal regimes from past centuries to employ Stasi-like tactics. Each time, whether it be the Spanish Inquisitors, the Stasi or Scientology, they used the power of secrets to assert absolute control over their people.

Stasi museums in Berlin are fascinating for their James Bond-style spy gadgets. Imagine if the Stasi were around today, making use of biometric watches, smartphone apps and mind-reading scanners. It's a frightening proposition. The cyclical nature of history suggests such oppressive regimes will keep coming back, which is scary given the rate of technological growth. In fact, we don't have to use our imaginations. China's techno-authoritarianism lurks in the background of every political discussion. It's an unsaid aside that parenthesizes every claim with: '. . . providing China doesn't . . .'

That's because not only does China spy on its own citizens, but it is believed they're watching the rest of us. In 2023, as concerns around China peaked due to speculation about its role in the Russia–Ukraine war, the US Air Force shot down a high-altitude balloon owned by China. President Biden alleged that it contained 'two box cars full of spy equipment'. Biden claimed Xi Jinping was upset about the incident because the Chinese leader didn't know about the existence of the spy balloon. Biden quipped: 'That's a great embarrassment for dictators. When they didn't know what happened.'

British former Conservative Party leader William Hague – who also served as foreign secretary – writes of his concerns that, as technology advances, surveillance states are beginning to take the upper hand on the global stage. Democratic countries have a harder time containing leaks, such as when whistle-blower Edward

Snowden revealed 'military defence and intelligence programmes of great interest to America's adversaries.'

A more recent breach was carried out by twenty-one-year-old Jack Teixeira, a computer specialist who wanted to show off to his gamer buddies by posting highly classified military documents. These kinds of leaks not only give an advantage to the likes of Russia in their war with Ukraine, but erode trust with America's allies. As Hague writes, British ministers 'raise the other eyebrow about how President Trump could allegedly hang on to top secret intelligence reports at his Mar-a-Lago estate without anybody asking where he'd put them – not something I could ever imagine being able to do as British foreign secretary'.

The States have enough concerns about spies from other countries, without wanting to worry about their own people too. Teixeira's leaks showed that Russian operators were claiming to be 'far more successful than previously thought at manipulating social media and search engine rankings to boost lies about Ukraine's military or the alleged side effects of the vaccines.' Egypt was considering passing a secret supply of weapons to Russia, and China was delivering them to Putin under the guise of 'civilian items'.

President Trump tried to ban Chinese social media app TikTok, citing national security concerns. When asked if TikTok had been spying on American citizens, the company's CEO Shou Zi Chew replied ominously: 'I don't think that spying is the right way to describe it.' TikTok has also admitted that employees at its parent company ByteDance had used the app to track the location of journalists who criticized the app. Meanwhile, TikTok continues to wage a public relations campaign using beautiful, smiling American influencers. It's all a bit creepy.

In China, surveillance is a fact of life in what is being described as a technology-inspired twenty-first-century authoritarianism. Forget the Stasi's enormous paper trail: Chinese state surveillance makes use of 'mobile apps, biometric collection, artificial intelligence, and big data, among other means to control 13 million Turkic Muslims,' alleges Human Rights Watch. Digital currency is fast being employed by the central bank to get a better sense of exactly how citizens are spending their money. 'Safe cities' are being constructed to predict and prevent fires, natural disasters . . . and political dissent. Blacklisted people will be denied certain services unless they comply with orders about exercising, healthy habits and other government policies.

It occurred to me while researching China that I have to account for my own bias. China is a far-flung nation that seems scary to me: partly because it's so different; partly because it genuinely *is* scary; and partly because all the news I get about it comes from Western sources. Our own authoritarian moves may not seem as frightening or egregious, but they exist.

The West is also moving towards a lighter form of a digital currency, simply by aspiring to a cashless society. Our financial transactions can also be tracked by governments, who can then grade us and punish us for holding the wrong views. That may seem a little *Black Mirror*, but it's what Canadian Prime Minister Justin Trudeau did in 2022, when he froze the bank accounts of anti-vaccine mandate protestors. It also came at a time of world-wide crisis, when nobody knew what the right course of action was. Still, I was amazed how quickly one leader was able to take away his citizens' access to money for holding dissenting views. As with many authoritarian measures, the intentions appeared to come from a good place: to get anti-vaxxers out of the street blockade and to encourage the country to vaccinate against COVID.

In 2019, Chinese citizens were made to download the 'Study Xi, Strong Nation' app, which forced them to study the president's philosophy, participate in quizzes, and compete against others. GPS locations are recorded to make sure that the country's poorest are diligently going about finding work to rectify their economic predicaments. The country has one of the lowest press freedom scores in the world, and is one of the least democratic nations, too.

It's terrifying to think of how China might use new technological advances to further tighten its grip over its people, and the rest of us. It is already having an impact on how the West develops tech. For example, many in the West are calling for a pause on all development of AI. The fear is that AI will take over the world, and we'll become at best, obsolete, and at worst, extinct.

Scientists want to halt production, while they work on 'alignment' – coding that ensures that AI's 'aspirations' align with our own. The first issue with this is that many computer scientists believe that it is unachievable, or that it would take decades to get right, by which time it may be too late. The second is that it's unlikely that Western powers will put technological advances on the backburner while China and other rivals forge ahead. It seems we're in a bind.

Despite these lessons from history and the present about authoritarianism, many of us still want a government that observes and scrutinizes its people. Like the former East Berliners with their nostalgia for a simpler time, some of us pine for an easy life, where our decisions are made for us, and we turn a blind eye to interference from government in the secret or private affairs of our neighbours. It's a fine balancing act between a ruler that fights crime with efficiency, and one that impinges upon the freedom of individuals to keep secrets. It seems we'd rather they continue monitoring the potential terrorists, criminals and child molesters . . . just as long as it doesn't get in the way of our own freedoms.

7

SECRETS, CULTS AND STATUS

As I delved further into secrets, one topic kept cropping up time and time again: cults. I wondered why, until it clicked. Cults represent a quintessential element of secret-keeping: its relationship with status. On my YouTube channel, I've interviewed experts on coercive control and cult mentalities, and defectors from such extreme authoritarian sects as Scientology and NXIVM. I've also spoken with those who consider religious communities into which they were born 'cultish'. These people come from extreme branches of Mormon, Jehovah's Witness, Islamic and Hasidic Jewish sects, among others.

The comments from viewers usually amount to some variation of: 'I would never be so stupid as to join a cult.' (But with expletives and all in capital letters.) Sometimes I do live interviews, and my subscribers raise this point in the live chat as part of a Q&A. Typically, my guest – who probably *did* join a cult – explains that *anyone* (including you, the viewer or reader) can be hoodwinked by one. Their argument is, the more certain you are that you wouldn't fall for it, the more likely you are to be susceptible. Perhaps my guests – having been subsumed into one themselves – *have* to believe that. I'm not sure I totally buy it myself, but there is perhaps some truth in it.

Steven Hassan is an author, educator and mental health counsellor who devised the BITE model for recognizing authoritarian control. It lists the signs that an organization might be a cult under the headings of Behavioural Control, Information Control, Thought Control and Emotional Control (hence BITE). He is seen by many as the go-to cult buster. *Salon* described him as 'one of the world's foremost experts on mind control, cults and similar destructive organizations.' He holds multiple academic qualifications, has given talks on cults and has written many books about them. He is intelligent and self-analytical.

He was also fooled into joining the Unification Church (a.k.a. the Moonies), a 'new religious movement' derived from Christianity and founded in South Korea. This came before – and influenced – the career he devoted to deciphering cults. Still, how could someone as smart as him be fooled into joining a group of people called the Moonies? They devote themselves to a man called Reverend Moon, who considered himself the second coming of Christ, and claimed to be creating a human lineage free from sin. You may have seen footage of the huge mass weddings, part of Moon's methods for keeping the cult insular and interwoven. If somebody told you they were literally Jesus, you'd keep a wide berth, right? Not Dr Hassan.

There is evidence that intelligent people are actually *more* prone to lapses in judgement. It's because they are bright enough to come up with convincing narratives to explain away any of their biases and ideologies. Science writer David Robson wrote in *The Intelligence Trap* about Arthur Conan Doyle, the author of the Sherlock Holmes detective books. As the creator of the character known as the master of deduction, one might assume that Doyle would have his wits about him. But in 1917, two girls, Elsie (aged sixteen) and Frances (nine), played a prank by making photos of 'fairies'. This was at a time when people absolutely did not believe in fairies, but Doyle still fell for it. Some of the public did, too, and interest in the photos reignited in the 1960s after a reporter tracked down Elsie, who again suggested the fairies were supernatural. Only in the 1980s did the now-octogenarian twosome admit they had forged the fairies using cardboard cut-outs.

Doyle had been had. His convincing narrative? The pins in the navels of the fairies (to hold the faked images up) were holes indicating belly buttons: evidence that fairies could give birth. His friend, magician Houdini – with whom he later fell out – said: 'As a rule, I have found that the greater brain a man has, and the better he is educated, the easier it has been to mystify him.'

Another victim of the intelligence trap was Nobel Prize winner Paul Frampton, a pre-eminent physicist who was 'fooled into carrying two kilograms of cocaine across the Argentinian border'. According to Robson, 'Intelligent and educated people are less likely to learn from their mistakes, or to take advice from others.' They have been found to have a 'bigger bias blind spot' and are less able to see 'holes in their logic'.

It is quite possible then for intelligent people to fall into traps. They may even join cults purporting to bring enlightenment, and overlook (or explain away) red flags that seem glaring to most of us. But I'm sceptical as to whether this could happen to just *anyone*. Sure, none of us are immune from traps and scams. Yet, to join a cult – an extreme authoritarian sect – requires other quite specific traits and experiences. For example, you have to be seeking community. Somebody who feels more comfortable as an individual is less likely to be driven to join a sect. Cults also seek out people who are at a point in their life when they feel they need direction. Scientology asks prospective new members about their 'ruin' – any undesirable issue that is holding them back. Defectors often talk to me about having been at a low point in their lives, before a cult came in and offered them advice, and a path to financial and spiritual enlightenment.

There's another key element. I was beginning to find a relationship between cults, secrecy and status. A prime reason people join cults is the pursuit of status. So much of the allure of cults is the idea of being the holder of secrets to which lower-status individuals have no access. This is why I don't believe that just about anyone could join a cult. It needs to be someone who – at a particular moment in their life – has a burning desire to stand out and feel special.

English marketing exec Alex Barnes-Ross joined Scientology not once, but twice. He grew up in a secular household, away from religion, and had a normal life, so he went against the grain when he first joined Scientology as a teenager. He'd seen journalist John Sweeney's BBC *Panorama* documentary, infamous for a scene in which Sweeney, tired of Scientology's mind games, has a screaming fit. Most viewers came away with a good idea of how unhinged the cult was. Not Alex. He tells me: 'Being someone who is quite critical of a thinker myself, I wanted to make up my own mind. I went in, asked them all the tough questions: "Do you believe in aliens? Do you believe in Lord Xenu? Do you disconnect families?"' He thought it might not be as bad as people said, like how someone might leave a bad review at a restaurant because of a uniquely unfortunate experience.

'It was about spending time with people who were like-minded, people who were trying to achieve a goal,' he adds. 'There's this goal in Scientology that is trying to clear the planet. Trying to rid everyone of their reactive mind. It's really important, we have to do it now. It was my purpose, what I wanted to do with my life.'

Beneath all the mythology, Alex is explaining two issues – or 'ruins' – in his life that he hoped Scientology would address. First, *purpose*: saving the world gave him a raison d'être and the chance to feel good about himself. Second, underlying all of that, is *status*: he wanted to play the role of the progressive critical thinker, in contrast to the vast majority of non-Scientologists who had a 'reactive mind'.

Scientology gives those who may not feel special – or haven't had their specialness recognized – a chance to role-play at special. So enthused by this was Alex that he signed a one-billion-year contract. Scientologists believe that your Body Thetans [mini souls] live on and go into other bodies after you die – the contract is designed to continue with your next body, though I don't know of any stories of people turning up and claiming to be the soul from a previous body. 'On the surface, it sounds insane and mad,' Alex admits. But he was hooked. He tells me about returning to school to complete his A-level exams as a teenager, and trying not to use the secret lingo he'd picked up in Scientology too much. At the same time, he went around school evangelizing, trying to cure his fellow students of their reactive minds, and sign them up to the sect.

'How did that go?' I ask, imagining not so well.

'Not so well,' he replies. 'You're just that weird kid, aren't you?'

But it didn't bother Alex, because he was on a path to right-eousness. He thrived in Scientology, and even worked alongside Tom Cruise's daughter Bella, as his status soared within the cult. He was going out selling books on Edgware Road, targeting people who didn't speak fluent English. Scientology believed foreigners would be easier to fool, since they were having to navigate in a second language. Alex and fellow members also brought Arabic pamphlets about Scientology's philosophy. People from non-Western backgrounds were less likely to know what Scientology was, or to have heard the bad press.

Bursting with the enthusiasm of the evangelist, Alex seemed like the perfect Scientologist. But they kicked him out. This devas-tated him. He's not sure why they made him leave; just that he was a 'potential trouble source'. One possible reason was that he hadn't given enough money to the cult. He recalls some mention of him trying to get auditing (Scientology's version of therapy) for free. He spent a couple of thousand pounds on the courses, but also got some parts 'for free' in return for selling books. Scientology often tells its members they are getting courses for 'free', neglecting to mention that these sleep-deprived devotees are working round the clock for them. What Alex spent is a drop in the ocean compared to many others, who waste hundreds of thousands of dollars taking the courses. But it's still a fortune for a teenage boy.

I asked Alex if he'd still be in Scientology if he hadn't been kicked out.

'One hundred per cent. I was fighting to stay.'

Scientology treated him terribly. At one point, they locked him in a room, while he cried because Scientology wasn't working for him. They accused him of having a hidden motive to destroy the church, and didn't allow him to leave until he admitted it. This is a common tactic in Scientology. I spoke to another British former Scientologist who goes by the name Kelli Copter. She was locked in a room by her own parents day after day, as they pushed her to admit to conspiring to break up their marriage. She convinced herself that she was as bad as they said, and made herself come up with reasons for wanting to hurt her parents. She was six years old.

Like Kelli, Alex eventually fabricated something, and wrote it down. 'I'll do whatever he wants just to get out of this place,' he remembers thinking. They call this confession of secret malicious intent a 'source of trouble declare'. He confessed (falsely) that he didn't always pay the exact money when he bought food in the Scientology cafeteria. He was finally allowed to leave, feeling defeated and upset. He was booted out . . . but came running back for more not long afterwards.

Why? He told me something I suspected; something I'd heard from others who had joined cults: it made him feel special. 'It's empowering,' he explained. I thought back to a young Alex pros-elytizing at school, using a secret language and feeling like he was saving the world. Yes, smart people can join cults. But not anybody.

Cults feed on vulnerable people who desperately seek status, purpose and community. Those three elements are enforced by a hierarchical secrecy – you find out more secrets as you progress. Scientology – with its crusade to save the planet and its special Celebrity Center glowing with the star power of Tom Cruise, John Travolta, the late Lisa Marie Presley and the late Kirstie Alley – hits the spot.

In addition to exploiting the glamour of A-list celebrities, I was finding that cults confer status to their members through secrecy, isolation and division. Kelly Thiel, former member of the fashionable lifestyle cult NXIVM, explains to me that the first step was to separate the men from the women. Confused and excited, new members of the cult attended classes cluttered with New Age wisdom on how to be happier, more productive and more charitable. These were packaged up as exclusive and secret courses, and aimed primarily at affluent suburban housewives with time and money to spare.

The lessons on how to be charitable may not appear to suit the goals of the cult. It's no good if the members donate to causes outside of NXIVM. However, this ambition appealed to middle-class housewives who obtain recognition from their peers through charity work. Inevitably, 'charity' meant transferring large sums of money to NXIVM.

Based in New York, NXIVM – pronounced *Nixiam* – was a cult that dressed itself up as a multi-level marketing (MLM) company. MLMs are so close to cults that, really, they were hiding in plain sight. Members were paid and rewarded with social clout for recruiting other members . . . to recruit other members . . . and so on. They raced one another to the top of the status table.

NXIVM had an enigmatic leader – Keith Raniere – who was himself high-status. He surrounded himself with celebrities to raise his profile and attract wealthy members to the cult. He even held audiences with the Dalai Lama and business magnate Richard Branson.

Raniere wasn't acting alone. He gained status from his famous assistant, *Smallville* actress Allison Mack. With her wide smile, celebrity and kindly nature, she made for the perfect recruitment foil to Raniere's ponytailed, bespectacled New Age wisdom persona. In 2018, Mack was arrested on charges of sex trafficking and forced labour, among others. She pleaded guilty to racketeering, and was handed a three-year sentence. Keith Raniere went down for a range of crimes including sex trafficking of children, and was sentenced to 120 years in prison.

In their creation of NXIVM, Raniere and Mack were heavily influenced by Scientology. In Mack's defence against charges of blackmailing members with nude photos for forced labour, she even cited a 2009 case involving Scientology. Two of their former members had been unsuccessful in their attempts to sue the cult for similar offences.

To understand what secrets and status can do to a person, look at cults. Cults run on secrecy. A mysterious leader convinces you that they have secret knowledge that will bring you to a higher plain of consciousness, or just make your life better in general. You are given secret tasks, and made to disconnect from friends, family, and anyone else outside the cult. You take countless tests and immerse yourself in the cult for years before getting your hands on the promised secret knowledge.

You don't learn about Lord Xenu, Scientology's alien dictator of the Galactic Confederacy, until you've made it past various obstacles and, importantly, handed over your life savings to the Church of Scientology. By that point, you've not only completed hundreds of hours of gruelling personality tests, but also administered the examinations to others, and recruited new members to a sect known for its alleged bullying tactics.

By the time you find out about the ridiculous secrets, you're in so deep that their absurdity is irrelevant. Your shame around the secrecy and your dependence on status are so profound that the crazy folklore around the cult *has* to be true. Otherwise, you did all those bad things to innocent people for no reason.

By this point, you've also achieved a level of status in the cult that you're unlikely to reach on the outside. You learn about Xenu at OT (Operating Thetan) Level III, which is higher up and more difficult and expensive to reach than it sounds. As you rise up the ranks, you grow in status. They even believe that you begin to take on magical powers.

L. Ron Hubbard, the sci-fi writer and cult founder, is expected to reappear in the body of another at some point. Former and current Scientologists have spoken to me of Tom Cruise having God-like status and even appearing in one woman's dream to recruit her to the cult. It is well-documented that – after Tom Cruise and Nicole Kidman divorced – Scientology went on a secret mission to find him a new girlfriend of suitable status. The process – which Scientology denies took place – is said to have involved dozens of audition tapes for a 'training film' from eligible women under the guise of a 'special project'. One of the questions in the so-called audition tape was: 'What do you think of Tom Cruise?'

The winner was not Katie Holmes – she came later – but Nazanin Boniadi, an attractive, Tehran-born actress. A fellow Scientologist, she was extensively prepped, and given a makeover to (in their view) bring her up to Cruise's level. Her hair was made darker, her teeth enhanced. Confidentiality agreements were signed. For a month during the auditioning process, high-ranking Scientologists asked her intimate details about her sex life and innermost secrets. She was made to break up with her then-boyfriend. Scientology is alleged to have shown her unflattering private details of him to speed up the process, although they deny this.

In November 2004, Boniadi was flown to New York to meet Cruise. According to *Vanity Fair*, that's 'when she first sensed that this was possibly going to be an arranged marriage.' Very early on, Cruise is alleged to have told her: 'I've never felt this way before.' Then she was given a second confidentiality agreement to sign, only able to tell her worried parents that she was away on a 'special Scientology project'.

The first month went well. By the second month, Boniadi was 'found wanting'. As a true believer, Cruise takes the strict rules of Scientology seriously. Whenever he found fault with Boniadi, he reported her to Scientology staff, who took her through the auditing (therapy-like) process for it. Her biggest mistake was telling him 'very well done' after he achieved his Scientology Freedom Medal of Valor. It's a popular phrase in Scientology, but is only supposed to be used when speaking to people of equal or lower status. Her other major faux pas was saying 'excuse me' to the cult leader – and Cruise's best friend – David Miscavige. Clear communication is pivotal in Scientology, so her failure to understand his thick, machine-gun-style Philly accent suggested he couldn't communicate well. This was a cardinal sin.

She was also unable to keep up with Cruise's public displays of affection. He is purported to have told her: 'I get more love from an extra than I get from you.' She was made to spend two or three hours daily purging herself of 'negative thoughts about Tom'. They lived together already, but she was swiftly moved out, and was told that Cruise wanted 'someone with her own power – like Nicole [Kidman]'.

Boniadi broke down and confided in a Scientology friend who – as a good cult member – reported her. Boniadi's punishment was to clean toilets with a toothbrush and dig ditches in the night. Scientology denies all of this. I've heard it first hand from former members who were in place at the time, and it was reported by journalist Maureen Orth in *Vanity Fair* as well as in memoirs from ex-members, such as Mike Rinder's *A Billion Years: My Escape from a Life in the Highest Ranks of Scientology* (2022).

I wrote previously about language as manipulation, and no one exploits this more egregiously than leaders of cults and ideological sects. They obscure meaning and isolate outsiders through their use of in-group language. Mastery of that language makes for high status; but, fail to understand it, and you go from Tom Cruise's girlfriend to scrubbing bathrooms in the blink of an eye.

Elements of cults can be found in every corner of society. Think even of today's populist politicians, as well as fitness fanatics, jumbo juice gurus and suicide pact cults. As those go, Heaven's Gate was particularly macabre. While many cults dress up their self-interested goals in terms of worship to an alien overlord, or adherence to a new political utopia, this cult 'recast death as something aspirational', according to cult and language expert Amanda Montell.

There were still aliens involved, but death became the aspirational status symbol for members of Heaven's Gate from the 1970s to the late 1990s. The leader of Heaven's Gate, Marshall Applewhite, never used words like 'dying' or 'suicide'. Instead, he clouded his intention in exclusive and vague terms, such as 'exiting your vehicle', 'graduation' and 'a completion of the changeover'. Like many cultists, he changed the names of his followers. He called himself Do. The followers lost sense of their former identities, and obsessed over some obscure secret knowledge and status that lay beyond death.

They became consumed by the concept of accessing a hidden higher plain. In the first week of spring in 1997, Do and thirty-eight of the Heaven's Gate devotees got together in a rented mansion in California, and evacuated Earth for ever. They took barbiturates and alcohol, before placing bags over their heads. That's how their bodies were found. In the members' 'exit statements' – which you can find on YouTube – they talk of their excitement about ascending to a higher 'kingdom level' through secret passages provided by extra-terrestrials. Each member died beside their own little bag containing a few dollars to be used as transport tax on their voyage to the new kingdom.

In shock value, the Heaven's Gate cult suicide is only equalled by the Jonestown Massacre in 1978, where 909 people died in what seemed like a group suicide. In reality, not everyone was willing to die. It is thought that those who changed their minds – or simply didn't agree to kill themselves – weren't allowed to leave. Guards with guns patrolled the limits of the camp, possibly shooting anyone who tried to escape. It's believed they later turned the guns on themselves.

Cult leader Jim Jones had become gravely ill. Convinced that he and his operation were about to be shut down and that he would be arrested, he took everyone with him in a mass suicide. Heaven's Gate and the Jonestown Massacre stand out as two of the most deplorable and deadly cults of all time.

Cults and – in the wrong hands – religions have long used status and secrecy to wield power over the masses. They've woven intricate tapestries of folklore around their cores, evoking images of aliens, ascensions, second comings and immortal beings. These distract new worshippers from the insidious dynamics at the core of the cult.

What interests me about the cult of NXIVM is its lack of lore. There are no aliens, no second comings and no miracles. This suggests that religious backstories may just be window dressing when it comes to coercive control. The allure of these sects really comes from their promise of secrets, status and purpose. The promise of clandestine knowledge lures you in, and makes you feel that if you just delve deep enough into the cult, you'll possess secrets that make you more righteous, dominant or successful.

Secret truths will grant you status and self-belief. These promises are made amid a show of love-bombing that melts your guard, so that you go all in. You then give up your own secrets, which – in the case of Scientology and NXIVM – are used against you if you ever try to leave or speak out (or if the cult requires your girlfriend to leave you for Tom Cruise).

In Scientology, secrecy is king. Former Scientologist Mike Rinder describes having to spend hours every day encrypting and decrypting communications for the cult. Founder L. Ron Hubbard's letters were sealed 'in envelopes with special tape that was then baked in an oven so it was impossible to steam open or tamper with'. Rinder writes: 'A lot of the information about [Hubbard's] life was hidden or embellished to make him seem like a perfect man.' When Rinder met with Hubbard, he was blindfolded for the journey to his hideaway. All this serves to enhance Hubbard's status. Secrecy made a legend of the man.

Members aspire to his status, slowly climbing the ranks. They are made to sign contracts before starting a new Operating Thetan level, and told it's integral they keep the secrets to themselves because exposure to high-status secrets could cause low-level members who hear them to die. The reality is that only by insisting on secrecy can these levels retain high status. If outsiders knew the doctrine, as many now do thanks to *South Park* and Wikileaks, the expensive courses and levels would lose their lustre and, therefore, their financial value.

And yet, when members finally attain the secrets, they are often left disappointed. Mike Rinder writes, 'Many who had spent decades and hundreds of thousands of dollars to reach the pinnacle of the Scientology Bridge were so disgusted when they finally got there that it was the last thing they did in Scientology.'

Secrecy and status interplay in the real world beyond cults. Take Ben Gunn. He was fourteen years old when his 'life started'. His mother had recently died, and he'd been placed in a children's home in Brecon, Wales. One day, he escaped the care home with an eleven-year-old friend called Brian, and wandered around an empty school. There, they had a play fight with chair legs that they'd discovered in a pile of broken furniture.

But that's not where it happened.

At around seven p.m., as the pair began to make their way home, Ben revealed a secret to his young friend Brian. He was shocked that he'd let it out, as he had never told it to anyone else (and still hasn't revealed what it was). It was a secret he had been keeping for an entire year. Writes author Will Storr, who investigated the story for *The Status Game* (2021), 'If anyone found out, he imagined that he'd be rejected by all of society, that people would spit on him in the street. But, that evening, he blurted it out.'

In Ben's mind the secret was so potentially damaging to his status and so all-consuming, that, once out, he felt he had no choice. 'I was overwhelmed by emotion. Within a second, I was hitting him with a chair leg because I knew I'd destroyed myself.'

What stood out to Ben after he attacked his friend was the silence. A ringing oblivion, alone with the draining vessel of his secret. 'I'd killed another human being and survived it. It's such an immense taboo. The fact you can do that, and nothing in the great universal sense is inflicted upon you.'

This was the 1980s, so Ben went to a nearby phone box to dial 999. 'I've killed a boy. I hit him with a stick and I think I strangled him.' Such was the intensity of the attack that emergency services found Brian – still alive – with a part of his skull missing. It was as if Ben had to break into Brian's mind to get his secret back.

'Well, you know it's going to be murder now. He's died. Did nobody tell you?' This was how Ben knew for certain that he was a murderer. The subsequent days are sketchy in Ben's memory. Crying in the corner of a room. Being interrogated by officers.

His sister bringing him sweets. Being sentenced in his school uniform. The judge telling him: 'You killed a boy without rhyme or reason. You brought his life to an end without any motive in circumstances which you know amounted to murder . . .'

Except there *was* a reason: status. Storr writes: 'The dread behind his secret revelation – so feared, it drove him to kill – was that its discovery would make him hated, marked, a social pariah.'

Here's the crazy thing. Once imprisoned, Ben's life took a dramatic upturn. He speaks of his life as beginning at fourteen: with a murder. In three decades in prison, Ben's status steadily rose. He was seen by fellow inmates as a maverick with integrity. One time, guards came in for a routine check, and threw all his belongings on the floor. He refused to tidy it up, despite their threats, and was sent to solitary confinement.

This kind of rebellion can win a prisoner admirers. He 'disappeared into his intellect', reading books from the prison library. He swatted up on military history, Buddhism, politics, physics, and everything in between. He even began a blog behind bars that was longlisted for the Orwell Prize. Ben took up a role as general secretary of the Association of Prisoners, and obtained a PhD in criminology while still in prison. 'I became known as the subversive, the political animal, the jailhouse lawyer.'

He was a dissident, and believed he was fighting for moral rectitude and individual freedoms. He was often involved in brawls with other prisoners and guards, and once embarked on a hunger strike for forty-three days, remarking on the sensation of his eyeballs drying out.

He fell in love with a teacher in the prison, but told her that he never wanted to step outside its walls. Prison was a cult to him, and he thrived. It gave him a level of status he could never attain on the outside. His refusal to comply with authorities delayed his release by twenty years. Eventually, he was made to leave, and moved into a cottage in the Cotswolds with the teacher.

But he found it tough to acclimatize to the outside world. Rather than taking long, leafy walks with his lover, he stayed inside smoking, mimicking his life behind bars.

Psychologist Sissela Bok believes we primarily keep secrets out of concern for the social consequences of our revelations. Secrets play a complex role in our social evolution. There is a delicate balance between the need to keep a secret to protect status and the desire to quell the fever and confess. This is true, for example, of sexual assault victims and incest victims, who list concern about social embarrassment and consequences as their primary reason for keeping secrets.

In a 1998 study by psychologist Catrin Finkenauer, 92.8 per cent of reasons for keeping a secret involve protecting the 'self' and any relationships with others from undesirable social consequences. Among women who had an abortion, it is largely societal stigma that predicts secrecy. In social groups that are predominantly pro-choice – and therefore less likely to negatively judge those who have an abortion – women are more likely to reveal the truth.

Known by her detractors as the Crazy Baby Lady, Mariana Rodriguez Varela was the face of the pro-life campaign in Argentina. Videos of her haranguing women who were attempting to terminate their pregnancies went viral. She became a figure of fun (and fear) for progressive pro-choicers, and a beacon of hope for the country's traditional Catholic factions. With each viral video of her, arms outstretched and bearing plastic and rubber models of foetuses, her reputation as either crazed bigot or righteous saviour grew on both sides of the political spectrum.

After months of talks, Mariana agreed to allow me to be the only journalist to follow her for a documentary about her campaign. She trusted me as an international journalist, who didn't bring the inevitable political baggage of a local reporter. I thought her divisive nature would make for an intriguing microcosm of a country split in two. Abortion was illegal at the time in Argentina (legislation to permit it finally passed in December 2020). I found Mariana eccentric, but also warm and friendly. We disagreed on some aspects of the morality of abortion, but she was kind and welcoming enough to take me on the school run to pick up her six kids, and make me and my production team food and chocolate milkshakes in her home.

She lived with a kind of secrecy that resembles something called the 'phantom effect' – the way secrets are passed down through generations. French-Hungarian psychologists Nicolas Abraham and Mária Török write of the phantom effect as a 'transgenerational haunting'. 'What haunts are not the dead, but the gaps left within us by the secrets of others,' they write.

They see secrets as ghosts who continue to haunt future generations in families. This is something we all sense. It's why the ghosts of our stories (*Ghost, The Sixth Sense, Casper*) tend to have to make things right to reach the afterlife. Secrets must be let out, unfinished business finished, and loose ends tied up. Otherwise, the secret – and the trauma and shame it causes – can pass down through generations.

When I interviewed Austrian Friderica Magdalena Wächter-Stanfel, granddaughter of leading Nazi Otto Freiherr von Wächter, she explained: 'I never heard anyone talk about the Nazi past.' This was disorientating for her, because she could tell in her childhood that something was amiss; something went unsaid. 'The silencing was practised all around me for all my life, and led to deep health problems.'

As for Mariana – the Crazy Baby Lady – her father Alberto Rodriguez Varela had been a colleague and close associate of Jorge Rafael Videla, a brutal dictator known – among other things – for dropping opponents alive and drugged into the ocean from helicopters. He also 'disappeared' students and stole babies from parents detained by the regime. These babies had their identities changed, and were then sold or given to wealthy military families. So numerous were the secrets piled upon secrets during that era, 1976 to 1981, that the entire country is experiencing a kind of united phantom effect and intergenerational trauma.

The recent past has left a stain on Argentina's collective psyche to the extent that the entire country gathers in public squares to celebrate when one of the grandmothers of the Plaza de Mayo – who fought for years to be reunited with their children – finds a relative. When a new reunion makes the news, it sparks a moment of intense shared emotion unlike anything else I've experienced. I'm welling up just writing about it now.

Mariana's father wasn't the main man, and had no criminal convictions. But the fact that he served as justice minister during the military coup that disappeared babies made her, in my opinion, an inappropriate choice for the pro-life campaign. Asking her about this ignited an irreparable argument between her and me, and the eventual end of what had been a bumpy but fruitful journey of mutual respect.

Before the law changed in Argentina, it is believed that pro-lifers found ways of procuring illegal abortions just as often as those on the pro-choice side. Due to the stigma involved, it's impossible to find reliable statistics. But Dr Gabriela Luchetti, Chief of Gynaecology at Neuquén Hospital explained to me: 'All women have abortions. Catholics, evangelicals . . . but they don't talk about it'. In 1976, the dictatorship banned the sale of contraception in Argentina. Dr Luchetti explained: 'But the birth rate stayed the same as in England, Spain, Italy. So, what's behind that? *Abortion.* Where are these abortions? Secret. Totally secret. When a woman doesn't want a pregnancy, she'll do absolutely anything not to have it. I've seen stalks of parsley, wire, knitting needles.'

For conservatives and Catholics, if their abortion were revealed, it would have severe consequences for their social standing – even though many of their peers had the same experience. At the other end of the spectrum, pro-choice activists tend to be candid and, at times, passionate about their abortions, even though the abortion itself can be traumatic.

At the extreme end of Argentina's pro-choice advocates, abortion is a progressive status symbol; one that signifies collective trauma and victimhood. Some women I met even appeared to weaponize their abortions, many of them finding ways to send photos of their aborted foetuses to Mariana. For these women, abortion is not a secret like it is for conservatives, which shows the subjective nature of our experience and the fuzzy line that exists between privacy and secrecy in different cults, communities and political sides.

I was beginning to see how status is a primary driver of secrecy. It shapes the communities and political tribes we join, whether pro-choice/pro-life, or cults such as Scientology and Heaven's Gate. Few venture as far as Ben Gunn, but we go to drastic lengths to keep our secrets and our status intact. Losing status is one of the most painful things that can happen to us. Our brains had to incentivize us to be seen by others as dominant, righteous or successful in order to rise in reputation and assure our place in the tribe. Status got you more food or shelter, and better enabled you to survive to pass on status-hungry genes.

For fourteen years, one of the most popular programmes on British TV was *The Jeremy Kyle Show* – a British take on Jerry Springer, where members of the public settled their private disputes in front of a baying audience. In 2019, it was taken off the air after something terrible happened. The show had already been labelled as exploitative for publicly humiliating some of its guests. Producers admitted that many were mentally ill. *The New*

Statesman described the guests as 'poor, mainly white, always working-class families' and criticized it for painting a 'morbidly chaotic picture of a British underclass – for those watching at home to scoff and sneer at – with the veneer of helping them'.

Its host Jeremy Kyle riled up the crowd, as he berated guests for their alleged misdemeanours. One appearance on that show could ruin someone's reputation for ever. As families tore themselves apart in front of our eyes, the ambiguities of the he-saids and she-saids always seemed to be decided by something concrete: the lie detector. Its results were brought out at the end, its verdict indisputable. The audience waited with bated breath to discover which of the participants had been telling the truth about their purported affair or marital abuse.

Jeremy Kyle read the results from an envelope, although you suspected he already knew them. He was rarely wrong about whom he sided with before the reveal. Often, Kyle would read out the charge that confirmed suspicions about an affair. The participant who failed the lie detector test then sat shaking their head in disbelief. But any protestation was met by Kyle and the audience with outrage and ridicule. The lie detector is divine (even though Kyle himself admitted that it was only 96 per cent accurate). The truth was very different, as we'll see. Millions of us watched as the dumbfounded purported cheater and their broken-hearted victim fell to pieces. We watched, too, as the cameras rushed after tearful and distressed victims backstage, seeking soundbites and tears of trauma in real time. And we watched as the events that led to a tragic death were packaged as entertainment.

In 2019, Steve Dymond, aged sixty-three, appeared on the show after being accused by his fiancée Jane Callaghan of lying and cheating. He denied the accusations, but failed the lie test. Kyle raged at him, calling him 'a serial liar' in front of a live audience and TV viewers across the UK. It was humiliating. When the show ended, Dymond told show researchers, 'I wish I was dead,' and sent his fiancée messages stressing that his life was 'not worth living'.

A few days later, his body was found in his rented room in Portsmouth. The show was taken off air, and it was revealed to surprised viewers that the accuracy of their lie detector test was likely not 96 per cent, but far lower – possibly as low as 66 per cent. Given there were 3,320 episodes of the show, and that the test was typically administered to at least one guest per episode, it is likely that hundreds – perhaps thousands – of guests were dressed down and condemned in front of millions of viewers for transgressions they hadn't committed.

In the case of Steve Dymond, coroners determined that 'acts or omissions' by Kyle 'may have caused or contributed to' his death. Dymond's son Carl told the *Daily Mail*, 'He had gone on the show solely to clear his name, but he said it had gone wrong because of the lie detector test. He was adamant that he did not lie. He was so upset that he wasn't making much sense, but he just kept repeating: "I haven't cheated, Carl, I swear I haven't cheated."'

In *The Status Game*, Will Storr writes about the concept that all of us are wrapped up in a game for which the prize is a stellar reputation. He argues that these plays for status are going on unconsciously, and that many of us convince ourselves we are not participating. Instead, we tell ourselves that we choose our ideologies and groups because we are good people.

It is difficult to admit that we actually do good things because our evolutionary psychology compels us to earn status. Storr believes this doesn't have to be viewed as selfish: 'It's astonishing that our species has evolved a system for rewarding ourselves and each other when we're virtuous. The result is courage and altruism.' If we do good things, our underlying motivations don't matter.

'The qualities we value most in humanity are nudged into existence by the status game.'

We can see examples of the status game taking root in childhood. Roughly 75 per cent of arguments between toddlers aged eighteen to thirty months are about possessions. If only two toddlers are involved, the figure climbs to 90 per cent. It is a 'means to establish where you are in the nursery pecking order' states developmental psychologist Professor Bruce Hood. 'Owning stuff is all to do with status among competitors.' Children have also been found to reject one prize token if it means another child will get two. They'd rather they both go without, so as not to fall behind the other child in the pecking order. As we grow older, status remains important to us, more so than wealth and power on their own. Like children with their prize tokens, wealth and power mean more to us when compared to others.

Studies show that most employees would accept a higher-status job title over a pay rise. One found that 70 per cent of UK office workers would choose status ahead of financial incentives, with creative assistants preferring such shiny new titles as 'chief imagination officers' and file clerks opting for 'data storage specialists' over improved salaries. Storr concludes, 'Assuming we have enough money to live, it seems relative status makes us happier than raw cash.'

Status is not the only reason we do things. Other drivers, such as sexuality, love and compassion, also influence our decisions. You'd probably save a drowning dog even if nobody else were around to witness it. You would most likely choose to have sex with somebody you're attracted to, even if sworn to secrecy. So, status is not everything (although you might feel an urge to tell others about those stories to gain status).

Yet, a sudden loss of status – as experienced unjustly and publicly by Jeremy Kyle's guest Steve Dymond – can *feel* like everything. Sociologist Dr Jason Manning points to rapidly declining status as a key contributor to suicide (among other complex factors). Suicide 'concentrates among those who experience an increase in their social inferiority'. It often happens 'when people fall below others. The greater and faster the downward mobility, the more likely it is to trigger suicide'. Suicide is a way of quitting the status game. Dr Manning believes it is not actual failure, but falling behind others – losing status – that often prompts it.

Desire for status is a fundamental aspect of human nature, one that can be manipulated by cult leaders to create a sense of belonging and purpose in their followers. Storr writes: 'The brain feeds us distorted, simplistic and self-serving tales about why they are above us and they are beneath.' Think of our marketing exec Alex Barnes-Ross, who told me he joined Scientology to help save the world from reactive minds. It sounded like a noble pursuit, but it was also about gaining status by aligning himself with the few progressive minds whose task it was to better humanity and teach the regressive minds.

A version of what Alex was told by Scientology appears in the movie *Pulp Fiction*, in a quote purporting to be (but not actually from) from the Bible.

> 'The path of the righteous man is beset on all sides
> By the inequities of the selfish and the tyranny of evil men
> Blessed is he who, in the name of charity and good will
> Shepherds the weak through the valley of darkness.'

As in Scientology, we're left with this sense that a good Christian has a mission to save the world. They are 'righteous', while others are 'weak'. That Samuel L. Jackson's *Pulp Fiction* character Jules is able to wave a gun around, while yelling this about righteousness at a few harmless, unarmed youths shows how powerful status can be. It enabled Jules to see himself as the righteous person in the room.

In Will Storr's book, righteousness is one of the three main status games, along with dominance and success. In tribal times, if you couldn't dominate your group, or be particularly successful in hunting or helping, then you might not get a share of the spoils – unless you showed yourself to be pious, helpful or caring. It's why Jules is believable as a character in that scene. It makes sense that he would like to think of himself as virtuous, despite murdering on behalf of a gangster. Before pulling the trigger, he exclaims: 'And you will know my name is the Lord, when I lay my vengeance upon thee.' In Jules's mind, he has become God. His righteousness and high status across the board (he is also dominant, successful in his profession and commits these assassinations while dressed in a designer Perry Ellis suit) clear his conscience. He is effectively in a cult or high-control group.

Cults, by their very nature, create an environment where the pursuit of status is intensified. Huxley's *Brave New World* portrays a dystopian authoritarian future where speakers beneath the cots of babies whisper to them in their sleep about why they are better than lower-status humans. Cult-like groups have a hierarchical structure, with the leader at the top and the rest of the members jockeying for position below. The promise of elevated status, coupled with the sense of community and belonging that cults provide, can prove irresistible.

Will Storr pinpoints 'secret knowledge' as one of the principal creators of status. Secrets reinforce the hierarchical exclusivity and special knowledge for a chosen few. Think of how high-level Scientologists aren't allowed to tell low-status members about the doctrine. Being privy to new snippets of secret information gives members a sense of constantly moving up. As Storr writes, 'No game – not even a cult – can survive when every player but one feels hopeless and useless.' They have to have something to aspire to: a greater level of respect and status within the cult.

Storr also writes of 'tight players' of the status game. These are people who adhere strictly to societal codes in order to 'earn status from precisely correct moral behaviour'. They join a cult to bathe in the glory of its secrets, preferential treatment and unyielding codes.

Heaven's Gate cult leader Marshall 'Do' Applewhite enforced many such rigid rules. A member called Swyody (his cult name) had been going through a rivalry of righteousness with another member called Srrody. For years, they had been rivalling one another for devotion to the Heaven's Gate cause, and the former found the latter 'always too eager to please Do'. They competed to show Do how good they were at following his strict directions. It's similar to the competitive modesty experienced by ex-Hasidic Jew Julia Haart, when she competed with friends at school over the length of their dresses. Swyody and Srrody competed for something far darker.

Among the most difficult rules for the male members to follow was the order that they refrain from sexual urges. When they struggled with this, Do suggested members get a DIY removal of testicles from a former nurse in the cult who had worked under a doctor who performed these procedures. Swyody and Srrody raced to put their hands up to volunteer as the first test subject. It came down to a coin toss, and – to Swyody's chagrin – Srrody won. His would be the most righteous and high-status genitalia (or lack thereof).

The former nurse performed the operation in a room with the title 'Mexico' on the door, so that they could honestly tell authorities, if questioned, that they performed the castration in Mexico. But once she stitched him back up, he started to swell up. 'Srrody's sack was as big as a baseball,' Swyody recounts. He took his rival to the hospital, explaining that Srrody was a monk and had gone to Mexico for the operation. He healed completely.

'I was disappointed that I didn't have the procedure,' said Swyody.

This – and the fact that the majority of the Heaven's Gate members killed themselves in a show of unity to ascend to the next level – shows how far 'tight players' will go for status.

But what of cult expert Steven Hassan, and the mystery of how an intelligent man with his wits about him could be enticed by the Moonies? In the 1970s, Hassan was in need of not just status, but community, direction and purpose. He had just been dumped by his girlfriend in college. 'I was a little lonely, and these three women flirted with me in the cafeteria, pretending to be students,' he tells me. The women were carrying books, and asked if they could join Hassan's table. 'It was three on one but I was happy because I thought I could get lucky with one of the three. I had no idea that they were going to try to recruit me into a destructive fascist right-wing cult. But that's exactly what happened.'

Storr writes, 'Players attracted to [cults] are often those who've failed at the games of conventional life. Alienated, injured and in need, their brains seek a game that seems to offer certainty, in which connection and status can be won by following an absolutely precise set of rules.' That's how Hassan was sold the dream of piecing together the broken fragments of his life through the rigid rules of a tight game.

The tight game may be enticing to tight players, but cult life – and the secrets it entails – can wear you down. In 2016, suburban California housewife Kelly Thiel was finding life a little monotonous and devoid of meaning. Her husband had a high-status career, but she needed to find her own righteous and meaningful path. She was looking for purpose and status, much like Steven Hassan. She wanted to become a 'happier, better person'. She sought connection, and a chance to be a better humanitarian. That's when she found out about NXIVM. It's also when she began keeping the secrets that would tear her life apart.

Initially, the in-group mentality, secrecy and sense of community in NXIVM appealed to Kelly. She talks to me of the 'love-bombing', which is a typical cult method. They shower newbies in love. Kelly says that you start to think: 'I must be pretty cool if these people think I'm worthwhile.' And then you start to learn the rules. 'There was this whole mission and whole set of regulations and secrets that were involved in being part of this community,' Kelly recalls.

In addition to the Derren Brown-like mind-play stuff they were doing, Raniere and Mack also branded people. Like cattle, members of the cult were prodded with sizzling branding irons. Their scars remain large, red and bulbous today. Members were informed that the branding was some sort of Latin symbol. But even this was laced with secrecy and deception. Members later realized that if you look at the symbols sideways, the initials KR or AM reveal themselves. Keith Raniere and Allison Mack were branding their followers – without their knowledge – with their own initials.

The branding took place as an initiation ceremony into something Raniere called DOS. This was the mysterious inner sanctum of NXIVM; its equivalent of Lord Xenu and the Operating Thetan levels in Scientology. If you're looking for the leader's secret motive, it's in DOS that you'll find it. After taking many classes, and coaching other new members into the clan, attractive female members were invited to DOS. To enter, they had to give up all their secrets to the cult. This step was called 'collateral'.

Raniere and Mack worked to get DOS victims into a place where the cult consumed their lives. Members had cut off most contact with the outside world by this point, and had invested too much time and energy into NXIVM to turn their noses up at the prospect of advancing into its obscure inner circle. It was the sunk cost fallacy, combined with the fear of reverting to their comparatively empty or low-status lives on the outside.

And now they were being asked for their biggest secrets as collateral. If you didn't have secrets that were juicy enough, you had to reveal something incriminating about your husband, parents or kids. Make it up, even, so long as it is out there as a recorded document; a means to get you to stay quiet, no matter what you find in DOS, the inner sanctum of NXIVM.

This was when Kelly began to retreat. Many others went ahead, finding their secrets exposed, and a sword of Damocles over their heads. It was from this vulnerable position that they were told they would be branded and forced into sexual slavery. Secluded away from their families in the darkest circle of NXIVM, women were coerced to have sex with Keith Raniere.

NXIVM was a cult that Raniere established with the goal of excavating secrets from women, and using them as blackmail to fulfil his sexual fantasies with high-status creatives. To take followers to such a vulnerable place, he used a combination of secret language and hypnotic techniques. But he also left members – who had come into NXIVM with the best of intentions – with their own stacks of secrets.

And that's why Kelly fell ill.

Kelly was left with so many secrets that she started living a double life. 'This became so hard to maintain,' she tells me, 'that I eventually began to suppress all my emotions and was like a robot.' Despite being in the dark about the sex enslavement, Kelly felt something was wrong at the heart of the cult. She felt responsible: 'I enrolled a lot of people, people who were open to evolving in this way, who were basically like me, needy. Needy seekers. Open to anything because they were in pain or wanted to evolve.'

This left her in an awkward situation, having to hide some of her suspicions from others in NXIVM. When lower-down members asked her about some of the malicious rumours they'd heard, she'd retort: 'Do you have any *data* on that?' This is a thought-terminating response common to cults that the leaders often use. It shuts down conversation and inquiry. She explains, 'I was doing the same thing that was being done to me.'

Kelly also felt she had to pretend to her family and friends that she was OK. Her parents didn't know anything about her involvement in NXIVM. Her husband had initially attended a NXIVM class with her, but opted not to continue. Now, she feared causing him concern and embarrassment, or starting an argument with him. To certain people, she claimed she was still fully 'in', so she could continue trying to fill in more blanks about the cult. To others, she had to talk as though she were 'out', to find out what *they* knew. 'I was in survival mode and trying to find a way to rationalize the lies, secrets and disinformation.'

But keeping all of this turmoil secret had grave effects on Kelly. 'I could actually feel my two worlds coming together. It started to feel almost schizophrenic, like there were two of me.' Kelly became physically ill. She couldn't sleep, and had a hard time functioning, always worrying about 'slipping up' by revealing the wrong information to the wrong person.

'I began to have nightmares, headaches, stomach issues. My body was screaming out for help, which I didn't listen to even as the symptoms became stronger.' She developed a rare form of paralysis, whereby her whole body went numb. Neurologists did tests on her during this time, but couldn't put their finger on the problem. 'If I put my hand on my nose, I didn't know where it was. My arm had no energy. The muscles were lacking. That went on for a while – I had balance issues, I had brain issues. They never figured out what it was. I wasn't able to be in the world in the same way.'

She and I look through photos of her during her most secretive period. Gaunt and pale, she resembles a terminally ill patient in their final weeks. 'Holding that secret started to make me sick. I look like a different person [now] to how I did in the cult. [Back then], I look like I've been through a war, it's a totally different person. It has a physical effect on the body.'

Although leader Keith Raniere is now in prison, the FBI are yet to recover the file containing the secrets used as collateral by NXIVM. 'Women were coming up with all kinds of things,' Kelly says. 'It's full of secrets. Naked pictures, deeds to houses, bank accounts. Anything you can think of . . . secrets.'

Attained with the enticement of status, but laced with the hidden motives of sex and submission, somewhere out there on the internet is a Dropbox account packed with secrets that could tear careers, families and lives apart. We can only hope that it doesn't fall once again into the wrong hands.

Inside or outside cults, impact on your status is vital in deciding whether or not to reveal a secret. We know there are mental and physical benefits to revealing secrets. We've seen how confessing is like curing a fever. It assists the tribe – and therefore the individuals within it – when people feel a need to confess their secrets to others. But there is a delicate balancing act between airing your secret to quell the fever, and keeping it in to protect your status. One way to have your cake and eat it is to wait until you die to reveal your secrets. That's where the Coffin Confessor comes in.

'If you don't want to listen to it, fuck off,' he says, in a rural Australian accent. He is telling me what he said to a gang of bikers. He crashed a gang member's funeral to reveal that the deceased had been a closeted homosexual.

'You know? And they go: "Well *you* fuck off."

'And I'm like: "Yeah, I'll take me client with me, then."

'They go: "Oh you can't take . . ."

'"Yeah, I can! I've got another hearse; I've got another undertaker over there. I can take the client any time I want."'

The Coffin Confessor's real name is Bill Edgar. He is a private investigator from Queensland, Australia, who crashes funerals to relay the secrets of the dead. As a child, he was abused by his schoolteachers and his grandfather. Nobody believed him when he spoke up, and this sparked an obsession with outing the truth. The motto on his Facebook page reads: 'He tells those you loved how much you loved them and those you loved to hate to fk off.'

Clients approach him in their dying days or weeks with a secret they'll pay him ten thousand Australian dollars to reveal at their funerals. It's a lot of money, but it's a big responsibility. Sometimes, the dying person communicates the nature of the secret to Bill in advance. Others pass him a sealed envelope that he opens when he steps in front of the mourners, the secret as fresh to him as it is to them. Whatever the secret entails, it's something his clients don't feel they can reveal. At least not while alive.

Bill's funeral revelations are a novel extension of the famed 'deathbed confession', a term so engrained in our collective psyche that we rarely pause to consider what it means to have a 'deathbed'. For a great many of us – a deathbed (be it at a home, hospital or hospice) is out there somewhere biding its time. Perhaps we'll make our own confessions there. Bill moves that confession beyond the deathbed, a key difference being that the confessor is no longer alive to witness the impact of their secret's revelation.

I was intrigued to find out what makes people reveal their secrets before (and after) they die. If you don't believe in an afterlife, the stakes are off. If you're about to die, social ostracism is no longer a barrier to revelation. You might as well reveal. On the other hand, the burden of holding onto a secret won't bother you much longer if you choose not to confess. You might as well hold it in.

People might resist revelation on their deathbed for fear of tarnishing their legacy, something that holds sway with some. This is protection of status. Shakespeare's sonnets are so admired because they speak to that almost-universal desire to live beyond death through something, whether it be a living heir, a lover or the written word. Those who hold stock in the concept of legacy might withhold indiscretions on their deathbed. Where they're going, they won't have to worry about the stress of mind-wandering and rumination.

Others don't buy into the importance of posthumous reputations, so might choose to reveal a deathbed confession. For them, tying up loose ends in the physical world – relieving any 'fever' and rumination accompanying them into their last moments – supersedes concerns about legacy damage. They might also hold religious beliefs, and hope to enter the spiritual plain with a clean slate.

It's hard to put a number on deathbed confessions, because most go unreported. A popular literary and filmic trope is of an elderly patient awaiting their penultimate gasp to reveal a child was adopted, or came from an extramarital affair.

Deathbed confessions can be horrifying. Construction worker Frank Thorogood was said to have confessed to a friend on his deathbed to having murdered founding member of the Rolling Stones, Brian Jones. Jones drowned at home in his swimming pool. His demise was put down to 'death by misadventure', but Thorogood had been the last person seen with him, and two books were published accusing him of murder. As to what prompted him to confess on his deathbed, we can only speculate. It's possible he enjoyed the idea of going down in history as the man who murdered a Stone, without having to face a stretch in prison. It might have been a lie for bravado, or from delusion. Otherwise, if true, the confession might have simply felt like a relief before he died.

One of the glitziest deathbed confessions is that of silent film star Margaret Gibson. After a heart attack in 1964, she confessed on her kitchen floor to her neighbour (no priest could be summoned in time) that she had killed film director William Desmond Taylor in a botched blackmail attempt. At the end of her life, she converted to Roman Catholicism. Now that she had little to fear from mortal matters, it made sense to Gibson to confess her sins, and start off on the right foot in the afterlife.

Before making an incriminating deathbed confession, you had better be sure you won't make a recovery. A 'dying declaration' has proved admissible in courts to get convictions. They're enough to reopen cold cases. That's what happened to a 'quiet and humble' Oklahoma man called James Anderson. Popular in the community, he was 'deeply religious' and led the Bible study in the local church. With death in his sights after suffering two strokes, he confessed to police that his real name was James Brewer. Brewer had been on the run since 1977 – thirty-two years previous – after murdering his neighbour Jimmy Carroll, aged twenty. He believed that Carroll was trying to seduce his wife.

To his great misfortune, Brewer survived. Upon recovering, he and his wife promptly sold all their possessions, and he surrendered to police. He might have faced the death penalty, but the district attorney decided not to go to trial due to Brewer's diminished physical state. Religious belief was the main motivator behind Brewer's deathbed confession. Believing he was about to die, the prospects of prison or corporal punishment no longer concerned him. The detective who interviewed him at the time said: 'He wanted to cleanse his soul, because he thought he was going to the Great Beyond.'

Many dying people reveal secrets to get their affairs in order or even for justice or vengeance, and to settle old scores. But while alive, they may not want to face the ignominy of admitting to embarrassing indiscretions. Also, they may not feel physically or mentally strong enough to challenge those who wronged them. That's where the Coffin Confessor steps in, taking the deathbed confession beyond the veil.

'I'll be honest with you,' he tells me. 'It started as a joke. I just told a dying gentleman that I'd crash his funeral for him, and lo and behold, he took me up on the offer, and he paid me well to do so. And since that funeral, it just went nuts! I did another funeral, and another one. And it was all by word of mouth.'

When he's not confessing beside coffins, Bill is a private investigator by trade. Much of his work comes from exposing theft in companies, particularly hotels. He strolls into a hotel, and tells the manager that he is so sure that he can uncover stealing that he will pay them if he fails to find evidence. He then spends eight weeks working as a security guard or cleaner – performing all the tasks the role demands of him – while snooping out theft.

'I don't mind folding sheets, making beds and all that, because at the end of the day, I'm interacting with these employees that are doing the wrong thing,' he explains. 'It's funny sometimes. I'll be making a bed, and they'll be making the bed with me, and I'll say, "You know, I wouldn't mind some of these sheets!" and they'll say, "Oh yeah, well just put them in a big bin bag, drop them down the chute, and tell Terry the security guard that they're down there, and he'll put them aside for you for when you leave at the end of the day." And I'll be like, "Thanks mate, no worries."'

He laughs, which prompts me to ask if he fears retaliation from those he reports. 'Yeah probably,' he laughs again. 'I've got more enemies than friends, and I haven't got a friend in the world, to be honest with you.' He adds: 'I don't really care. I'm here for a time, and my time's what I make it. If anyone wants to come after me, come after me.'

His first client as the Coffin Confessor was a terminally ill man called Graham, who had previously hired Bill as a PI to prove that his accountant was stealing from him. Bill found the evidence, and forced the accountant to pay it back. A few weeks later, Graham got in touch. He told Bill he was concerned that his best friend had intentions for his wife. From his sick bed, he caught glimpses of a one-sided flirtation instigated by his friend whenever the door was ajar. Bill and Graham discussed writing something to be read out after the latter's death, but believed it would never get done. Then, Bill joked, 'I could always crash your funeral for you.' They laughed, and left it at that. A few weeks later, Graham contacted Bill to ask him to reveal everything at his funeral. He'd pay him AU$10,000.

Bill had to be sure of the facts. With Graham's permission, he installed surveillance cameras around the house: 'Fuck me if it wasn't true.' Sure enough, the best friend was coming to the house without seeing Graham. He flirted with Graham's wife, who spurned his advances. The friend kept 'persisting and persisting', and trying to 'be there for her'. 'His best mate did the dirty on him, and was trying to sleep with his wife, which was really belittling and hurtful for Graham because he was on his deathbed.'

'He was a dog,' Bill continues, 'and the best thing that I ever did – for Graham and for her, and even for myself – was to be able to stand up, interrupt the funeral service while his best mate was giving the eulogy, and tell him to sit down, shut up or fuck off.'

Listening to Bill, I was starting to see how status could affect secrecy even after death. Graham didn't want to reveal his friend's attempts in real life for fear of the consequences. But once he was no longer on this planet, it was important to him to make a social pariah of the man who had wronged him.

Motivated by justice and revenge, Graham's case is an innovative take on the age-old posthumous confession. Traditionally, this might be done by suicide note or other written evidence, which brings to mind the eighteenth-century French novel *Dangerous Liaisons* – its dénouement has the deceased Valmont's letters exposing the spiteful schemes of antagonist Merteuil – or the brilliant ending of *Cruel Intentions* (1999), an American high school version of the French classic. In the movie, copies of the late Sebastian's journal are distributed throughout the school – to the tune of The Verve's 'Bitter Sweet Symphony' – to expose the abusive behaviour of Kathryn, played by *Buffy the Vampire Slayer* actress Sarah Michelle Gellar.

Her necklace with cross is revealed to contain cocaine, and she is presumably expelled (the principal looks livid at the end of the film) and, worse, socially ostracized. In death, Valmont and Sebastian achieve a sense of closure and justice that they were not able to pursue in life. Their status rose at the expense of Merteuil and Kathryn.

As for bedridden Graham, he felt too weak and ashamed of his condition to confront his best friend. Instead, he kept his feelings secret, and employed Bill's services to exact revenge and humiliate the man in a very public way. A few weeks after making their deal, Graham passed away. True to his word, Bill stood up at the funeral when Graham's 'friend' was one minute into delivering the eulogy, and told him: 'Excuse me, sit the fuck down, shut up – the man in the coffin has something to say.' He then read from the letter Graham had written about his friend's indiscretions. Graham not only had the last word, but his was a funeral that none of the mourners would soon forget.

There is more to a deathbed or posthumous confession than status. It is a practice that has been engrained in us for thousands of years by the stories we tell each other. Confession (and the deathbed variety) is hardwired into our religions. Whether this urge to confess developed out of evolutionary necessity (passing knowledge down through tribes), was artificially introduced into our culture by authoritarian leaders wanting to know our secrets, or is simply a logical way to feel at the end of a life, it is prevalent across belief systems. Catholics believe that their sins must be confessed to a priest before they die. It is the most indispensable factor in reconciliation with God. One is reminded of the ostensible hypocrisy in

Mafia movies, where confession to a priest is like clearing one's browser to the murdering mobsters.

In Judaism, the Viddui is a deathbed confessional prayer that 'acknowledges the imperfections of the dying person and seeks a final reconciliation with God.' Unlike in Catholic confession, it is unrelated to one's place in the afterlife. Pauses are permitted at certain points in the prayer, to allow loved ones to respond, ideally with love and forgiveness.

When a Muslim is close to death, they are invited to ask for forgiveness for wrongdoings. Their offences are not said out loud, but are supposed to remain between them and God. Since men are considered fallible, there is no Muslim equivalent of confession to a priest. The imam is human, and therefore unable to grant forgiveness in the way that God might. In fact, it is forbidden to confess to anyone but God. The deathbed confession for Muslims is not, then, about posthumous status. But God's exclusive role in the confession reinforces his status as divine, and reminds humans of our place in the hierarchy. Across belief systems, the focus on confession underlines the importance we place in sharing secret information – with deity or mortal – before it disappears for eternity.

After Bill's first funeral confession, the word spread about his unique services. Now, many clients ask him for strange and unusual things, such as to pin-prick their bodies once they pass away to check they're definitely dead. Once, he allegedly buried a Harley-Davidson motorcycle (which wouldn't be legal if he officially admitted to it) with a client. And he often tackles 'vultures' who try to steal their dying parent's money. Bill even helps to enforce late changes to the will to guard against said vultures.

The demands can be really strange. 'I was starting to get requests to go to people's houses and clean them out before their families and friends found certain items. It could be guns, drugs. It could be sexual items. It could be anything they're embarrassed about and didn't want their loved ones to find. Even web browsers.' The only time Bill can remember refusing a client was a request to kill the dying man's dog and bury it with him. Bill refuses to hurt animals. Since the dog was sixteen years old, it died not long after its owner anyway.

One time, an eighty-eight-year-old man asked Bill to clear out his basement after he died. The dying man didn't divulge any more information. After all, if you have something you believe to be so embarrassing that you don't want a single soul to know about it before or after you pass on, revealing it all to Bill before-hand would be an unnecessary risk. When Bill arrived at the man's house after his death, he was confronted by a sex dungeon, complete with masks, toys and a massive swing.

The more I researched, the more mesmerized I was becoming by that fuzzy line between secret and private matters. It occurred to me that – if it were acceptable in polite society for an eighty-eight-year-old man to be the proprietor of a basement sex dungeon – then he might not have felt the need to keep it secret. It'd be private, no doubt. But not something that could ruin his post-humous status. Despite presumably breaking no laws, it is likely that the man lived with a great deal of shame around the discrepancy between the self he presented to the world (his friends, children and grandchildren), and the one stepping down to the dungeon in a gimp suit and chains.

That's not to say that a society in which sex dungeons are part of polite conversation is necessarily preferable. I'm just intrigued by that line of acceptability that distinguishes the private from the secret. In previous decades, we've seen that line move dramatically around such themes as mental health and sexual liberty (pensioner dungeons exempted). Depression was, not long ago, a dirty secret that – if out – might damage a reputation. Now, it might still be considered private, but many people are now open about their struggles, and the societal stigma around it continues to weaken. In some circles, victimhood appears even to enhance social status.

As for the dungeon keeper, his status is intact. Bill got rid of the sex equipment before the family could find out. They may even be reading this right now, none the wiser about the kinky side of Gramps.

8

SECRETS AND ESPIONAGE

In the late 1950s, Mike was a troubled sixteen-year-old boy often found smoking or drinking at his summer school on the remote Scottish island of Scalpay. He was a likeable enough young chap, but, like many troublemaking pupils at the time, couldn't seem to escape the cane. Whether it was due to his illicit habits or the sheer cheek of the boy, he was always receiving corporal punishment. Such was his regularity with it that prefects – his fellow pupils – were burdened with picking up the slack, and ensuring Mike received enough beatings.

This continued for several summers, with 'the troubled teenager in shorts and long socks' ostensibly a glutton for punishment. At least one other student found him 'a bit odd', and it reached a point when suspicions arose that he might have been enjoying his punishments. This was confirmed, after it emerged that he had been paying other pupils to hit him with the cane. One of those students admitted he was 'surprised' to be asked to do it, and noted that Mike 'never evinced any grudge' after his punishment.

Despite what might have been a bit of an impediment in the popularity stakes, Mike's apparent masochism didn't make him a recluse. He even socialized with the other pupils outside school – as well as with their families. The other pupils didn't meet Mike's family. And he was strange to look at. But letters from his legal guardians and his uncle assured the school of his credentials.

One summer, a new private tutor called Michael Green – a former army chaplain – came to teach at the school. Green's arrival spelled the beginning of the end for an illusion unlike any other that I've come across. When the new teacher saw Mike, he immediately asked the boy to see him privately. Later, Green spoke to Mike's fellow pupil David Campbell – one of the boys who had been hired by the powers that be to 'supervise' and cane Mike.

'This has to stop,' Green told the boy. 'Do you know who Mike actually is?'

I felt like I was getting a pretty good handle on secrets and the strain it lands on their keepers, but I wondered: what happens when it's taken to the extreme? What happens when someone devotes their entire life to a secret?

It turns out that those of us who are able to see life as a play are better equipped to handle the strain of such dramatic secrets. There is artifice involved in every social interaction. We are like actors reading out a script. Just think of the different ways that we might touch and smile at one another while getting a point across. The end goal of these acts is acceptance from the audience (everyone we meet and interact with). Success is achieved when the audience perceives the actor – you – as the character you intended to portray (just like the concept of matched and mismatched).

This can be as simple as coming away from a dinner party having left the impression that you are as suave and sophisticated as you'd like to be. This concept – that we are always acting – is called dramaturgical theory. Literary theorist Kenneth Burke first presented his principles of 'dramatism' in the 1940s, believing that life was like a play. Later, sociologist Erving Goffman advanced the theories. The key difference was that Burke genuinely believed that life was theatre, whereas Goffman took the philosophy as a metaphor for a way of approaching life. Like an old-fashioned life coach, he advised that you approach life as though you're the director of a great play. The school on Scalpay is what happens when you take it to the extreme.

Mike was acting – he wasn't who he said he was. He wasn't even a teenager. He was fifty-four-year-old Lord Brendan Bracken, Churchill's wartime minister of information and the founder of the modern *Financial Times*. He set up the school to satisfy his desire to be caned by prefects. How was he able to get away with it? First, he was a master at inventing stories. Just as a good method actor starts to become the character, Bracken appears to have believed in his fictions, and felt little remorse. He'd had previous experience with inventing different personas and lives. For example, despite being the son of an Irish builder, he – after spending time in Australia – posed as an Australian and said he was four years older than he was. He also lied that his parents had died in a bush fire in the Australian Outback.

After moving into publishing and politics, he became close to Winston Churchill, and worked as his chief of propaganda in 1941. A decade later, he started his own school on a Scottish island, and began attending it. From the briefest glance at a photo of Lord Bracken with pupil David Campbell – who later composed a memoir exposing the whole affair – it's clear something is amiss. To me, he actually looks older than his fifty-four years.

He told fellow pupils, teachers and staff that he had a premature ageing condition. I was reminded of how, since we are typically honest, we expect others to be. When someone lies with conviction about something as outlandish as an ageing condition, we don't always think to ask questions. 'Part of me was stunned,' explains Campbell. 'Part had already begun to unpeel the cataract of credulity that had let myself, tutors, companions, cooks and housemaids in successive Scottish grand house "schools" become part of the masquerade.'

It is believed that Lord Bracken never touched or molested the other boys. He simply enjoyed the fantasy and the masochism from the canings. Campbell – who was actually around one third of Bracken's age – wrote: 'It just seemed to be this strange fantasy we were all sucked into. Yes, you think that's really odd, but he made a friendship with me and my family and after a while you came to accept it.'

It does seem odd. But honesty is the norm, deception the exception. This is particularly true with identities, as very few of us are able to fake our identities over an extended period of time. Bracken constructed a fantasy world around him, filled with forged letters from fictional guardians, lawyers and even a made-up uncle. All of this supported his premature ageing invention.

This is another example of a secret or deception that would be harder to pull off nowadays, due to advances in technology. Bracken and Churchill were so close that it was rumoured that the former was the prime minister's illegitimate son. Had they had access to something like the internet, the pupils and teachers would have recognized 'Mike' as one of Churchill's right-hand men. But Bracken's schoolboy ruse lasted several summers without coming close to being found out.

'He is Lord Brendan Bracken,' tutor Michael Green disclosed to Campbell. 'You can imagine the feast the press would make of the set-up here, the nature of the implications they would draw. I've spoken to Lord Bracken and he has, of course, agreed. The matter is at an end.'

Bracken paid off Campbell, before covering school and university fees for him and his brother, and even buying a house in Edinburgh for their mother. A year after the school was shut down, Bracken died of throat cancer. He was fifty-seven. Campbell writes that regardless of any potential masochism or paedophilic interest, what he believes Bracken most enjoyed was 'the manufacture of drama'. He explains: 'The elaboration of his fantasy was a work of genius'. I wondered if that ability to invent and act might be the key to escaping mind-wandering and shame. If we're most burdened by secrets relating to our identity, then our best bet is to change our identity.

'All the world's a stage, and all the men and women merely players.' Shakespeare's words would have made for a fitting motto for Bracken's school, which turned out to be nothing but a vehicle through which Bracken could indulge his fantasies. The pupils and teachers were merely unwitting actors and stagehands that enabled the show to go on. There is something to be said for seeing the world as a stage. It reminds me of the advice – when giving a speech – to imagine the audience naked. You are reminding yourself that clothes are part of an artifice to allocate different roles in society. We are all acting in some way.

Lord Bracken's act was as shocking as it was successful, but it was just a warped extension of what we all do every day of our lives. We are all presenting a slightly different version of ourselves to the world. A 'dramaturgical' act is an attempt we make to be viewed by others in a certain light; to enhance or modify the impression we make to the public, and keep secret what we believe to be our real self. Often, shame can arise from the disparity between the self we portray to the world, and that which we keep deep down. To ward off the shame, you must truly convince yourself that the world is just a stage.

I wanted to know more about Goffman's theory of dramaturgy to better understand how some people are better able to keep big, identity-related secrets. In Chapter 2, we looked at the three main types of secrets: immoral, relational and aspirational. Oscar Wilde's hidden homosexuality covered all three. These distinctions are about the motivations and settings of the secrets, whether they be related to our professional environment, our relationships, or our moral compasses. But Goffman categorizes secrets in relation to the audience. These are secrets that we actors must use to prevent the audience – or other people around us – from finding out our secret intentions or who we really are. 'Dark secrets', for example, comprise information that would let the audience know we are different from the selves we are portraying.

In Lord Bracken's case, a dark secret could be that the documents he provided were from a fake guardian. Were that secret to get out, the whole act would fall apart. On a simpler level, a dark secret might be the fact that you are not as confident as you want the world to think you are. Perhaps, when giving a talk, an unavoidable hiccup or voice wobble would give that dark secret away. The audience would see through the act.

'Strategic secrets' are another kind. They symbolize the actor's hidden motivations. Even now, those of Lord Bracken remain secret. But we can imagine they might relate to sexual desire. His goal was to get a caning from the teenage pupils at the fake school. He created the summer school as a ruse to hide this strategic secret.

A third set is 'inside secrets': those that are shared by a *team* of actors. Perhaps Bracken had a friend who was in on the whole scandal. This would have enhanced the feeling of intimacy between them, creating a sense of 'us versus them'. Inside secrets play a huge role in cults and can be negative, but they can also be positive, as with the bonding inspired by preparing a surprise party for a friend. Or, on a sneakier level, when one friend nudges your leg beneath the table at dinner to imply that a second friend is talking twaddle.

There are other kinds of secrets, including 'free secrets'. These are the secrets of another, which you could reveal without giving up your own secrets. When tutor Michael Green spotted Lord

Bracken among the pupils, he had a free secret that he soon revealed to the others to break the spell.

Goffman goes into depth about the roles of secrets on the stage of life. He sees every micro-interaction as a dynamic between a performer and an audience. Audiences only know what the performer has revealed to them, wittingly or not. There are all sorts of roles in dramaturgy that people can play on the stage of life. For example, an 'informer' – such as a spy or traitor – will put on a performance to fit in with one group of people, only to reveal that group's secrets to another audience.

A 'shill' is another example, and covers a person who is acting on behalf of another interest without disclosing it. Journalists are often accused of being shills or sell-outs for asking certain politicians 'easy' questions or being in the pocket of, say, the tobacco industry. Examples of alleged shills include conservative commentator Armstrong Williams, who was discovered to have received payments from the US Department of Education to promote a policy without disclosing it in his columns. Then, there's the 'spotter', who sits on the side and analyses the performers. These are critics and social commentators. To an extent, I'm taking on that role now by writing this book.

In the play of your life, Goffman writes of the 'non-persons' who make up the background. These are most waiters, cleaners, doctors and chefs, who are essential-yet-bit-part players in your life. Elevated to the part of 'service specialist' characters are the hairdressers, plumbers and bankers who are given exclusive access to private parts of your life, even if they don't play large roles themselves. Then, there are colleagues and confidants who play larger parts in the story of you. But all, says Goffman, are playing out roles.

I wonder to what extent we adopt the roles that we think others want us to fit into. On an almost unconscious level, we act out the versions of ourselves that make for a happy dynamic. Nobody likes to think of themselves as studied, affected or fake, but I know that the 'me' that speaks to my wife is different to the one who interacts with my family, friends and colleagues. And that's not to mention those clichés I mimic when speaking other languages. I even notice myself imitating the colloquialisms and speech patterns of the people I interview. We all do this to different extents.

I think of the role that people in the service industry – particularly in the US – are expected to play while at work. No matter how rude customers are to them, they are expected to go on, stoically smiling and chanting the mantra: 'The customer is always right.' Many of us have – or know people who have – worked as waiters or receptionists. We know then that we are far from the personas we have played in those roles.

Unnervingly, I recently experienced this with a New York hotel receptionist who had a fixed smile, and continually said my name whenever I entered the lobby. One time, I arrived to find him talking with a colleague in hushed, conspiratorial tones. He looked annoyed and downtrodden. I imagine he was complaining about work or relating bad news.

As he caught my gaze, the corners of his mouth lifted into a beam: 'Andrew! How was your day, Andrew? Did you see Central Park, Andrew?' His colleague also fixed me with a toothy smile. Something about that interaction left me cold. I felt like a child who had stumbled upon a Mickey Mouse entertainer at Disneyland with his costume head removed. Sure, he popped it back on quickly enough. But I had come too close to the artifice, the 'Truman Show' that lies behind every interaction. Later, when I checked out, I did my best to avoid eye contact, as I hadn't left a large tip after running out of cash. I visualized him searing a dollar-shaped hole into the back of my head with his eyes.

Just as we act to present our best – or most work-appropriate – sides in our careers, we perform around our friends to give off the impression that we live up to the tribe's expectations. Social media is a stage, where we curate the best parts of ourselves to convince others of our performances. Our followers are spectators. We control which secrets they are privy to. To do this well, we must convince ourselves of the lies. We become method actors. We make ourselves the heroes of our own stories.

For this reason, suspicion often grows on both sides of a secret or a lie. When we are lying, we denigrate the image of the people we're lying to, so that we can still be the 'good guy' in the dynamic. Research indicates liars trust those they deceive less. It's self-protection. The more potentially damaging are our lies, the less we trust, or even like, our victims. We believe our own performances. We all know that feeling of being caught in a lie, only to feel not humbly disgraced, but indignant. 'Yes, I lied, but they shouldn't have been snooping in the first place!'

I imagine Lord Bracken embracing a whipping at the school, while mired in mistrust and disregard of those around him. Since he died so soon afterwards, and the truth about his fake identity wasn't revealed until decades later, we'll never know what was going through his mind. But we can ask others who have lived a double life about their own experiences.

It is true that we all conceal aspects of our true selves, accentuating certain traits while downplaying others. However, except for psychopaths, criminals, and notorious figures like Lord Bracken, it is uncommon for someone to fully assume an entirely different identity. Nevertheless, some do. Throughout history, the notion of hiding in plain sight has evoked images of undercover officers in plain clothes and enigmatic double agents. As I came to find out, some have fallen further than you can imagine into the identity of another.

I was looking into how secretly living another's life can impact one's psyche, when I came across a group of people who were told to go into a supermarket and smear the fruit with poison. To this day, the British undercover police officers who took this top-secret role are unsure whether they were actually supposed to do it, or if it was just some sort of mind game. Surely, it would constitute murder?

Completing this task – and none admitted to having done so – may have affected their chances of getting into the Special Demonstration Squad (SDS). Even today, a lot of confusion surrounds the SDS, an undercover unit of Greater London's Metropolitan Police Service, set up in 1968 to infiltrate protest groups. Part of the counter-terrorism Special Branch, it officially ran until 2008, recruiting a particular kind of psychological profile. One of its instructors explained: 'They have to be utterly trustworthy but also have to be able to live a lie.'

The training took – or takes, if it's still secretly running – would-be spies to weird and unexpected places. They're never on solid ground, never entirely sure of what is abstract and what is real. One exercise has the hopeful recruits telling one another life stories. Some use stories from their real lives, while others make up false narratives. No one is sure what is being asked of them. Those who make it as spies for the SDS – mostly men – are told to totally change their lives. Entire backstories are created for them; they are almost exclusively to be left-wing hippies. Glasses, beards, earrings and new haircuts are crafted for each spy until they look like the police's idea of environmental activists – think Shaggy from *Scooby Doo*. Bold checked shirts and jeans; sloppy jumpers; a hat. Whatever least resembles the spies' actual taste.

They choose their names by leafing through old death certificates. The trick is to find the name of a child who died in an unspectacular way, so that it hasn't been reported in the newspaper. Also considered is whether the deceased child had family that the spies might run into. This might seem cautious, but stories have emerged of at least one spy who was caught out and confronted with his own apparent death certificate. Some undercover cops are said to have visited the graves of the children whose names they took, as part of a 'macabre ritual'.

Next, backstories are invented: fictitious uncles, strained relationships with mothers, and so on. It has to check out. If you create a fictional experience, the spies are told, make sure you can live up to it. Don't say you used to live in Mexico, unless you speak Spanish. Don't say you were a concert pianist if you can't even play 'Chopsticks'. They say that the bigger the story, the harder it is to remember. I was learning: if I ever want to live a second life, best to keep things simple. A former recruiter said: 'You have to be a different version of yourself. To maintain a complete deception is much harder than just having a slightly shifted version of yourself.'

For years, the SDS had the upper hand. They arrived at the protests before the leftists, ready to prevent any destruction. The activists couldn't understand. They were frustrated at every turn, even turning on one another as they sought out moles. None was found. Yet, all along, they were looking the answer in the face every day. It was the first thing they saw when they woke up, and the last before going to sleep. It was taking their children on the school run, cleaning the dishes after dinner, and sharing their most intimate moments with them. After a gruelling recruitment process, the final step for the male undercover cops had been to ingratiate themselves with the female activists. In the 1990s, British spies from the police started romantic relationships with left-wing environmental activists.

This is not the only time that romance and sexuality have been used by authorities to get secrets out of political opponents. In 2021, it emerged that some of President Donald Trump's allies engaged female spies to serve as honeytraps. They were paid

$10,000 to seduce high-profile targets and record their views on Trump.

Politics has long been a breeding ground for secrets and double lives. And if you're feeling judgemental, remember that it is not just politicians, but voters, too, who are deceptive about their politics. Think of the silent Tory vote, aka the 'Shy Tory' factor. In 1992, polls had 38 per cent voting Conservative, suggesting a narrow Labour victory. In the end, the Tories got 42 per cent, and won their fourth successive election. In 2015, no polls saw the Tories' 6.5 per cent winning margin coming. Many polls predicted a hung parliament, while several had Labour ahead. People keep secret their intentions to vote for the Conservatives, even from anonymous polls. The undercover cops of the SDS represent the extreme end of our willingness to deceive for political or tribal gain.

The SDS is an example of a state-sponsored secret. Conspiracy theorists get a bad rap – and usually rightly so – for spreading paranoia through unfounded allegations. But we need to have a certain number of them in our societies to expose secret injustices and abuses of power by the people who are supposed to be looking out for us. Watergate is the conspiracy that coined the 'gate' suffix. But we've been misled by state-sanctioned secrets many times. Yes, we have flat-earthers barking up the wrong two-dimensional trees, but we also have true stories of extraordinary deceptions by those in charge.

From the start of the 1950s, for twenty years, the US government's MKUltra programme secretly experimented with mind control and chemical interrogation methods. The CIA performed illegal experiments – including the use of hallucinogenic drugs – on humans, and committed all manner of psychological and physical abuse on participants. They wanted to see if they could enable humans to unlock magical powers, such as psychokinesis, levitation, and the ability to walk through walls. As far as we know, they were unsuccessful.

Plenty of countries have engaged spies and undercover cops to report on their own citizens. We've already discussed the Stasi, but the KGB in the Soviet Union were also known for targeting political dissidents and employing intense surveillance of the public. Some claim that the current FSB (Federal Security Service) in Russia is just another iteration, with its harassment of journalists and human rights activists.

Some state-sponsored secrets are particularly damaging to innocent members of the public. In the 1970s and 1980s in the UK, 4,689 people with haemophilia and other bleeding disorders were infected with HIV and hepatitis viruses when blood products – many imported from the US – were used in their treatment. Neglectfully, much of the blood came from high-risk paid donors in the States. This included the blood of drug addicts who sold their samples to fuel their addictions. The blood donations were pooled together to create factor concentrate, which was made from up to 40,000 donors. Just one donor with infected blood would contaminate the whole concentrate.

As a result, more than 3,000 people have died. More than 1,243 were infected with HIV, including 380 children. Others were infected with hepatitis C, which causes liver damage and liver cancer, and can be fatal.

The contaminated blood was the result of a series of accidents and negligence. But the secrets here involve the ensuing cover-up. Records of the hepatitis C contamination were destroyed. Although it was possibly done by 'an inexperienced member of staff', the Contaminated Blood Scandal was covered up for decades, and only in 2022 were 3,000 surviving victims awarded interim compensation payments. These secrets were kept to preserve the status of those who were culpable in a disaster that led to thousands of deaths.

The Tuskegee Syphilis Study is another example of state-sponsored misconduct and deception. It was conducted by the

United States Public Health Service and the Centers for Disease Control, and ran from 1932 to 1972. They studied 400 African American men with syphilis, who were promised free medical care in exchange for taking part in the study. The men weren't actually told that they had syphilis, but rather 'bad blood'. They were misled.

But the worst part is that they weren't actually given penicillin, despite the fact it was widely available from 1947. Instead, the men were given placebos and other ineffective care. They were kept ignorant of the scientists' true purpose of the experiment: to observe the natural course of untreated syphilis. More than 100 of the 400 men studied died as a direct result of this deception.

What led the scientists in their pursuit? They believed that the knowledge gained would be good for the whole of humankind. Even this argument is flawed, because the study continued for nearly thirty years after a cure was available. But it speaks to those familiar concepts of a higher purpose and a need to feel special, which have led countless humans to Scientology, radicalized sects and even – in the case of the SDS undercover police officer – to trick left-wing activists into something unthinkable.

As the agents fell deeper into their new leftist family lives, the line blurred between real and fake. Some of the agents straddled that line precariously. Others flew past it, landing head-first at the point of no return: they married and had children with their victims. In 2010, in one of the most infamous cases yet uncovered, victim Lisa Jones was enjoying a 'blissful holiday' in the mountains of Italy with her boyfriend – who she believed to be fellow environmental activist Mark Stone.

While looking for her glasses in the glove compartment of their van, she felt the leather cover of a British passport. It contained a photo of Mark. But in one of those 'glitch in the matrix' moments that make life seem suddenly incongruous, the name alongside the photo read: 'Mark Kennedy'. That was the real name of the undercover cop posing as her boyfriend. Beside the passport lay a mobile phone with emails from two children Lisa didn't know. They referred to the phone owner as 'dad'.

'I just remember that the mountains were pulsating and swimming around me,' Lisa recalls. Her world fell apart at the seams. When something so deceptive and traumatic happens to a person, it can be hard to trust the people around you, or your own reality. Just imagine your own partner, family member or friend weren't who they said they were. The stories of the deceived women are harrowing, and give us an insight into the irrevocable effects of having secrets kept from you. Many have been unable to form relationships again. One woman ended up traipsing the streets of South Africa – she suspected her boyfriend originally came from there – showing photos of him to strangers in the street in the hope of tracking him down. She even contacted a private detective. She believes she developed shingles from the stress.

As for Lisa, she missed out on having children because of the undercover ploy. She wasted years in a relationship with Mark Stone – actually Kennedy – and wasn't able to trust anyone enough to start another relationship. Another victim said she had to get pregnant through IVF because she couldn't trust another man enough to have sex with them.

When Lisa broke the story, it exposed Kennedy and collapsed several ongoing trials of climate change activists who had been prosecuted for conspiring to shut down power stations. Police tried to claim Kennedy had been a rogue officer acting alone. But it was revealed that they had been setting mostly female activists up with undercover cops since 1968, starting with protestors against the Vietnam War. Only the top tier of the police knew about the undercover officers, who were nicknamed 'The Hairies' due to the fuzzy, hippy appearance of the agents. As is similar in cults and other secretive organizations, new language was developed for the spies. Their victims were called Wearies.

The Duff meant the undercover cops' home life away from the spying.

Across more than four decades, at least 139 police officers adopted fake identities to monitor more than 1,000 political groups. They convinced the women of their undying love and devotion to 'the cause'. They kept up the ruse for many years, despite often disagreeing with the activists' views, and sometimes actively detesting them.

How does somebody take on a double life? How do you deceive and keep secret a second life from a person you marry? How do you continue along that deceptive path even after raising a family? It appears that not everybody can do so without remorse. In fact, Mark Kennedy – the man busted by Lisa – is one of the few undercover cops we know about who actively showed remorse.

Upon being exposed, he telephoned another of his targets (some of the spies had multiple victims), a climate scientist. She recorded the call, as he exclaimed: 'I fucking hate myself so much. I betrayed so many people.' If we are to take Kennedy's words at face value, it's an indicator of what comes from the discrepancy between the person we claim to be, and the person we have been showing to the world: shame. We can only speculate as to how other under-cover officers grappled with their consciences after misleading women into sham marriages and phony lives.

The SDS was officially disbanded in 2008, with one senior officer admitting they had 'lost their moral compass'. A more cynical reading is that the spies were disbanded not because of any moral reason, but because they were caught. Long-term infil-tration continued after the spying was officially cancelled under a different name. The only difference was that it was no longer known as the SDS; it was now an integral part of the National Public Order Intelligence Unit (NPOIU).

In some cases, the shame felt by the agents living double lives became deeply engrained. Some swapped sides. An undercover cop called Bob Lambert took the name of a seven-year-old boy – Bob Robinson – who had died of a heart condition decades earlier. He began to sympathize with the leftist cause. For him, the act – the new life – became reality. In the 1980s, he allegedly set fire to a Debenhams department store as part of a left-wing protest. He denies the charge. He also fathered a child while in the role. Bob was promoted to a senior manager, and received an MBE for 'services to policing'.

One of the recruiters, Neil Woods, has spoken about the guilt and the difficulties many spies have had with living split lives. He suffers from sleepless nights, panic attacks and a fear of loud noises. These are symptoms you might associate with Post-Traumatic Stress Syndrome (PTSD).

Peter Francis, an agent who blew the whistle on the SDS, also claims he doesn't know who he is any more. Host of *Bed of Lies*, a podcast series about the scandal, Cara McGoogan explains to me: 'We don't want to be too sympathetic because a lot of these men harmed a lot of women. But I think there are definite feelings of moral injury and PTSD among them as well. And a kind of dissociation with who they are. Mark Kennedy came out of being undercover, and said, "Those were my true people and I really believed in the work they were doing in the end." Whether he means it, we'll never know . . . is it just part of the lie? You definitely have got to be a good actor at least.'

On the PTSD exhibited by some of the spies, McGoogan says, 'You've not necessarily been through a traumatic event, but you've done something that's so at odds with who you think of yourself as a person and your idea of self . . .' She pauses, 'That's come more from a sense of self being damaged by the work.'

As established, secrets hit harder when they are wrapped up in our identity. If you can convince yourself that you are simply a cop following orders – or that your new identity really is who you are – then you might be able to pull off the double life. As wartime code-breaker Alan Turing said, 'Advice about keeping secrets: it's a lot easier if you don't know them in the first place.'

Actually, I can't find any evidence that Turing said that, but his avatar – played by Benedict Cumberbatch – does so in the 2014 biopic, *The Imitation Game*. Considered the father of computer science and artificial intelligence, Turing helped turn the tide of the Second World War in favour of the Allies. His work on code-breaking machines helped unravel the secrets of the Nazis, enabling British Armed Forces to predict and prevent planned attacks in the air and sea.

It is impossible to know exactly how many lives Turing saved. However, historians believe he brought the war to a close two or three years early. Each year of war averaged 7 million deaths across Europe, so he may well have saved between 14 and 21 million people.

Turing was a man consumed by secrets, perhaps like no other in history. Not only did his work centre around the extraction of Nazi secrets, but his own life was shrouded in them. Much like Oscar Wilde, he was a gay man at a time when homosexuality was illegal. His secret was central to his identity. I can't help but wonder whether the burden of keeping his secret is what drew him to a life of exposing them.

In 1952, Turing was arrested for having a relationship with a man, and he was forced to admit to 'acts of gross indecency'. As part of his punishment – and a substitute for prison – he had to receive chemical castration. This involves anaphrodisiac drugs that reduce your libido and sexuality. He also lost security clearance and was forbidden from continuing his work in code-breaking for the government, a fall from grace and a loss of status that must have been excruciating.

I can't begin to fathom the grief and frustration he must have felt at having to hide being a gay man who had sex with consenting adults. Living a double life is all-consuming. You become engulfed by the secret new persona, but can never totally commit to it. For Turing, the sense of injustice in criminalizing an act that has no bearing on the freedoms of others will surely have added an extra layer to the difficulty of keeping his secret.

In 1954, just two years after his conviction and forced chemical castration, Turing was found dead from cyanide poisoning; likely suicide. He was forty-one. A law legalizing homosexuality for two men in private over the age of twenty-one was introduced thirteen years later. It is estimated that about 49,000 people were convicted under homosexuality laws, and many more had to live with the shame and burden of a secret that should never have been one. Homosexuals were hiding in plain sight – but they were forced to suppress and hide something at the core of their being. In 2013, almost sixty years after his conviction, Turing received a post-humous royal pardon, and in 2019 he was featured on the £50 note. Nevertheless, Turing's story is a stark reminder of the terrors that some people endure and how devastating secret-keeping can be.

Some of the undercover cops of the SDS, however, were able to act out second lives without shame. If we see life as a great play, then the commands from superiors are the closest we get to receiving orders from a stage director. McGoogan says, 'They were being told to go out and do it, so I think although you might have people who also had sociopathic tendencies within that, they're being told to do it and being supported, and I guess in some ways they're not lying to their superiors, are they? So, they think they're doing the good thing.'

The idea of following orders made me think of the Nazis once more, and of Hannah Arendt's 'banality of evil'. This is the idea that anyone can do horrific things, not out of deep-seated hatred or evil, but thoughtless obedience to authority and societal norms. We've seen how well-meaning people have joined malign cults, and done terrible things in their names. Arendt's thoughts on the

Nazis were echoed by Canadian psychologist Jordan Peterson in an interview with Piers Morgan: 'There's a bit of Hitler and Stalin in everyone.'

'A bit of Hitler in everyone?' responds Morgan, incredulous.

Peterson's face turns to stone: 'There's more than a bit. Why would Nazism have spread the way it did?' He explains Swiss psychiatrist Carl Jung's assertion that, in a truly totalitarian state, everyone has to be willing to lie all the time.

I had seen how one way of avoiding rumination, mind-wandering and shame, while hiding who you are, is to convince yourself – and everyone else – that life is a stage. You have to act as though the secret 'you' – the real you – doesn't exist. We're not all brilliant actors. But humans are adept at following orders. It begs fascinating questions about the essence of being human, and why good people do bad things.

How did seemingly ordinary people willingly commit unspeakable acts in Nazi Germany? Does evil lie dormant within us all? Given the right set of circumstances, could we do as they did? Given what history tells us about the sheer number of people who fell in line with abhorrent ideologies over the centuries, the answer to the final question is: probably, yes.

That doesn't mean that we are all capable of committing horrors and slipping on a new personality like a uniform at the behest of those in authority. Plenty of objectors formed resistances during the Second World War, and many Germans harboured Jews in direct dis-obedience to the Nazis and at great risk to their own lives. But many of us – including those of us who believe most vehemently we couldn't be swayed – could be susceptible. Among the reasons I believe this to be true are two vital experiments in the twentieth century that can likely never be repeated because they were so fraught with ethical dilemmas.

The Milgram Experiment was carried out by Stanley Milgram at Yale University in 1961. The psychologist was fascinated by our obedience to authority figures, and wanted to see how far people would stray from their convictions simply because they were told to do so by a man in a white coat. Participants were told they had to administer electric shocks to a 'learner' in another room. The Milgram Experiment sent shockwaves – both figurative and real – through the scientific world, because the results found that most people – when ordered – were willing to administer lethal levels of electricity to the 'learner' (fortunately, these were actors who went to another room, from which pre-recorded sounds of pain were played). Milgram found that most of us will simply obey, if an authority figure gives us instructions.

The experiment came just a few months after the trial of Adolf Eichmann in Jerusalem. Eichmann, a Nazi on the run, had been found hiding in Argentina by Israeli agents. Milgram asked the question: 'Could it be that Eichmann and his million accomplices in the Holocaust were just following orders? Could we call them all accomplices?' While the Nazis are the go-to example for horrors committed by the masses, we've seen it time and time again through history. I've spoken to countless survivors of cults over the years, and am always struck by how fine the line is between perpetrator and victim.

Former *Smallville* actress Allison Mack – known for her innocent demeanour and pleasant smile – is the high-ranking member of the cult NXIVM that I described earlier. She carried out horrific crimes, blackmailing fellow members into becoming sex slaves for Keith Raniere, and branding them with her initials. In many respects, she was simply following orders: many of the most sadistic ideas appear to have come from Raniere.

Each former Scientologist that I interview speaks incredulously of the abusive acts carried out by the cult. They seem amazed by the lengths that some Scientologists will go to in the name of their leader, David Miscavige. And yet, just months or years earlier, my interviewees were carrying out those very acts under the guise of righteousness. They speak to me as if their former behaviour – spreading vicious lies about detractors, turning up at their houses to 'fair game' them (Scientology's harassment policy), and carrying out cruel punishments on fellow members who transgressed arbitrary Scientology rules – were not them, but someone else.

They were playing out roles dictated by their directors. These dynamics of authority were further explored in the Stanford Prison Experiment, conducted in 1971 – ten years after Milgram's test. Led by psychology professor Philip Zimbardo, the experiment split male-only participants into teams with different roles: prison guards and inmates. Guards were dressed in uniforms that were meant to rob them of their individuality, and inspire group-think.

Extraordinarily, real Palo Alto police officers brought the prisoners in, and the guards were instructed to prevent prisoners from escaping. The participants who were unfortunate enough to have been assigned as prisoners were stripped naked and 'deloused', to add to their humiliation and to create further disparity in status between guards and inmates. They were also made to wear smocks that looked like dresses without underwear.

Participants were purportedly forced to stay, even after asking to leave. In the first five days, the guards' behaviour became so erratic and abusive that another psychologist confronted Zimbardo, forcing him to end the experiment prematurely.

Much like the Milgram Experiment, Zimbardo's work both fascinated scientists the world over, and raised questions around its morality. It caused universities to improve their ethical requirements, which is why the two experiments stand out as ones that can likely never be repeated. It's said Zimbardo inserted himself into the experiment, and that many of the guards believed they were supposed to act and be dramatic. Milgram's experiment is now picked out for its lack of rigour and allegations he manipulated the results. They are flawed, unethical pieces of work that nonetheless give us insight into the power of authority and following orders when taking on a secret second self. If you have a convincing director, it's easier to act, or – as the saying goes – 'there are no bad actors, only bad directors.'

We see this with the SDS undercover cops. Despite many of them claiming to have developed PTSD, many were able to carry out second – and even multiple – lives. They became close to the women who were the victims of this decades-long ploy, and even raised families with them, all the while working for the other side and splitting their personality.

As they were following orders from their superiors, there is a morally grey line between victim and perpetrator. Some developed PTSD from the strain, while others negated the effects of rumination and shame by disassociating themselves from the real them. Like Lord Bracken in his fictional school, they had to play a role to perfection. But what made it easier for many of the spies is the fact that they were only following orders.

But what if you weren't following orders? What if you were born having to play a role? What if you could never tell anyone – not even your closest friends and family – who you truly are, and what you're really hiding? What if you had to keep the worst secret in the world? What would happen to you then?

9

THE WORST SECRET IN THE WORLD

I didn't feel like I could truly grasp the power of secrecy until I'd seen it at its darkest. I wanted to get an idea of what it felt like to keep the most burdensome secret imaginable; the kind that you'd be tempted to take to the grave. From what I'd learned in my secrecy research, the worst secret in the world – the one that would affect its holders most egregiously – needed to be tied up in its keeper's identity. Rather than simply following orders, it had to be something that defined them as a person, but couldn't be shown to the world. It would be even worse if the holder had low self-esteem, and worried that releasing their secret could get them ostracized or even killed. I was on a mission to find a secret that could cause societal stigma, lose its possessor their friends and family, and provoke wild and feverish rumination and mind-wandering.

My pursuit took me to a tiny village in northern Germany. It made for the strangest and most disturbing day of my life. I will just warn the reader now that – as you might expect from the darkest secret imaginable – what follows makes for difficult reading.

Some secrets might be better left unknown.

*

'I have to tell you something,' says Ruby, her voice quivering. 'I don't like men.'

'Oh,' says her mother, a devout Lutheran from a German hamlet. She pauses, her disappointment palpable. 'Don't tell me you like women.'

This isn't going to be easy.

Ruby takes a breath, readying herself to utter the words that will confirm her as a freak of nature to her mother.

'Um . . . no,' she says. 'Actually, little boys.'

Her mother narrows her eyes.

'Very little boys.'

Horrified by her own desires, Ruby is a non-offending paedophile. For many of her twenty-five years, she has lived a sad and lonely existence, hidden away in a village in northern Germany. Last year, her isolation was disturbed by love of a most unconventional nature. Two years her senior and living in the same village, Sirius is a fellow 'minor-attracted person' – a clinical title that attempts to distinguish non-offenders with the affliction from paedo-criminals or abusers. They met through an online forum for non-offending paedophiles.

As an attractive and seemingly well-adjusted young woman, Ruby is an anomaly in a paedophilic world dominated by men. Rarer still is a love between two non-offending paedophiles. As far as I know, they are the only couple of their kind in the world. I'm curious to see how they live with their secret. It is one they can't reveal to others unlike them (aside from Ruby's mother . . . and now me). I've been chatting online with Ruby for more than a year. Her pseudonym comes from the Latin for Little Red Riding Hood.

'People think I'm the little girl,' she tells me. 'But actually, I'm the wolf.'

'Don't you mean the other way around?' I ask. 'I mean, people who know about your . . . condition . . . might think you're an offender – a wolf – who preys on children. But you're actually the innocent little girl . . . right?'

'Umm . . .' she pauses. 'Yes. I forget which way round it is. I guess I just like the name.'

We stay in touch from afar, both staying vigilant. She worries I might be a paedophile hunter, intent on outing her. And I worry about getting too close to someone with her inclination, orientation or mental illness, as though it were catching. With time, Ruby comes to trust me, and invites me to meet her and Sirius. I take a train from my base in Berlin to northern Germany, my heart pounding, as I move between fear and curiosity. Paranoia reigns, as the train chugs past wind turbines and reddish-yellow autumnal forests, before a jumble of factories and gabled cottages pull the village into view.

Just as I wonder how I'll recognize them, they emerge on the platform, looking like high-school emos dressed in black hoodies and loose jeans. Sirius is twenty-seven, with bright blue eyes and thinning, slicked-back hair. Ruby has a round face and red cheeks curtained by blonde locks. I'm checking to see if there is a physical manifestation of their condition. Before me on the platform, they stand petrified and mute. They shake, looking this way and that, as I approach them. Ruby begins to sob uncontrollably right there on the platform. I'm aghast. Sirius can't meet my gaze, and kicks the floor. I feel the weight of being privy to such a dark secret; one that could get them not just ostracized but killed. I feel the burden of the secret of others. It's one thing to read about paedophiles online, and see them as statistics (1 per cent of men, according to sexologist Michael C. Seto). But to see these young, confused human beings in front of my eyes – and to worry about looking like a co-conspirator – is all too real and daunting.

We sit tentatively in a cafe making cheerful chitchat with a waitress who wouldn't be so amiable if she knew what our meeting was about. Ruby and Sirius each take long toilet breaks, leaving me in painful silence with the other. I wonder if they have gone to vomit, because they come back looking even paler and gaunter than before. Their visceral pain is not just about the strain of keeping the secret, but also the fear of what letting it out to this strange British journalist might do to their status, security and survival. Having confessed to me, but not to others, they're now living with both the burden of the secret and the fear of the ramifications of having confessed to me. I've made things worse.

Later, we walk together through a park. They begin to trust me and open up about their Age of Attractions (AOAs) – the age of child that they are attracted to. They insist they'll never act on these clandestine desires. AOAs, I learn, are how paedophiles introduce themselves to one another online. In a far darker way, it's used like 'Age Sex Location' was in the chat rooms of the 1990s to find common ground.

Out of the many paedophiles I'd considered meeting to find out what it was like to keep the world's darkest secret, there were two reasons why I chose Sirius and Ruby:

1. It was important to meet with *non-offenders*. I didn't like the idea of spending an afternoon with somebody who has – or wants to – abuse children. Despite the non-invasive role of the journalist, I would want to turn them in to the authorities. Sirius and Ruby were determined that no adult should ever touch a child sexually, nor should they download child sexual abuse material. They were committed to activism online against it, and regularly argued on message boards against proponents of adult–child relations. Sirius and Ruby spoke of these people with the same contempt that the rest of us do. I imagine that this made it even harder for them to live with their secret.

2. Finding a female paedophile who'll agree to meet a journalist is exceedingly rare. In fact, it is almost unheard of. I imagined that the stigma of being a paedophile combined with society's expectations around maternal instincts might make it an even worse secret to keep for Ruby.

Ruby's AOA is even more alarming. She is attracted to boys from age seven down to just one year old. 'But only boys,' she insists. 'And the babies have to have hair.' I investigated this topic for more than a year, but this is one of the most disturbing things I heard. As she tells me about it in the quaint park in the heart of her home village, I do my best to hide my revulsion, lest she break down again in tears.

'That young . . .' I say, trying to keep my composure. 'And only boys? How do you know the sex?'

'It depends.'

'What if someone told you a baby girl were a baby boy?'

'I suppose I would be attracted to it,' she snaps.

This seems to me like she has a compulsion to tell herself she has such an attraction. It doesn't seem like actual sexual desire.

I tell her so.

She glares at me.

I'm intrigued to find that she is offended by my remark. It says something about how closely she links her desires to her identity. 'At first, I thought it might be obsession. Or maternal feelings. But now I'm 100 per cent sure these are real sexual feelings.'

Ruby didn't have much of a childhood, and her father made her feel unwanted. She first realized something was wrong after becoming aroused by Japanese anime depicting young boys, and using it as a substitute for porn. She knew she couldn't tell a soul, and this weighed on her. The secret became so oppressive that she closed herself off from society, and sought only the company of others like her on dark forums. Ruby told her ex-boyfriend about her attraction, and even persuaded him to role-play as a baby. But it turned out he'd been abused as a child. The role-play was traumatic, and he left her.

Soon after, Ruby and Sirius met and fell in love, despite neither of them being attracted to adults. Being able to talk about her secret urges with Sirius lifted Ruby's burden. They each tell me that this is what saved them from suicide. Now, they take turns during sex – which they have at least once daily – to be the baby. Nauseating though it may be, it's a more palatable alternative to the couple acting out their desires on real children.

They tell me they want to raise a family together. I don't ask if they are worried about abusing their own children. Given their anti-offending stance, the question would break the trust I spent a year building with this uniquely dark couple. Perhaps they'd take it as though I were asking a non-paedophile if they were tempted to molest their siblings or parents. Still, I find the idea of them raising children together deeply uncomfortable.

It is a source of dispute between the two of them. Sirius believes that – as non-offenders – it is only right to tell their future kids their secret: 'We have a responsibility to help normalize this. We're hypocrites if we want to remove stigma, but continue to hide it from our children.'

Ruby disagrees: 'It's not right to use our own kids as experiments.'

If they do as Sirius suggests, the kids will have to live with the burden of another's secrets. Not just *any* other, but their own parents. And not just *any* secret: the worst secret in the world. Should they decide, however, to follow Ruby's logic by not informing their kids, then the children will live with the phantom effect: the passing of things unsaid through generations. They'll be haunted by the gaps between words. They'll always know deep down that something isn't quite right.

Every country has a torrid relationship with paedophilia. Its offence rates are similar throughout the world. In terms of prolific and sensational cases, just as the UK had TV presenter Jimmy Savile and the US had island-owning financier Jeffrey Epstein, Austria had basement fiend Josef Fritzl and Australia had a paediatric nurse called Boris Kunsevitsky, who abused at least forty-seven boys. Germany has a particularly gruesome tale of state-sponsored horror. In the 1970s and 1980s, Berlin had two major problems that the senate were looking to fix:

1. Too many homeless boys.
2. Too many paedophiles.

Renowned psychologist and sexologist Dr Helmut Kentler suggested solving both problems at once . . . by placing the homeless boys in the foster care of paedophiles. Remarkably, Dr Kentler believed that these men would make for extra-caring foster guardians. Even more remarkably, the state agreed, and implemented what is now known as the Kentler Experiment.

For thirty years, children were sent to a foster home run by a known paedophile. Even now, much of what happened to the homeless boys – and how it was allowed to happen – is being kept under wraps by the senate. Many of the politicians involved are still in office, and the country's Green Party – which long had public links to extreme far-left groups with paedophile sympathies – has never fully recovered. The horrors of the Kentler Experiment came to light in the 2010s, and more is still being discovered. The men who as boys were placed on this scheme are too damaged to properly speak about it.

I was beginning to see how the worst secrets in the world – ones involving such taboo topics as paedophilia and rape – would always have far-reaching consequences on both sides. Just as Ruby and Sirius are compelled to keep an excruciating secret about their darkest thoughts, secrecy also engulfs everyone, from enablers and neglectful authorities to victims of offenders and their families – as I saw with the story of Madeleine Black, who was brutally raped by two American teenagers.

The Berlin homeless debacle is today a black stain on the nation's recent history, but a liberal ideology continues to influence its stance on treating paedophilia. In most countries, including the UK, reporting paedophiles to authorities is mandatory. A doctor would be struck off for not reporting predatory inclinations to police. In Australia and the US, it is more severe: doctors in those cases could serve time in prison for not reporting. Not so in Germany.

Run from Berlin's Charité Hospital, the Don't Offend clinic invites 'minor-attracted persons' (MAPs) to come in and talk without fear of being reported. It's controversial: it means letting some known sex offenders back on the streets, where they could abuse children. The clinic counters that this is the only way to get paedophiles to come in for therapy. They believe by helping them to control their urges, they save countless children from sexual abuse. Ruby and Sirius are among the thousands who have attended the therapy.

Statistics are difficult to prove, but one estimate finds one in nine girls are sexually abused by adults. Despite our understandably emotional reaction to paedophiles, you can't simply lock up and kill them all. Even if you tried, it would be impossible to find most of them – and more of them are always being born (or made, depending on how and why the attraction forms, on which there is no real consensus).

Instead, the idea with Don't Offend is to get to these people before they offend, so that therapy disabuses them of the notion that child sexual abuse is acceptable. This may seem obvious, but offending paedophiles often gather in secret online forums, where they convince one another that society has it wrong, and that sex with children can be consensual. It's a cognitive bias that Don't Offend seeks to eradicate.

As I looked deeper into the topic, I was shocked by how pervasive attraction to children is in our society. In 2003, Mike Freel, of the UK's Child Protection and Review Unit, found that fourteen out of ninety-one male childcare workers (15 per cent) expressed a sexual interest in the children they were employed to protect. As for female care workers, ninety-two were asked, with four confessing to child-related arousal. As established, the more conservative estimates by Dr Michael Seto rate the prevalence of exclusive paedophiles (those with zero attraction to adults) at one per cent. It may seem relatively low, but it's a significant portion of society. They're our friends, family members and teachers. And they're sitting on deeply troubling secrets.

I meet Don't Offend's Maximilian von Heyden in his office at the back of a traditional Berliner courtyard. I'm keen to find out how the therapy helps paedophiles deal with the weight of the worst secret in the world, and whether this might make them less likely to offend. Even though the taboo topic of paedophilia is quotidian to him, I find I'm nervous to bring it up.

I ask, 'How does this work? Presumably, they never lose that longing for children, even after attending the Don't Offend clinic?'

He replies, 'No, but some of the patients we see have high ethical standards. They come to therapy to improve their lives and try to cope with this better. To be better socially integrated. But they would never abuse a child.'

I ask, 'Would you let your kids hang around with someone who'd been through this therapy?'

He gazes out the window. 'That really . . . I mean . . . I wouldn't leave my children with someone I don't know. We have quite a good success rate when it comes to establishing behavioural self-control, but we don't succeed all the time, so there's always a risk. But in general, if I have a good relationship with a patient and he's opening up and telling me about his sexuality . . . I'd probably be more cautious, but wouldn't suspect he intended to abuse my children.'

He explains the clinic's own findings: 'Up to around 4 per cent of the general population include an attraction towards minors.' It's a harrowing thought. It means one in twenty-five of the people you pass on the street, your work colleagues and your family and friends, are keeping this dreadful secret. He continues, 'There's a difference between exclusivity and non-exclusivity. If you're exclusively a paedophile, you probably have a hard time because you can never act out your sexual fantasies without committing a crime or hurting someone.

'But if you're non-exclusive, you will be satisfied having sex with a partner in the normal age range. You might become aroused by a child running around naked, but you're not obsessed with it.' I wonder whether Ruby and Sirius are exclusives. They enjoy sex with one another, but require role-play. Later, I mention them to Maximilian's boss – and the head of the programme – Professor Klaus Beier. I'm intrigued to find that – even after years of study in this area – he considers Ruby an extremely rare find.

Maximilian believes the research and clinical data point towards paedophilia 'being stable over the life course'. This is the dominant theory, and suggests that it is possibly unchangeable. Some disagree with that consensus. The head of the UK's Stop It Now! programme, Donald Findlater, told me he considers it a curable illness. Don't Offend, however, focuses its attention on trying to prevent paedophiles from acting out their desires.

They talk with patients about risk factors, such as drinking alcohol, being near children and stigmatization. Maximilian says, 'You're left alone with [your attraction to minors]. Everyone hates you, and it becomes part of your identity: "Society hates me, so why not do what I want?" So, it's really wrong to stigmatize people with attraction to children just because they're born that way. But of course, it's very important to point out clearly that abuse can't be tolerated. That's the red line, right?' he asks.

I nod.

That word 'identity' reminds me of how burdensome the secret is for these people. The stigma that Maximilian describes is exactly the kind of thing that makes secret-keeping so difficult. Many of us have an urge to punish paedophiles, even if they have never offended. Just the fact that they are thinking that way about children is revolting. But here's the problem with venting our repulsion from a secret-keeping perspective.

Typically, secret-keepers are desperate to reveal everything to the world, so that they can feel better and recover from the fever model. But there are certain topics – such as paedophilia – where confession is not an option due to the severity of the consequences. They have to live with their secret. But by stigmatizing them (outside the Berlin clinic, 'Hang the Paedos' is scrawled in graffiti), we are hitting at the core of their identity. This makes it even harder – impossible, even – to live with the secret. But they can't come clean. So, there are only two mechanisms they can employ to quell the pain from the build-up of secrets and the attack on their identities: suicide . . . and cognitive bias.

By cognitive bias, I mean that many of these non-offending paedophiles – after being told that they are monsters – will do anything to feel better about themselves. This leads them away from normal society, and down the rabbit hole of the forums of the dark web. Here, they meet twisted people who love-bomb them; who tell them that their identity is fine, and that it is everyone else who is wrong. These dynamics can also be found in cult members, conspiracy theorists, and radicalized terrorists. I've spoken to several non-offending paedophiles who have joined such groups, and subsequently told themselves that child sex abuse is a victimless crime. That's very dangerous, because it gives those who never intended to offend a free licence to do so without feeling bad about their identities.

The clinic in Berlin has its work cut out trying to bring those people in, and convince them that child sex abuse is extremely damaging to children. One of the standout lessons I'd learned from investigating cults, and spies following orders, is that we must never underestimate the power of cognitive dissonance, especially when a person's identity and self-appraisal are at stake.

Maximilian adds, 'We're interested in the well-being of the children. We know there are severe consequences for victims.' This is true. Victims of child sexual abuse are four times more likely than others to abuse drugs and experience PTSD as adults, and three times more likely to experience a 'major depressive episode'.

This is hammered home to the paedophiles, who the clinic separates into types. There are those who would never offend, and don't necessarily need help. I hope that Ruby and Sirius belong in this category. There are others who resemble psychopaths. Little can be done about them at the clinic. But where the clinicians make the greatest impact is with another type: ostensibly well-meaning paedophiles who are in danger of letting cognitive biases sway them.

Maximillian says, 'Working on cognitive biases is a big part of what we do. They think, "Oh the kids want it, they love it, they tease me." But they have to realize some normal behaviour from children isn't sexual, and even if the child is teasing you, which sometimes happens, it doesn't mean you're allowed, as an adult, to follow that impulse. There's a huge power difference, so there are philosophical, medical and psychological reasons to not abuse children; period.'

Don't Offend has enquiries from prospective patients around the world, with many moving to Germany for the therapy. This shows how serious they are about getting help and finding a therapist who can listen to their secrets without being forced to report them to police. It is the firm hope of Don't Offend that letting a person get their secrets off their chest without stigmatization might just save a child's life.

Jenny lies in a crumpled heap on the floor. Her world, and everything she thought she knew about it, has turned upside down in an instant. Her husband Sam kneels beside her, a little unsure and off-kilter. He has just revealed that he sexually abused their two children multiple times. He stares through damp eyes at his feet, overwhelmed by the guilt of what he has done to his kids and wife.

Somewhere deep down, there is also relief. The secret infested his body and mind for years. At last, it is out there. Things will get harder at first, he believes. By revealing the secret to Jenny, Sam has hurt her – perhaps beyond repair. He has risked not only his status, but his liberty. Given his crimes, he could – and should – be locked up for a long time. But he has spoken truth. He got off his chest a secret so dark and rotten that it *had* to come up for air, lest it fester within. Now they can begin working together towards some semblance of healing, whether that be together or apart – or after a spell behind bars.

The only thing is: Sam's confession is false.

After hearing Sam's revelation about what he had done to their children, Jenny did one of the most difficult things a parent could ever do. She sat her children down to ask them about the abuse they suffered at the hands of their dad. But they had no idea what she was talking about. This was no case of repression of hurtful memories. They were adamant that their father had never behaved inappropriately with them.

Sam didn't know it, but he was suffering from a severe form of Obsessive Compulsive Disorder (OCD). Back when Jenny was pregnant with their first child, rather than celebrate, he obsessed over the idea that the baby wasn't his. This obsessive behaviour continued after his son was born. 'Obviously he can't be mine because his eyes are blue,' he thought, before researching the probabilities of those differences. Then, he didn't sleep for months, convinced his son would suffocate in his sleep. He took full control of things like baths and feeding, obsessing over whether he had 'contaminated the bottle' with too many scoops of powdered feed.

A few years later, his daughter was born. His obsessions and compulsions – still undiagnosed – were compounded, and, after a few years, he fixated on the idea he had sexually molested his children. After all, hadn't he *insisted* on taking full control at bath times? Hadn't he spent *all that time alone* with them? Surely – his mind told him – he had done the worst thing a father could do in those private moments?

False memories of molestation began to creep into his mind. Invention and self-flagellation are surprisingly common in sufferers of OCD, and part of 'intrusive thoughts'. We all have them to an extent. It's like standing on top of a building and worrying you'll jump off, or that you'll swear at the top of your voice during a school assembly. Sam's intrusive thoughts were so vivid that he was unable to tell the difference between reality and his darkest fears.

This all comes from the dread that either you are – or people think you are – the worst thing in the world. Another OCD sufferer, a journalist I know, told me he convinces himself that everybody thinks he is a serial killer. He is a mild-mannered and sweet-natured writer. The idea that he is a serial killer is preposterous. But no amount of convincing assures him. Once while out, he burnt his clothes at midnight because he thought they were contaminated. He walked home naked.

At times, he has also worried that others might *think* he is a paedophile. This is as unfounded as the idea that people could think he's a serial killer. I sense that many men share this fear, and it's a large part of why we shirk away from discussing it. We feel on some level that even talking about preventing paedophilia will arouse suspicion. This is despite the fact that just 1 per cent of men are exclusively attracted to children. The paedophilic patients I meet don't tend to talk about how to stop paedophilic acts . . . they talk about *children*.

The fear of being accused of it is so common among OCD sufferers that it has its own name: Paedophile Obsessive Compulsive Disorder (POCD). Those with the condition think of the worst thing imaginable – being a child abuser – and make it real in their minds. Sam explains, 'The images were so strong and real that I actually believed I had done that. So, I confessed.'

He tried to suppress the intrusive thoughts. But the cruel irony – as discussed through the rebound effect we came across in Chapter 3 – is that this makes things worse. 'Thought suppression *causes* intrusive thoughts,' write psychologists Julie D. Lane and Daniel M. Wegner. 'People who try to stop thinking of a white bear cannot seem to do so'. This is why somebody with OCD is so susceptible to the compulsion to divulge, and reduce the fever. They are afflicted by intrusive thoughts, and no matter how many times they confess them to others, more keep coming.

When I was a teenager, I suffered from OCD. As a child of divorced parents, I lived just with my mum and little brother. By the time I was thirteen or fourteen, I felt responsible for the security of the home, and it is thought that OCD can sometimes develop or become accentuated in those with a chronic need to control their environments. Night after night, while preparing for GCSE and A-level exams, I went through a long list of safety checks.

It began small. I twiddled the knobs of the hob to make sure the gas wasn't on. I pulled down hard on the front door handle to ensure it was locked. As the months went by, my list developed into hundreds of checks. I'd have to count the packets of crisps in the cupboard; make sure every window was jammed shut; and ensure every curtain covered gaps. If I did anything in the wrong order – or if any safety check didn't feel quite *right*, I had to start over.

I spent hours doing this every night, and at its worst, it continued outside, so that I was standing barefoot in my pyjamas in the snow pulling at my car door handle (I guess I must have been seventeen by this point). From months of pulling at it – because I never trusted my own assessment that it was locked – the car door handle came off in my hand. I had to enter through the passenger side for weeks. Standing in the snow at 3 a.m. with a car door handle in my hand, I knew I needed to get help.

I was fortunate that my own variant of OCD proved easy to solve. I learned a lot about my need to control my environment. And how liberating it can sometimes be to just completely let go. Some OCD sufferers can benefit from learning to embrace the randomness and lack of control. You almost have to learn to obsess about not obsessing.

All of this is to say that I can understand what happened in Sam's mind. Seconds after pushing down on an unmoving locked door handle, I could still feel the pressure in my hand. And yet, I doubted my own memory. I believed the worst outcome – that I hadn't checked properly, that the door was actually unlocked. I'm fortunate that my type of OCD wasn't that imaginative. Unlike many others, I didn't believe that, by not doing a check, bad things would happen to me and my loved ones. And I didn't invent false narratives of criminal behaviour.

But Sam did, and it took him to a cliff edge. He was thinking about ending his life. Here is where self-esteem comes into play. 'Individuals with low self-esteem are increasingly likely to divulge the (typically negative) concealed information.' Sam clearly had very low self-esteem, and was dealing with a (made-up) secret that directly affected his self-perception and identity. After coming down from the cliff edge, he continued to self-flagellate by not eating for two weeks. He lost two stone. People with low self-esteem are far more likely to reveal their secrets, both to confirm negative feelings they have about themselves, as well as to seek consolation.

People with anxiety-related psychological disorders are also more likely to confess secrets. As part of his OCD, Sam suffered from neurosis, anxiety and depression. Remarkably, he hadn't actually been diagnosed with the disorder at this point. He approached the Samaritans, and got the help and understanding he needed. It came as a 'great relief' when a psychiatrist explained what was going on in his brain.

What interests me is not that Sam had such horrific intrusive thoughts (although I do find that intriguing and deeply upsetting). It's that he felt such a strong compulsion to confess to a false crime. Guarding the secret – which Sam believed to be true at the time – would have been the best way to protect his status as well as his relationship. He could have lost his family, friends and freedom. He could have been locked up and placed on the sex offenders register, his life never returning to normal.

Yet, a life with those consequences of confession became preferable for Sam to a life with the secret. It was eating him alive. Then, as Edgar Allen Poe poetically put it in 'The Imp of the Perverse', 'the long-imprisoned secret burst forth from [his] soul.'

I found Sam's story fascinating as far as secrecy goes, because his OCD heightened the anxiety, rumination and fever that we all experience to varying degrees. Such was the force of the fever that it made a man reveal an awful secret that could have torn apart his life . . . even though it wasn't true.

No secret I've encountered has been darker or more burdensome than that of Ruby and Sirius. If the world were to learn about their attraction to babies, their safety – even their lives – would be at risk, not to mention their jobs and social ties. I feel the weight of knowing their secret; the secret of others. Even as I write, I'm careful not to give away identifiable information. A wrong choice of words might see them killed.

As we walk side-by-side in the park, I ask Ruby why she told her mum about her secret. She and Sirius smile knowingly at each other. 'That's the thing,' she says. 'This is not just our sexual preference, it's our identity. And it'd be a relief to come out and talk.'

It's a shock to hear about the pride involved in being a non-offending paedophile. Up until now, I've skirted around the p-word in their presence, expecting it might offend them. But rather than shy away, they are desperate to talk about it, and spread their non-offending stance in their community. This open discussion helps them to control their urges and, they believe, will help others do the same. Perhaps Don't Offend, then – with its attempts to open the conversation – is onto something, providing that stigma remains in place around any form of acting on their desires.

They walk me back to the train station in their quaint northern German town, and we run out of things to say. Their secret has consumed their lives to such an extent that there is very little to talk about besides paedophilia. Now that they have the chance to tell an outsider about their secret, they don't want to stop. For me, I'm a bit sick of it. The preceding hours are enough for a lifetime.

I ask them about hobbies, curious about what such an un-orthodox couple might do day-to-day. 'Do you travel?'

'No,' says Ruby. 'I don't like being in new places.'

'OK, so Netflix? Have you watched *The Handmaid's Tale?*'

'Never heard of it,' says Sirius, oblivious to the gigantic billboard promoting the series above his head.

'Sports?' I ask, reaching.

'Umm . . . sometimes I go swimming,' says Ruby. She pauses. 'But I don't enjoy it.'

After walking in silence for some time, something occurs to her.

She says, 'I like to draw.'

'Hey, that's something,' I say. 'Are you any good?'

'Umm.'

'I think she's good,' says Sirius, a beat too late.

'That was a beat too late, Sirius,' I say.

'No, no,' he backtracks.

Ruby breaks into feverish laughter, playfully hitting him on the shoulder.

'She can draw,' he admits, with the faintest hint of a smile.

For the briefest of moments, the shackles of their secret seem to fall away, and I imagine they look to strangers like the most normal couple on Earth. No one could imagine the darkness within. For those who will never again cross paths with this dark duo, perhaps this is one secret they're better off not knowing.

10

SECRETS AND US

'What would happen if you went all the way, being radically honest, totally transparent, exposing yourself to distant strangers. Why would anyone wanna do that?'

– Justin Hall

I'd delved into the worst secrets in the world, and seen how authoritarian governments and cults, from China's Wu Zetian to Scientology, spread fear and confusion through their own use of secrets. This, in turn, pushes civilians and members to keep their own secrets, and suffer the feverish consequences. But what about the rest of us, as we go about our day-to-day lives? How do we engage in the trade of secrets?

I saw how one way that we act and keep parts of us we'd rather others didn't see hidden is through dramaturgy – taking on certain societal roles. We also, I found, engage in a complex dynamic – dating back to prehistory – of lies, white lies, privacy and game theory to enforce hierarchical bonds and enhance social cohesion. But things have changed rapidly in recent years. Modern technology now allows all of us to manufacture our images on greater scales than ever, through choosing what we do and don't reveal on online platforms.

My journey into secrets has led me back to my own world, that of the influencer and the social media user. And not only is our place in the tribe at stake, but money. Lots of it.

Social media is a curiosity-quenching tool that enables us to find out the darkest secrets of people from other worlds, while trading our own secrets for intimacy, shock and fame. Our ancestors hunted and gathered in tribes of 150. Today's stars of social media lead tribes of hundreds of millions, dwarfing the estimated 30,000 people involved in Scientology or the hundreds of thousands who worked for the Stasi in East Germany. It makes status-rich multi-millionaires of those who perfect the art . . . but its stakes are so high, and its pits so deep, that it can lead to depression, suicide and cult-like megalomania. And – without ever setting out to do so – and without ever imagining my job description might be 'YouTuber' – I found myself right in the thick of it.

If I really wanted to understand the state of secrets today, and get to the bottom of why my listeners were sharing their innermost secrets with me, I had to uncover the roots of social media. I had to look at us. Who better to start with, then, than the patient zero of our social influenza. The person who kick-started our habit of revealing everything – from what we had for breakfast to our infidelities – to our insatiable followers on social media.

If anyone has led a life fit for the epitaph of the World's First Influencer, it's him. Androgynous and mesmerizing, he was the standout pioneer at the turn of the 1990s who laid down the clicks and beeps for everything that followed. The alpha blogger and HTML wizard to whom every YouTuber, Instagrammer and TikToker owes a debt. And yet, Justin Hall has been largely forgotten.

At the birth of the blog, I expected to find an affluent Silicon Valley geek more interested in coding than people. I had images in my mind of Mark Zuckerberg, Jeff Bezos and Steve Jobs. This was a mistake. Blogs are a platform for storytellers to share their most intimate moments. They're more human than computer. They came into being in the early 1990s, around the time that *Wired* magazine started splashing its front covers not with computers or . . . wires . . . but human faces. Blogging is a modern take on cave paintings and graffiti artists. It's saying 'I blog, therefore I am. Like and subscribe?' So, it makes sense that blogging pioneer Justin Hall wasn't a Bill Gates or an Elon Musk, but a modern-day Jack London, whose writing has been compared to that of beat (or gonzo) journalists Jack Kerouac and Allen Ginsberg.

In 1993, his website links.net became the world's first blog. At the time, the World Wide Web only had about 600 sites, mostly belonging to universities and the military. Links.net published and reviewed links to all the websites that existed. It's crazy to think that this was even possible, but at one point, Justin browsed the world's entire archive of websites in just one weekend. This was long before the first search engines, so his catalogue of links proved invaluable. New to the internet, a growing number of web surfers managed to find Justin's blog, which he made from a rare internet-enabled university computer he borrowed from a friend.

Justin was fascinated by his analytics. His visitors arrived at the blog from universities, military institutions and even NASA. He learned that – as curious as these academics and professionals were about his links and reviews of websites – they were mostly clicking a very specific category: his sex links.

These tended to be links to porn on other pages, but also . . . photos of Justin. The world's first blogger was, fittingly, an exhibitionist. In one iconic page of photos on his nostalgia-inducing 1990s blog (which is still up), he perches in a variety of poses, long blond hair swept across his forehead, and lower lip flipped, part-sultry, part-mock-self-pity. At the bottom of the photo, he's lifting up a red and swollen flaccid penis (his own) for the camera. In the column beside these photos are zoomed-in versions of his floppy instrument. 'Upon inspection, it appeared as though my foreskin had swollen lips around my dick,' states the caption.

Crude as it may seem, this image is a historical artefact worthy of a place on the shelves of an ethnographical museum. It's possibly the world's first online dick pic. It's also one of the first examples of the internet being put to good use through the sharing of intimate details. One of Justin's early readers was a doctor. He inspected the images from afar, and got in touch to let Justin know that it was nothing serious, and there was no need to go to a hospital. That night, as a result of this online exchange, another doctor's time was spared. Who knows? Perhaps the doctor saved a life in that time.

The image is also one of the early examples of porn (particularly of the bizarre fetish variety) and, most importantly, an early illustration of the absolute 'intimacy' that would soon be required of bloggers. Try as you might, you can't conjure up a more intimate and authentic image than what Justin still refers to today as 'Cat Dick'. Justin was the first in a long line of bloggers and social media influencers who volunteer their most private moments – flattering or otherwise – for public consumption.

As I learned more about Justin, I wondered why some of us are given to revealing even the grossest or least appealing parts of us. In Justin's case, there is a dark history at the root of his craving for intimacy and affirmation. When he was eight, his father shot himself in the head in a corner of their family home. Justin's father had been vacant and aggressive as long as he could remember, while his mother had also been absent. But he believes that losing a parent in such a dramatic way left an indelible mark. He grew up seeking the attention he never received from his parents. He sought a paternal figure who could listen and give advice. Like a warm hug, the online community became a father.

Justin has said his 'need for attention and coming of age somehow coincided with the dawn of participatory media online.' It was the perfect storm of advancing tech and a personality dying to broadcast itself for feedback and community. His site became one of the most popular in the world: by January 1995, he had 27,000 daily readers.

For a few years in the early 90s, links.net was the go-to hangout on the internet. Justin became the darling of the Web. He lived a life befitting of his burgeoning celebrity, attending crazed island parties, and even getting into a physical altercation with celebrated American author Kurt Vonnegut. He appeared on news features to discuss how the internet would broaden our horizons.

The blog offered something that TV couldn't do so smoothly: it was interactive. Visitors could upload their own links and comments, and get replies from Justin in real time. The commenters could have their own effect on the community and the wider world through the blog. Once, one of Justin's followers put up a link on links.net, purporting to be porn, which actually went to the official website of the Indiana University. It was a prank. Despite being just one of many apparent porn links on Justin's blog, it still managed to bring so many Web surfers to the university website that it crashed their servers. The university formally complained to Justin.

He pressed ahead, and began revealing all of his – and his friends' – secrets online. This was bringing in a lot of traffic, and included the time he picked up a sexually transmitted disease, and when he was arrested for getting caught up in a progressive protest. (He'd been swept into the crowd of protesters, and was falsely accused of arson.) For years, Cat Dick winked at the world from the corner of an increasingly popular blog, oblivious to how badly things would turn out for its owner.

The wave that Justin came in on in these heady early chapters of the internet comes from a modern take on parasocial interaction. Sociologists coined the term in the 1950s to explain the relationship that talk show hosts have with their viewers. Talk show hosts create the illusion of a two-way relationship with an unlimited number of viewers, each of whom feels an intimate link to the host. It is, however, an illusion. They may seem like our best friends, but they wouldn't know us if they passed us in the street.

In the 1950s, fans would line up outside the windows of television shops, transfixed by the faces they recognized on the screens. The best talk show hosts are enigmatic paradoxes, managing to somehow appear both intense and relaxed; friendly and out-of-reach, as they perch with kinetic energy in front of the camera. They present inhuman levels of composure, smarts and friendliness. They appear to be gazing at you, the viewer, but they're not even looking into the camera lens, but reading words from a teleprompter screen in front of it. Illogically, they perform rehearsed spontaneity and surprised omniscience around events that unfold on the show. We welcome these contradictions, because they allow us to bathe in the illusion that we have a friend on whom we can depend to keep showing up.

In extreme cases, this has allowed the talk show host to act with impunity in real life. Jimmy Savile was the host of the *Jim'll Fix It* show, and notoriously used his fame and access to institutions to sexually abuse hundreds of children. Less egregiously, after years of acting as the smiling face of equality and righteousness – and a proponent of the 'be kind' philosophy – talk show host Ellen DeGeneres was outed as an alleged bully by the people who worked for her. In 2020, *Buzzfeed News* ran an article about the real face behind one of America's pleasantest masks. She was accused of enabling a toxic work culture. 'That "be kind" bullshit only happens when the cameras are on. It's all for show,' said one disgruntled former employee.

It was a big news story. But you got the impression that people weren't really surprised. Two years earlier, Ellen had responded to similar rumours with the hint of a threat: 'The one thing I want is for everyone to be happy and proud of where they work, and if not, don't work here.'

Many weren't truly shocked by the allegations about Savile either, or the ones about talk show host David Letterman's abuse of power around women. We weren't entirely surprised to hear about the alleged toxic work environment under British presenter Phillip Schofield, who it was revealed had an affair with a boy he met at a school. The boy – now a man – went on to work as a runner on the show. Schofield maintains that nothing sexual happened until after the boy was of age. Dan Wootton is the GB News presenter accused by an investigation in the *Byline Times*, as well as articles in *Private Eye* and elsewhere, of living a double life. He denies the allegations, but admits 'errors of judgement'.

We enter into an unwritten pact with the talk show host. Deep down, we know that they're acting – it's dramaturgy on a wider scale – but we expect them to keep up the illusion. That is why most of the online scorn for presenters isn't reserved for DeGeneres or Letterman (who got a bumper Netflix deal off the back of the allegations), but Jimmy Fallon and James Corden. Their crime? Bad acting. They let the secret 'real them' out. They're still immensely popular, but countless videos and articles take aim at the 'phoniness' of these two presenters; their apparent false laughs and body movements analysed in minute detail by let-down viewers. To many, Corden and Fallon fail to keep up the charade of 'authenticity'. They ruin our game of make-believe.

This is not to suggest that all talk show hosts and influencers are Machiavellian agents of phoniness. But the more successful ones are those who – deliberately or not – cultivate a parasocial relationship with viewers. The biggest podcast host in the world is Joe Rogan. It is said that he has more than twice the number of listeners as the next most-popular podcasters. Search his name on Twitter, and – in addition to criticisms – you'll find countless references from supporters to his *authenticity*. Really, it's a meaningless buzzword that helped draw millions of voters to Donald Trump, who had significant parasocial interaction points in the bank from his role as a TV presenter and reality show host.

Says Singaporean journalist Melissa Chen, who was a guest on Rogan's show: 'Yes, I will die on this hill. You cannot buy authenticity and love. The reason people *love* Joe Rogan is because the conversations he has on his podcast reflect the conversations that people have in real life.' This is clearly not the case, since very few of us hold conversations with the pre-eminent astrophysicists, leading professors and famous comedians that grace Rogan's stage. That Rogan is able to give off such an impression is a mark of his authenticity as a host. Chen goes on to call his episodes 'long and searching', and 'not set up'. The implication is that many competing podcasters 'set up' their shows; they're too obvious in their acting. They're keeping secrets.

She also writes that 'his questions are free from the kind of corporatized, political establishment bias. That shit is contrived and people can smell it. That is not how real people speak or learn about the world. That is why Joe has 50 million views per episode vs CNN's top news show which gets 400k views.' Whether Rogan actually is all of these things is irrelevant. The fact is that the 11 million people (lower than Chen's estimate) who listen to his show believe to varying degrees in the parasocial relationship they hold with Rogan.

This pact entered into between viewer and talk show host has its pitfalls. Part of the job of the parasocial interactor is to make the audience feel like they are the host's friend. They do this by revealing secret and private snippets of their own lives, meaning that the line is blurred between their professional and private life. Their inner secrets become commodities that audience members consume. The movies *The King of Comedy* (1982) and *Joker* (2019) – which both feature Robert DeNiro – are extreme portrayals of what can happen when the frontier between talk show host and friend is muddled.

In the former, De Niro's character Rupert Pupkin becomes obsessed with talk show host Jerry Langford, failing to grasp that the friendship he perceives through the screen is part of the latter's act. Pupkin shows up at Langford's home, even bringing a date, before being kicked out. He descends further into his state of delusion, and kidnaps the talk show host.

In *Joker*, De Niro is the talk show host, and Joaquin Phoenix plays the Batman antagonist who develops an unhealthy obsession with the idea that the two can be friends. A similar story is told in Eminem's hit song 'Stan', in which a fan can't understand why the singer hasn't replied to his letters.

These stories draw from real life. Paul D. Zimmerman, the writer of *The King of Comedy*, was inspired by a documentary about autograph hunters and an article about an obsessive follower of talk show host Johnny Carson. Director Martin Scorsese was convinced to do the project after feeling alienated by his own relationship with his growing celebrity. Eminem's song about a fan who kills himself and his girlfriend after failing to get a response from the rapper was also based on his own experiences. The success of the song is why the word 'stan' has become synonymous for 'obsessive fan' online. Such is the pride involved in being part of an influencer's tribe, that 'stan' doesn't appear to have a pejorative connotation (even if it is often slightly self-mocking).

I try to leverage this parasocial relationship on my own podcast. Sometimes, I leave in mistakes and bloopers, aware that viewers and listeners enjoy these authentic snippets of my flaws. I post behind-the-scenes photos of me setting up my office. I initially replied to every comment on YouTube with a personal message, sometimes staying up into the early hours to do so. Due to the frequency of messages, that's now impossible, but I still check in and hit the heart button when I get a moment. I try to reply as often as possible. This is a modern take on parasocial reaction, and it was kick-started by Justin Hall and his bloggers. Social media and online platforms have enabled us to respond to our viewers and listeners, heightening the sense of community.

Responding to messages is a way that social media influencers are able to make that one-way relationship into a two-way. Parasocial interaction is being replaced by a bi-directional communication. You might also call this interactive or reciprocal social interaction. Typically, the larger the following, the less interactive the interaction. Owners of smaller channels have more time to engage with viewers and fans.

The more I looked into this phenomenon, the more I saw how much stronger this reciprocal social interaction is than the parasocial interaction of talk show hosts. Just like Britney Spears's 'Britney Army', Dr Who's 'Whovians' and Ed Sheeran's 'Sheerios', many social media influencers have tribes of fans who give themselves group names and fight with other tribes about their favourite influencers. The 'Jake Paulers' may lack originality in their name choice, but it's efficient for YouTuber Jake Paul. Influencer Javi Costa Polo has an army of so-called 'Luvs' at his beck and call. Fans of YouTubers 'The Vlogbrothers' are known as 'Nerdfighters', and those of Hannah Hart – a YouTuber famous for cooking drunk – call themselves Hartosexuals.

One day, one of my YouTube viewers suggested that those who are fans of my *Heretics* podcast – formerly known as *On the Edge with Andrew Gold* – be known as 'Edge Hogs'. The channel has hundreds of thousands of subscribers, many of whom tune in for the 'premiere' of new episodes to chat with me while watching it. I also do live streams and urge my viewers to ask my interviewees and me questions. I enjoy the communal feeling. Sometimes, they tip me when they're really enjoying an interview. Most of my income is through ads, but I know many YouTubers who are 'demonetized' (when YouTube considers their content too controversial to allow it to make money through ads), but make a fortune through these tips, which are known as Super Chats and Super Stickers.

Parasocial interaction – and by that token the *reciprocal* social interaction of social media – has benefits for the viewer. It has been shown to fulfil social needs and decrease feelings of loneliness in listeners and viewers. When people were made to stay at home during the COVID-19 pandemic, they had virtually no physical contact with others. They relied more than ever on this 'social surrogacy'.

My YouTube page has become that for me. I moved to another city with my wife, and – despite being here for three years – am yet to make real-life friends (aside from people I meet in sports settings). Yet, most evenings, I get to hang out with the Edge Hogs. I am able to reward those who have been with me a long time by making them moderators, allowing them to time out users who are out of line. One or two that I selected as moderators wrote about what a thrill it was; they'd never expected it, and it had made an otherwise depressing moment in their lives more bearable. Selecting a new moderator doesn't really do much, but provides them with status in the chat, because their handle will be blue. If my channel were a cult, it would be my equivalent to Scientology's Operating Thetan levels (although my users don't have to pay for the privilege, and are allowed to leave).

Listeners reach out to me to ask for my home address, which I don't give out. It is a nice thought, as they want to send chocolate and other gifts. When I decline, it creates a subtle rift in the para-social fabric. We act like friends. I respond to their messages and we joke and laugh together. If a friend asked for my address, I wouldn't hesitate. In not giving it to fans, I suppose I am inad-vertently saying: 'Our friendship is an illusion for the benefit of my business. Plus, there's a small chance you might lace the choc-olate with anthrax.'

That's not how it feels to me. I love talking with readers, viewers and listeners. But as my subscriber base grows, I am having to learn how to navigate this world, and where to set boundaries. I often receive angry messages from subscribers who can't understand why I didn't reply to their last messages and emails. Many want to come on the show. Most of the time, I didn't even see their message.

Some fans write emails thousands of words long, which I couldn't possibly find the time to read. On a scarier note, others reach out with veiled threats and anti-Semitic conspiracies. Some tell me of their disappointment about a position I have taken. They speak to me in paternal tones, as though they've known me for years. I suppose they have. But it's a strange feeling to get a message of disappointment from someone who has been listening to my voice for hours each week for years, but who is totally new to me. I remind myself: I signed the pact. The nice, supportive messages make up for the creepy ones. And without them, I wouldn't have access to the secrets that prompted this book.

Justin Hall also loved getting supportive messages from his blog readers. It's amazing just how interactive and influential it was. When some of his followers started messaging to complain that they couldn't tell what was new on the website, he changed the homepage to feature new articles at the top. It's something that seems so intuitive to us now, but was a ground-breaking move at the time, and meant that the freshest titbits about Justin's hidden life were always front and centre on the blog, just like online news publications today. He refused to advertise, believing it would take away from the *authenticity* and *intimacy* of the blog, which are key cogs in the business of parasocial and reciprocated interaction.

Advertising is no longer such a moral quandary for today's influencers, some of whom garble on about those two buzz words, while raking in millions from the brands they endorse. (For the sake of transparency, I should declare that I am just as guilty, and also make a living through ads on my podcast and channel.) Instead of ads, Justin asked readers for donations to offset the cost of his servers – like a very early Patreon (or a very late version of the arts patrons who supported the likes of Shakespeare centuries ago). Cheques and cash started arriving at Justin's house by mail. The money created a problem: there was now a pressure to continue revealing new, authentic secrets from his life to share with his paying subscribers.

In the next few years, the Web expanded rapidly. Even so, it still wasn't large enough to satiate Justin's need for intimacy and kinship. He wanted more people to be empowered to make blogs, tell their stories, and, vitally, interact with him. He loved how the internet was billed as the great equalizer, but believed that he was in a position of privilege, as a man from an affluent background with the keys to the blogosphere.

He embarked on a road trip across the States, staying at the homes of his followers, and teaching them HTML coding to make their own blogs. No number of new interactions and exchanges could satisfy him. He even stayed at 'a half-way house for the mentally ill.' He said, 'Giving someone the chance to share their truth online might help us understand people we might not see in our everyday life. I believed the Web could promote empathy. If we shared our truths, if people who weren't us published online, we could learn about each other.'

During his road trip, this digi-vangelist updated his blog with stories about the people he met. He profiled strangers and, in so doing, gave his readers a chance to learn about the inner lives of one another. Search engines such as Lycos came into play in the mid-1990s. People used them to look up their own names, and many were surprised to find they'd been written about on Justin's blog. They got in touch and invited him to parties, including one in the Caribbean. He blogged in detail afterwards about his sexual encounter with an accountant there.

This addiction to sharing had its drawbacks. Justin's mother explained to him how nobody in the family wanted to speak to him, for fear of being publicly written about and embarrassed on his blog. Friends began telling him they weren't happy that he mentioned them by name on his page. This had a profound effect on Justin. He never meant to shame anyone. He just wanted to see what other people were like on the inside; to get to the real, secret *them* within. An open book himself, Justin couldn't understand why friends were slighted by his breaches of privacy and trust. He took it badly.

He slowed work on the blog, and got a job at a TV channel called CBTV. He was doing well as an on-air host for a Web workshop, until a viewer from Mississippi wrote to his show's producer: 'I see you have this homosexual freak pornographer. He uses drugs and profanity. I'll boycott your channel.' (This is Justin's paraphrasing to me of what was written.) His bosses asked him to remove the pornographic links and adult material from his website, but the blog always came first. 'TV shows may come and go, but mature content is forever,' he told them, and left his job.

He may have acted facetiously, but this rejection and failure by his employers to act on homophobic abuse (Justin wasn't actually gay) deepened the wounds inflicted by the family and friends that were avoiding him, and the emptiness that sprang from his father's suicide when he was eight years old. Feeling dejected and misunderstood, he got as far away as he could. He moved to Japan as a freelance reporter to cover the launch of the first multimedia cell phones. At one point, he lived in an old-world bathhouse in rural Japan. He soon tired of his new life, and headed to California in 2005.

No longer sure which secrets he was allowed to write about on his blog, he fell into a funk. Having profiled his family, friends and fans across America, Justin turned the camera on himself, with a breakdown video in the mould of the Chris Cocker 'Leave Britney Alone' clip that came out that same year (2005). Justin stares at the screen, tearfully screaming the cautionary line, 'I PUBLISHED MY LIFE ON THE FUCKING INTERNET. AND IT DOESN'T MAKE PEOPLE WANT TO BE WITH ME! I CAN'T WRITE ABOUT PEOPLE. THEY DON'T WANT TO BE THERE! AND I HAVE NOTHING TO WRITE ABOUT . . . AND I HAVE NOWHERE TO GO WITH ALL THIS SHIT!'

His breakdown made the front page of the *San Francisco Chronicle*. The mental decline of a man whose father had committed suicide in his childhood home was, to many commentators at the time, a source of comedy and light entertainment.

By the mid-2000s, Justin was already becoming a curious relic from the dawn of the digital age. At twelve years old, his blog was like a half-forgotten piece of trivia from a pub quiz. It was a fall from the hedonistic, party-going pioneer of the digital plains he'd once been. The breakdown video found its way to eBaum's World, a website not unlike Justin's blog. It featured links to games, funny images and weird stuff from the back alleys of the cyberworld. The comments beneath Justin's clip were brutal:

'Just when you thought you couldn't hate emos anymore, they make retarded video blogs.'
'Hahahaha. Fucking classic. What a dick, what's with the perfect articulation on every word. It's so long too, Jesus Christ what's wrong with him.'
'that guy sucks at life.'
'this fag needs to get some real problems.'

Conjuring up Justin's childhood tragedy (perhaps unwittingly), the final comment read: '*cheers for suicide*'

But he didn't take his life. In fact, he is still active. He doesn't share as much as he used to about his most secret and private thoughts and moments. You'll find him back to basics, posting links on his retro blog, where he shares observations and articles. Depending on when you read this, you might find a photo of me at the top of the world's oldest blog, because he wrote a blog post about our conversation for links.net. He also updates Wikipedia entries to 'give something back to the community.'

Justin has a modest social media following: 5k on Twitter and 1k on Instagram. It's not a lot for the world's first blogger, especially given his fight with Kurt Vonnegut. But he feels he has learned to respect the boundaries of privacy, even if I get the feeling he isn't exactly enamoured by it. He says, 'Sometimes I miss not sharing my struggles in public.' Still, he tells me he values the intimacy he gets from his wife – he is happily married – more than he craves further input from online strangers.

If this is a warning to the rest of us, it's not one heeded by most influencers, who openly invite intrusion into their lives. On my podcast, I am comfortable talking about superficial aspects of my relationship, or the joys of moving to a new city. But you won't see me posting anything like Justin's Cat Dick. At least, not on purpose. It appears that Justin had a longing to share every part of himself with the world in return for judgement, feedback and, ideally, acceptance.

He inadvertently stumbled onto something that many social media influencers are deliberately taking advantage of today. They share every waking moment of their lives in return for clicks and affirmation. The more secretive and private the information, the more likes and shares they get; today, that means money from brands. This phenomenon is known as 'audience capture', and means that the viewers guide the influencers in their content strategy rather than the other way round.

Through our curiosity, thirst for gossip and craving for connection, we long to possess hidden parts of others. And while we are happy to play our part in the crafted authenticity of talk show hosts and podcasters, we're constantly looking for something 'realer'. Perhaps we don't want to have to keep suspending our disbelief, as we do with James Corden and Ellen DeGeneres. It's why we're so taken by reality shows featuring apparently ordinary people who broadcast the inner secrets and private moments of their lives on the dating circuit or while working as estate agents. We know the contestants and participants aren't being themselves; they're being directed by producers to create the illusion of conflict and plot. We don't see them, but there are multiple cameras and a crew in the room.

Although many point to the popularity of reality shows as a sign of the collapse of culture in the West, the irony is that these shows might be the last bastion in the fight to keep artificial intelligence from removing purpose from our lives. Elon Musk argued that AI 'will make life meaningless.' Yet, hope for humanity lies with the Kardashians. The fact that the Kardashians are far more popular than arthouse films might seem depressing, but it is evidence that we still prefer the 'authenticity' and 'vulnerability' of flawed real people than artifice (even if reality shows actually contain plenty of artifice). For that reason, we still watch chess played by humans rather than by more skilful computers. As *The Times* columnist James Marriott writes, 'We are addicted to personalities, not to disembodied excellence.'

We turn to social media for that hit of perceived authenticity. We hope to see and relate to flawed humans. Yet, Instagrammers have learned to create illusions of wealth, success and status. The fake lives of Instagram influencers have a real effect on the mental health of those of us who are watching and comparing their exploits to the mundanity of our own lives. In a sense, we want to believe that those kinds of jet-setting lives are more common than they are – we aspire to them – so the most successful influencers get away with faking or manipulating the look of their lives. But just like with talk show hosts, I feel we sort-of know deep down that it is pretence.

This is why we're so intent on finding something 'realer'. In 2022, an app called BeReal launched with a claim to being the most authentic app yet. Once a day, it nudges its users to take a photo with the front and back cameras of their smart phones within the next two minutes. It markets itself as an anti-Instagram app, with the claim: 'BeReal won't make you famous. If you want to be an influencer you can stay on TikTok and Instagram.'

Here, the concept of 'influencer' is portrayed negatively, as though a phony and superficial pursuit compared to the 'authenticity' of BeReal. But the app still gives its users two minutes to prepare and pose for a photo, which they can set up to look better than reality.

A friend of my wife has the app. She received a notification when we were sitting in a park, and hurriedly asked if she could take a photo of me. I obliged. I'll never know what that photo looked like, or whether that titbit of real-time exclusive access to this user's private life pleased her followers. I suspect that it was a little boring, like most of the app's feeds, which often feature nonplussed faces for the front photo, and desks and computers for the second.

What we really want is to see how others live when they don't know we're watching. We're voyeurs who want to know what other people get up to when social constraints fall away; to get to the essence of human behaviour unobserved. The weird habits, the sex fetishes, the lying and the cheating. It would be unethical to create such an app without the permission of those involved. And although I'd wager that some people would agree to feature in such an experiment, just by giving their permission, they'd have already lost authenticity. They would already know they might be being observed, and adjust their behaviour accordingly.

We want to relate to the flaws of others, and feel good about ourselves by comparison. That's why there has been a spate of YouTube videos by influencers in which they admit – often while crying – that they have no friends.

These videos are often presented by extremely attractive, young and fashionable influencers, with titles such as '18 years old – I have no friends'. From a marketing perspective, it's a great hook, because it inspires so many questions that can only be answered by clicking. Who would admit to such a thing? Do they really have no friends? Why not? Can I help? For that reason, these videos are ratcheting up hundreds of thousands, and often millions, of views. Ironically these friendless (if you believe that) content creators are building enormous followings off the back of this admission. The videos are not only clickable, but extremely powerful in creating longstanding relationships with viewers. Viewers think: if this person has no friends, they'll likely be extremely happy to get a comment from me. The influencer thinks: great . . . what can I reveal about myself next?

And so, the dance goes on. Social media influencers and talk show hosts keep acting and insisting they're revealing real snippets of themselves to us, and we keep pretending not to notice when the mask slips. Many influencers have noticed the public's desire to look behind the curtain. They make content purporting to show 'the real them'. This supposed authenticity flies in the face of traditional celebrities, who seem comparatively distant and unreachable. In fact, bloopers and backstage access have become the currency of the modern influencer, because it enhances the parasocial and reciprocal interaction. Viewers feel like these 'ordinary' influencers are sharing their secrets with them. This reinforces the trust fans have in their stars. And that is valuable to brands.

The more I looked into the way influencers work, the more it reminded me of cult leader dynamics. They – or should I say we –

reveal more of ourselves the longer a subscriber or follower sticks around. They feel a closer bond, and get to call themselves Edge Hogs and become moderators. Some subscribers seem to worship their influencer of choice, and become tribal and isolated from wider society. They send money to these influencers, and increase their pulling power with big advertisers. And it all comes off the back of an intricate relationship with secrecy, and feeling like you're privy to the YouTuber's secret world.

Psychologists have found that the more we feel celebrities are revealing secrets, the closer we feel to them, and the more money they make. For that reason, posts by one individual blogger create a 'higher purchase intention' for brands than online magazines run by a whole team.

One of the most popular forms of influencer is the sharenter: parents who give an apparently authentic look into their lives as a family. The ethical dilemmas are myriad. The parent exploits their children for likes and brand dollars, while the kids grow up in a *Truman Show* bowl, never knowing what is real and what is artifice. Some critics accuse the sharenters of forcing their kids into child labour.

I hated being asked by my parents to stop for photos during family activities. Imagine – on your breaks from schoolwork – having to sit for hours'-long tedious video shoots, read from scripts and perform or 'be funny' for the camera. The kids in these families grow up feeling they have to sing for their supper. They are often rewarded with transactional love and gifts or the promise of exciting excursions, providing they sit still for video shoots and reveal something private and secret.

In ambitious sharenters, this inspires abhorrent behaviour. The American sharenters FamilyOFive (originally known as DaddyOFive) became popular in the mid-2010s for Mike and

Heather Martin's pranks on their young children. At its peak, the channel racked up nearly 1 million subscribers on YouTube.

However, the couple were accused of physically and emotionally abusing their kids for likes and subscribers. The more people watched, the more carried away the couple became by the momentum of their channel. A tactic by dad Mike was to encourage the eldest child Jake to physically and mentally torture his younger siblings. In one video, teenager Jake throws Cody – who is about nine at the time – through a doorway. In another, Mike shoves Cody into a bookcase.

The parents also engaged in pranks in which they scolded their children for things they hadn't done. For example, they falsely accuse Cody and Alex (also around nine) of spilling invisible ink. After winking at the camera, the parents scream and swear while accusing their kids – who break down in tears – of lying.

Another video has Mike surreptitiously swapping Alex's Xbox for a fake, before smashing the latter up in front of him as a punishment for being bad at school. Before doing so, Mike explains to the viewer what he is going to do, before adding with a taunting smile: 'Sound familiar?' It's hard to watch Mike violently taking a baseball bat to the fake machine while his son cowers in the corner. Then he holds up a hammer, and yells at him, 'Are you gonna listen!? You gonna stop being bad at school!?'

When Mike finally reveals that it was a prank, there is no change in Alex's demeanour. He has been harangued and humiliated, aware that the video of his degradation will be available for the world to see on YouTube. He looks distraught, confused and tired, as his father continues shrieking: 'Do better at school!'

Social services were alerted to their videos. Two of the children, Emma and Cody, were removed from their custody. The parents were also charged with 'neglect of a minor', and sentenced to five years of supervised probation. It is widely agreed that growing up in a 'stable' environment is crucial for children. The FamilyOFive kids could never predict their parents' mood swings – and they never knew what was real.

Another channel I found is called Fantastic Adventures. Its owner, Machelle Hackney Hobson, adopted seven children, and taught them to perform tricks and recreate stunts from famous movies. One video mimicked a famous *Mission: Impossible* scene – a horizontal kid was lowered by rope from the ceiling to steal sweets. We were being given privileged access to the adorable inner lives of this 'perfect' family. Millions of viewers tuned in every week to view their new skits.

The reality was that Hobson abused and tortured the kids off-screen to get them to sing, act and dance. She withheld food and water when the kids didn't 'recall their lines' or perform 'as they [were] directed'. She sprayed them with pepper spray, beat them with a belt and locked them in a cupboard for days at a time. One of her daughters eventually reported Hobson to the police, who discovered the kids malnourished and dehydrated. Hobson was charged with child abuse and unlawful imprisonment, and her two adult biological sons were arrested on suspicion of failing to report the abuse of a minor.

In Britain, there is the Ingham Family channel, who have been selling replica dolls of their children. In one video, the parents are shown swimming in the sea without a care in the world. Yet, eagle-eyed viewers spotted their four-month-old toddler unsupervised in the sun on the beach in the distant background. Chris Ingham said they were 'literally no more than a few feet away from Jace at any one time', and blamed the wide-angle lens for making the baby seem further away. The father was also accused of sending explicit messages to the sixteen-year-old daughter of another family at a hotel resort, an accusation which he has denied.

Then, there's the Family Fizz, also from Britain, who homeschool their kids while they travel around the world. The videos increasingly focus on their teenage daughter, with the thumbnails featuring her in revealing outfits. Their most popular video is disturbingly titled '13 year old wears pregnancy bump'. With 10 million views, it seems likely the video touched upon a bizarre sexual fetish. Another of their top videos is 'I started my period mum'. The videos and thumbnails of the thirteen-year-old daughter are sexualized, and she is sometimes shown wearing nothing but a bikini. As well as her most intimate moments, her body is on show for the world to see. Her parents exploit her privacy, secrecy and sexuality in return for clicks (and a whole lot of money).

These sharenters are the extreme end of YouTubers in thrall to audience capture. Such is the pull of this phenomenon that it appears to override the paternal bond these YouTubers have with their children. A more innocuous version of this concept has had a hold on me. There are many ways to grow a successful YouTube page, but one philosophy that crops up time and time again is that you don't choose your content; YouTube and the viewers do.

For two years, I had few views and little growth on YouTube. But I did notice a slight trend. Whenever I posted a video that criticized Scientology, it got a few more views than the last. I wanted to keep my channel diverse, moving from evolutionary biologists and psychiatrists one week to true crime and bizarre stories the next. Occasionally I went back to Scientology as a theme. Each time, it did better, until eventually I found myself in a position where video after video featured Tom Cruise in the thumbnail and title.

With each new video, a flurry of new subscribers came to my channel. Soon, I came to find that videos about Meghan Markle had a similar effect. Eventually, I was able to get out of this pop culture cycle, because it wasn't what I wanted for the channel. But even now, there are many topics I'd love to cover, such as astrophysics and certain aspects of philosophy, that just don't appeal to my core demographic, and so I avoid them.

Many online content producers have spoken about the stress

of constantly creating content. A traditional TV channel might have a diverse panel of commissioners producing content across a variety of shows. Each show runs for a number of seasons before coming to a natural end, or being cancelled. But social media influencers *are* the show. They can't come up for air, lest their audience look elsewhere.

Zoe Sugg – known online as Zoella – and PewDiePie (Felix Kjellberg) are among the biggest YouTubers in the world. They've become rich through the medium. Both have spoken of the pressures to keep creating, leading to panic attacks and anxiety.

Social media star and model Essena O'Neill quit the platforms in 2015 at the height of her success. She had become an influencer at the age of fourteen, and Instagram consumed her life for the next five years. Audience capture led her to start posting a different version of herself. It seems to start gradually, with slight tweaks, but then it sneaks up on you. You become unrecognizable from the person who started out: 'Social media allowed me to profit off deluding people,' she says. 'I started seeing things that I didn't like in myself, and that was terrifying . . . so I quit, because I wasn't happy.'

In my own experience, constantly creating content is exhausting, as is the obsessive checking of analytics, and the panic over losing your audience. I'm fortunate that my page isn't about me or my family. I don't have to keep coming up with revelations from my life. But I can see what might lead a parent down a dark hole. Imagine you start your channel because you're proud of your kids. First, you just want to show your circle of friends, but unexpectedly, it becomes a huge success.

You upgrade your equipment, make better thumbnails and titles, and learn how the social media platforms work, as more and more likes and subscribes fill your notifications. You set up as a company, and hire a team of editors and producers. Big brands are in touch, and you're bringing in £50,000 a month, while paying the salaries of several employees. Now, you not only make ends meet, but pay off your mortgage and take luxury holidays.

A few years in, you begin to run out of shock revelations. Your kids reach an age where you realize that they'll soon fly the nest. They're around the house less. The money dries up fast. What was £50,000 per month is now £30,000, then £10,000. It falls further. You let a couple of staff go. You check your stats, and you see that – as depraved as it is – the videos where your kids reveal more of themselves do better. Much better. We're talking about the difference between, say, 1,000 views and 1 million views. It's the difference between £5 and £5,000 per video.

Many of us would draw the line at anything that involves our children. But others might fall back on desperation and cognitive bias: 'It's OK, I'm earning this money for *them*.' Before they know it, they've posted moments that should remain private and secret in a video about their thirteen-year-old daughter's period, and plastered revealing photos of her all over the internet. The exchange of private moments and secrets that are not your own for financial benefit is morally reprehensible. But – like joining a cult – it happens too slowly for the parents to notice.

Influencer researcher Crystal Abidin writes about 'the performance ecology of family influencers'. Regarding parasocial and reciprocal social interaction in family channels in the West, Abidin writes of 'anchor' and 'filler' content posted by sharenters. The anchor content is what the influencers are known for. It's their bread and butter: high-definition videos recorded with top-of-the-range cameras, audio mixers and lighting. It might comprise beautiful family photos or a reel of a trip to Disney World, mixed with editing tricks, slo-mo effects and the works. It's high-value production. Sharenters tend to schedule this kind of material to come out a couple of times per week. Examples of anchor content outside of sharenting include 'singing covers, comedic skits, and cooking and craft tutorials'.

Then, there's the filler material. Abidin writes that this is 'intentionally framed to convey the aesthetic of an amateur, such that the production comes across as being raw, unfiltered, spontaneous, and more intimate.' This is how influencers, including sharenters, look authentic, as though sharing something secret and unplanned. The filler content complements the polished anchor material by providing a look behind the scenes. They're your friends, fiddling with low-budget cameras.

In reality, the filler is just as studied and planned as the anchor material, but we go along with the idea that we are being let in on a secret inner life. University of Queensland Professor of Cultural Studies Graeme Turner notes that representations in the media increasingly tend toward the 'lived experience of the ordinary'. In filler content, calculated productions are passed off as seemingly authentic representations of everyday life. What we're actually seeing is micro-managed inauthenticity.

Often, these 'real moments' are behind a paywall – only the influencers' most loyal and privileged fans may bear witness to the secrets within. The more the viewer pays, the higher their tier, and the greater the level of secrets they unlock. If this is reminding you of my chapter on cults, and the way NXIVM and Scientology nab new members, that's no accident. The influencer world works in much the same way, though typically with far less drastic results.

I first noticed this link between influencers and cults when I enrolled on a thirty-day online course for YouTubers. The course I chose is popular, and has been used by some of the biggest YouTubers to help grow their channels. Each day of the course had a different theme or title, and the first week covered such algorithmic topics as search-engine optimization (SEO) and branding. Week 2, however, surprised me. It was setting me up to make a cult leader of myself. This is how each day's class was titled:

Day 1: Creation Story
Day 2: Creed
Day 3: Icons
Day 4: Rituals
Day 5: Sacred Words
Day 6: Non-Believers
Day 7: Leaders

One of the most useless and widespread pieces of advice that YouTubers give to aspiring stars is 'be yourself'. It's meaningless. The course teaches that to become a leading YouTuber, *real* authenticity or simply being yourself wouldn't do. You need to engage in a specific kind of false realness, using the same tricks that cult leaders use to enhance their own relatability.

I was instructed to create a genesis story around how my channel began, to place certain recognizable icons in the background of my shots and to create secret words that only my audience would understand. I was prompted to carry out rituals (such as starting and ending each video with a memorable phrase). To exploit the tribalism innate to us all, I was asked to speak of non-believers, or enemies; people who didn't believe in me, or had 'dissed' my channel. Finally, the course pushed me to look and act like a leader to my flock of viewers. The course was encouraging me, I realized, to start a cult.

These are all concepts that I find difficult to enact. Not just because it's morally objectional, but I don't consider myself a great actor or leader. I took some of the suggestions on board. You'll see lamps and LED lights in the background. I start each episode on the audio version with, 'You're on the edge of . . .' followed by the theme of the episode and the name of the guest. I have a bonus community on a platform called Locals where users pay for extra live streams and articles about what I learned that week. But there's more to it than the cultish aspects. I would like to think that I'm a good interviewer, and that I choose interesting guests, edit the episodes well, and so on.

Now that I know those seven cultish commandments, I see them in all kinds of influencers and brands. When you see YouTubers digging one another out, know that this is likely in-authentic and managed – part of creating the illusion of the 'non-believer' or enemy. This is often labelled 'Podcast Wars' and is particularly common in young, competitive YouTubers (who often seem to take up boxing to fight each other in the ring).

This earns them a lot more money, and forces you to pick a tribe. Think of how Catholics signed up to their religion despite not knowing the doctrine of God for most of recorded history because they couldn't read. There is a pressure to choose one identity, and for that identity to be tied to one organization. Like religions, brands and influencers are fighting for your attention.

The funny words they use that only you – and the YouTuber's other loyal viewers – understand are carefully picked out to create an impression of intimacy. And sure, it's not NXIVM, it's not Heaven's Gate, and it's not Scientology. Typically, members can unsubscribe from a channel at any time; they're not coerced into sex acts (although some high-profile influencers have been embroiled in such scandals); they're not forced by collateral to give up all their secrets, or to stay a subscriber. You (hopefully) don't lose your life savings to advance up the status game of YouTube channels.

But here's something to consider: Scientology is thought to have 30,000 members worldwide. My own YouTube channel has ten times that number in subscribers, and grows by Scientology's entire base each month. Comedian Russell Brand – accused of spreading dangerous conspiracy theories – has more than 6 million subscribers. In 2023, he was accused by several women of rape, and many more of inappropriate sexual behaviour. Some believe that – knowing for years that a documentary and article were being crafted around these accusations – he cultivated a messiah-like personality and groomed those subscribers to stick by him once the inevitable mainstream cancellation hit him. I tried to approach the Brand controversy on my YouTube channel with subtlety, but still received death threats from his fans. Donald Trump has nearly 100 million Twitter followers. He influenced an attack on the Capitol with nothing more than a few tweets.

Who can really say which is most dangerous: traditional cults or New Age social media sects?

'I wasn't Moses or someone,' says first blogger Justin Hall, when I video call him one morning at his home in San Francisco. I've called Justin to find out his thoughts about how audience capture – and the need for influencers to keep revealing secrets for clicks – has developed since his blog in the earliest days of the internet. He's preparing breakfast on screen, like some kind of foodie influencer. I wonder whether Justin is creating live filler content for me. 'I was a Johnny-Come-Lately compared to people scrawling on tablets to tell people what's important to them.' He means tablets in the biblical Moses sense. 'I thought, at the dawn of this tool, "This is gonna usher in a new era of commerce-free social exchange."'

'And did it?'

'Well, you could cynically say "they're all shills being puppet-eered by corporations and fashion lines". That "it's actually *more* commercial, everyone's learning how to exploit themselves for likes and it's all depressing". But you could also say "we have a tonne of social sharing in places like Reddit, where it's more about attention, not mediated through money". I still have a lot of fun on the internet.' He pauses. 'But I share a lot less.'

Justin now runs a marijuana company called bud.com, 'a California benefit corporation delivering recreational cannabis.' He's in his mid-forties and he has a child. The Justin of the 2020s I speak to is a much calmer iteration of the 1993 influencer I'd read about: the blogger behind Cat Dick and the tearful breakdown video. 'To me, social media interaction was a great opportunity when I was forming my identity. I could bricolage my identity from all these pieces I could find. I've had all kinds of amazing experiences meeting strangers on the internet, and it totally changed me. I was hungrier for a public approval or connection, but I've subsequently found that connection closer to home.'

'You sound like a new person,' I say.

'I needed attention . . . but I got married and had a kid. It's not *so* linear, but there is some truth to that progression. I've changed, I'm older.'

Every few months, Justin posts something on links.net, usually an essay or a poem about life. In one post, he describes me as 'a semi-public seeker in the United Kingdom'. I can't say I'm sure what that means, but I'm pleased to be on his page. His posts aren't regular enough to class him as a blogger. Not like he used to be. Finding out his friends and family had been hurt by his online writing had a profound effect on him. 'Now, I want to read [my posts] and make sure I'm not offending someone accidentally, and not revealing something that would hurt something else.'

He has mixed feelings about today's influencers, praising their ingenuity and innovation, while being aware of the phoniness and sadness at the phenomenon's heart. He is happy to have left blogging behind, and concerned for the influencers who seem to be stuck in a cycle, always having to come up with fresh new content that is juicy, alluring and secret.

'I cannot live my life for content, I will not be happy. Man, you see these people – my heart goes out to them – they have a crazy run being a social media public person and they flame out.' He impersonates a modern influencer: 'My friends are [video] *content*, and my house is [video] *content* and my neighbours . . . and everyone knows they'll be on the show if my camera is running. And I run the camera every day, because ratings were down last week.'

He adds in his normal voice, 'It's a recipe for personal grief in public. You need the grief for the ratings, and it becomes an insidious feedback loop.' Justin's depiction of today's social media influencer sounds stressful. It makes me think of the frantic final act of *Goodfellas*, when Ray Liotta's coked-up protagonist tries to do a million things at once to escape the feds, help his family and save himself from Mob bosses.

'When you started out, did you imagine it getting here?' I ask.

'Well, I didn't imagine it *not* getting here. I think there are almost moments many years ago of, "Why don't people think I'm more famous, why don't I get more recognition?" Oh, because I don't want it, I'm not ready for it, I'm not enough of a *performer*, I don't deserve it. And I'm glad. Once I realized that, it was about everything else in my life. I felt so blessed.'

Justin may not consider himself a performer, but he is certainly capable of adapting to people around him. In our call, he often refers to me by name. Despite coming from Chicago, he uses British terms with me – like 'mate' – and shows an in-depth knowledge of UK culture. He has even researched my work. He believes that my documentary filmmaking is difficult to sustain in today's social media world. In reference to my BBC exorcism documentary, he says: 'The thing is . . . what you do . . . who wants to pay for that story? The people in the church are embarrassed by it, Argentina doesn't want that story. And at the end of your story, you're not saying, "And I have a better story, buy this eBook."

'But that's the influencer path. I was very focused when I started on *integrity*. And like, I'm going to be "who I am" on the internet, and "I am Justin Hall, I'm going to create the transparent self on the internet." And now, I look at it and everybody's posturing.'

I'm reminded of a video I watched of American conservative influencer Brett Cooper – known for looking and sounding like a female version of right-wing commentator Ben Shapiro. She launches an impassioned attack on restrictions of individual liberties amid talk of a return to pandemic restrictions: 'We've done that. We don't want to do it again. Of course, they're going to tell us that it's good for us. It's not good for you! What is actually good for you . . .' She turns to look into another camera, smiles as if the previous segment hadn't happened and picks up speed, '. . . is a Good Ranchers steak! That is what you should be eating. That is what you should be focusing on. But I'm not just talking about your health! Financially, Good Ranchers is the healthy option!'

But it's not just about sponsors and money. Justin continues: 'All this stuff on Instagram, and Twitter, everybody's just like, "Look what I believe in. Look what I think is cool. Look at my dog." And I have sympathy for them, because I think they're lonely. They want people to think that they're notable and important, and their dog matters, and is especially cute. And that's human, right? We all want to matter.'

He hasn't entirely lost his 'transparent self'. We turn to audio-only for a better connection. Later, he stops responding. I check my phone: 'Call Muted'.

'Fuck's sake . . .' I murmur, believing I've done it with my ear.

His line picks up. 'Sorry. I'm in the bathroom.' It goes back to mute.

'Um . . . oh,' I say, hoping he doesn't think I aimed the fuck's sake at him. 'I'd better keep talking then while you go.'

I've never had a contributor go for a wee in the middle of an interview, so that ranks high for transparency. Then again, the Justin of 1993 wouldn't have bothered to mute the call. Despite his concerns for lonely influencers, Justin is optimistic about the future. 'If you like humans and the human project, you can find a way to like how people share online. I don't need it right now, but I'm not done with it. One day I might say, "Hey strangers on the internet, console me!" Now, I'd wonder how many of these people are real . . .'

'Ah, yes, the bots . . .' I say.

'Yeah, I think the robots are gonna get better. And I wonder if it matters. The influencer of the future is somebody composed of a few other identities, using artificial intelligence. They'll talk about, say, 70 per cent nature things, 20 per cent animal things and 10 per cent product things. They'll post in a regular cadence, but irregular enough that they seem human. What if one of those "people" reached out to me and said, "I really connected with your story?" It's getting zanier, as we have non-human entities that are likely to take part in that exchange.'

Justin suggests the influencer world is motivated by loneliness and a craving for attention; feelings he describes as *human*. But since big brands got involved, influencers are more interested in gaining likes and followers. The relative purity of Justin's era has been corrupted by dollar signs. The dystopian social media network that he describes – in which bots and AI take over – could be the final blow to our humanity on social media.

What does that say for our curiosity and pursuit of authenticity? Most of us would probably say we prefer acclaim and affirmation from a human than a computer. But Justin is fine with the bots. Maybe he is simply ahead of the curve, just as he was with blogging. Maybe, in the not-so-distant future, we will have our curiosities for secrets quenched and our desires for affirmation met by bots. We're already seeing the beginnings of this with the introduction of robots to care homes.

Before ending our call, I'm curious to know what really went down between Justin and writer Kurt Vonnegut.

'He gave a speech,' Justin explains, 'where he railed against the computer and the lack of intimacy that comes from electronic communications. I went up to him at a meet-and-greet afterwards, and argued with him. And then he sort of got frustrated, and moved on to talk to other people. And then I went back and continued arguing with him . . .'

I laugh.

'. . . until he grabbed my hair and shook me.'

'Oh.'

'He shook my head and yelled in my face, "Can you get this from a computer!? Can you get this from a computer!?" And stormed off.'

'Wow,' I say, trying to imagine Vonnegut – a pacifist with an Einstein moustache – in a rage against the machine. 'What a nutter.'

'Yeah. But what a great writer. So funny and smart.' He pauses. 'I was the nutter maybe.'

'Were you a fan?'

'Yes, yes,' he says. 'It was sad to see this guy I respected was shitting on my new medium. It was 1995, and I was like, "Why you gotta hate the internet so hard?"'

Kurt Vonnegut wrote time-bending narratives that served as cautionary tales about the perils of technology.

'Can you get this from a computer?' Vonnegut yelled in 1995, referring to real and impactful human connection.

Nearly thirty years later, on a video call over breakfast from San Francisco to London, Justin's answer is still: affirmative.

CONCLUSION –
JUST ONE MORE THING . . .

Louis Theroux: 'Didn't you spend time in prison, John?'
. . .
John Malpezzi: 'I'd rather not discuss that.'
                              Louis and the Nazis, 2003

After becoming the unwitting receiver of secrets from my podcast listeners, I set out to get a better understanding of secrecy. I saw how authoritarian regimes and cults used secrets to ensnare their members. I learned about the fever model, and its suffocating effect on secrets in our minds. Secrets and their revelation, I came to find, were essential to our social evolution.

I wanted to know why my listeners chose to bestow upon me their deepest, most clandestine thoughts and experiences. The intimate interactions with my online community go some way to explaining it. A benign cult, my community inadvertently establishes hierarchies, love-bombing and deference through parasocial reaction. Still, I wanted something more; something on an individual human level about what made people reveal secrets. Was I doing something without realizing that nudged my listeners to tell me?

From sex bot suppliers, spies and psychologists to police, priests and periodical 'paragraph' pundits, I scoped out a variety of professional secret extractors. They make use of audio devices, behaviour examination and bonds of trusts to bring hidden truths to the fore. But to understand secrecy at its most naked and vulnerable, I want to strip it all back, and get back to the human. Without these technological aids, how might you or I go about getting information out of a friend, colleague or family member? What makes some humans tell things to certain other humans? To examine the characteristics that make you seem like a safe receiver of clandestine information, I realized I'd have to turn inwards to my own profession: journalism.

Journalists don't have lie detectors and props like the fake Game Boy device used by Guantanamo Bay interrogator Lena Sisco. Nor can we make use of the sacred bond of a confessional booth or online secrets forum. Classes in journalism don't teach much about secret extraction. In fact, the very acknowledgement that our job depends on getting people to give up their secrets is taboo – it implies that interviewer and interviewee have conflicting interests, and that journalists take advantage of vulnerable people, poking at them to reveal things they'd do well to keep secret. We like to tell ourselves our paths are worthier.

Yet, making people feel comfortable enough to reveal secrets is one of the key qualities that separates a good journalist from a bad one. If something about your body language or speech makes people close down, then you won't last long. With that in mind, it's worth looking at the style of a good journalist; one who has been at the top of his game for decades.

Like Nick Broomfield and Alan Whicker before him, Louis Theroux has popularized the presenter-led (journalist visible on screen) documentary investigation that we continue to see in the UK, fronted by the likes of Reggie Yates and Stacey Dooley. Bringing fringe to the fore, he has become known for his Columbo-like knack of dragging the truth out of unsuspecting interviewees.

Much has been made of Theroux's faux naïf approach, thought to lull his subjects into a false sense of security. Such is his amiable presence and innocent veneer that interviewees overlook the presence of cameras, and reveal to him deep and dark secrets.

It's not a superpower. Louis can't *know* if someone is keeping a secret. When he interviewed Jimmy Savile, the latter came across as a congenial – though eccentric – character. After his death a few years later – as alluded to earlier – Savile was found to have been one of Britain's most prolific sex offenders. There were allegations of necrophilia and rampant child sexual abuse, with his youngest known victim just two years old. Louis had heard rumours at the time, and even touched upon them in the documentary, which delves into Savile's perennially single status, his obsession with his mother and his previous strange comments about children.

'Why do you say in interviews that you hate children?' Louis asks.

'Obviously I don't hate them. We live in a very funny world. And it's easier for me as a single man to say, "I don't like children", because that puts a lot of salacious tabloid people off the hunt.'

'Are you basically saying so tabloids don't pursue this whole: "Is he or isn't he a paedophile" line?'

'Yes! How do they know whether I am or not?'

That is as far as Louis gets to *knowing* what Savile is hiding. Louis later described meeting Savile as: 'The strangest and most upsetting event I've ever been involved in'. He told the *Independent*: 'If I did that story with a time machine and went back again, I would be armed with so much more information.'

So, he's not magic. Yet, providing he suspects a secret, he's adept at getting interviewees to give it up. Many put it down to that non-judgemental approach. This certainly helps, but the reality is that he is often judgemental. Take the following moment from the *Louis and the Nazis* documentary, when a neo-Nazi leader asserts that – because he is white – he is better looking than actor Denzel Washington:

Neo-Nazi: 'If I had the money and the power, making movies, I'd get ten times more women than him.'

Louis Theroux: 'Do you really believe that? That seems delusional.'

In fact, Louis judges his (usually racist) subjects throughout the episode, both in voice-overs and to their faces. He tells the same man that his 'brain is twisted' and 'you keep pretending that you're a revolutionary but the facts of your existence completely undermine that.' He also asks April Gaede, the mother of twin girls Lynx and Lamb, who were brought up to sing white supremacist songs: 'Do you realize what a handicap that will be for them in life?'

He's far from immune from judging. So, how does he get information out of those reluctant to reveal?

In a scene from *Louis and the Nazis*, public relations agent John Malpezzi appears alongside his client Tom Metzger – neo-Nazi leader and Grand Wizard of the Ku Klux Klan. Rather than focus on skinhead Tom, Louis surprises Tom's agent John by inquiring about *his* background. He asks if John has spent time in prison. Caught off guard, and disinclined to discuss his ignoble past, John becomes defensive: 'Wait a minute! What is this? Louis, come on!' Then, he changes the subject: 'Come on out here boys, and let me show you the view.'

John begins to lead Louis past the swimming pool in his garden, looking to divert attention to the colonial cabins and cacti of the arid Mid-Western hills framing the vista. Then, Louis does something unexpected; odd, even. From behind John, he breaks into an offhand half-jog along the top of the patio's exterior brick wall to intercept him down on the concrete pool deck. Nonchalantly, he now walks ahead of John. It's a rude thing to do when somebody is showing you their garden. Louis continues walking briskly, yet insouciantly, ahead, not even turning his head when he speaks to John. He is assertive but unenthused.

Louis' stance and demeanour seem counter-intuitive for a TV presenter. We're told to do everything we can to keep our faces on camera. It's hard work, because you have to remain vigilant of shadows encroaching on your face, while making sure everyone else is in shot. But here's John having a conversation with the back of Louis' head. This lasts for ten seconds, and is part of an offhanded demeanour Louis often exhibits when dealing with reticent interviewees.

Once John catches up, the pair stop to talk on a viewing deck at the edge of the clifftop garden. The dynamic has changed. Now, John seems to will Louis to ask him again about his past, and Louis casually obliges.

'I was looking at eighty-five years,' John divulges. 'So, a life sentence. And I wound up doing three and a half years.'

'What was the conviction?' Louis asks, hiding how pleased he must be at his guest's unravelling.

'Cocaine trafficking.'

Exactly one minute of uncut footage passes between John's insistence that he will not discuss his secret, and his confession. It's possible that Louis behaves in this way unconsciously. Regardless, in one short scene, he climbs from the role of 'impertinent inquisitor' to 'cool kid in the playground', while John cascades from cautious to needy. He wants to confide and impress. If you're interested in how to get secrets out of interviewees, and what kind of approach from interrogators might leave you vulnerable to exposing your own, study Louis.

Research shows that when asked what kind of people we *believe* we reveal secrets to, most of us say polite and enthusiastic people. Given Louis exhibits neither of those traits in that scene, why does his conduct work so well? It turns out our assumptions are all wrong. Enthusiasm and politeness are actually predictors of being confided in *less*. When you break it down, polite just means obeying rules and adhering to societal norms. The Bolsheviks were likely bursting with polite people, but you could be making a fatal mistake by confiding in card-carrying members – by polite, I mean that they adhered to the societal expectations of the Party, and those expectations were that the polite thing to do with a secret would be to report it to authorities. What may seem like civility and good manners really means obedience to these norms, which can change quickly. Politeness is similar to orderliness (wanting everything to be just right) – in Nazi Germany, it was considered both polite and orderly to report a Jew to the Gestapo. Neither quality makes others confide in us.

Dictatorial regimes rely on polite and orderly supporters, and rules of decorum have been set up to legitimize and support slave trading and other practices that we now consider abhorrent. Politeness is subject to the whims and fancies of time and place. Think of the way swear words – those that transgress societal politeness – have migrated over the centuries from religious (heck, hell) to bodily (fuck, shit) and, more recently, to identity (the n-word and other identity group slurs). These words reflect the sacred themes of their times.

Linguist John McWhorter believes that this will change again, but we have no way of knowing in which direction. When I push him, he posits 'climate change' as a potential challenger to identity for the next sacred group of words. Perhaps, he suggests, in a hundred years' time, you'll call someone a 'windmill'. I imagine a future where a roomful of polite people shudder upon hearing me call someone a 'real dirty piece of charcoal' or an 'old fossil fuel'. I think these are better bets for negative slurs than 'windmill', but opt not to tell the world-renowned linguist that.

All that said, the changing nature of politeness doesn't mean that there is anything inherently immoral about it. Politeness is good. Societal traditions and practices are integral to our social cohesion. It's just that you might do well to avoid giving too much away about your societal transgressions, including secrets, to those who live by and for the very rules that draw up that society's moral boundaries. As for enthusiastic people, they don't seem serious enough to actually help with your secrets.

The reality is, we confide not in the polite and enthusiastic, but the *compassionate* and *assertive*. These are the empathetic rule-breakers who are caring, non-judgemental and motivated to help. This brings us back to the second chapter, and the truth-obsessed philosopher Immanuel Kant – the world's worst secret-keeper. He asserts that truth is right and moral in all circumstances. It's very polite, but it doesn't chime with the popularity of the rule-breaking protagonists, resistance groups and plucky underdogs from our favourite movies and TV shows, from *The Godfather* and *Scarface* to *Catch Me If You Can* and *Breaking Bad*. The more rules our heroes break, the more we like them – providing they show compassion (which is why *Breaking Bad*'s Walter White character is so brilliant, keeping us invested while testing our loyalty to him).

I ask the Coffin Confessor – the Australian who reveals secrets of the dead at funerals – whether there is something about him that makes people want to tell him their secrets. 'I didn't think so at first. But now, absolutely. I think I've got that persona about me that people can trust,' he replies. 'When they meet me, I think they just realize that they're going to get what they pay for, what's done for them without care or concern for those left behind.'

The Coffin Confessor is brash, profane, and shows disdain for polite societal conventions. It makes sense that his clients trust him to get back at their family members and friends, because they know he's assertive, and won't show too much concern for the feelings of the living. He's impervious to peer pressure and communal fashions. He's bolshy and rude enough to go full steam ahead, and do 'the right thing'.

When I put this to him, he laughs: 'Come on Andrew, fucking hell. I don't swear that much, do I? Oh mate! Oh Jesus!' He insists there's a lot more to it: 'There's empathy, sympathy, looking into the actual truth of the matter. There's a lot that goes into it. My integrity is everything. It really is.' He seems to care about his clients. There's that compassion to complement the assertiveness.

As for Louis Theroux, he is awkward when he first asks John about his prison time. But by taking the reins, and walking ahead of John in his own garden, Louis is assertive and makes a performance of being unenthusiastic. A quick glance at Louis' oeuvre will assure any viewer of his compassion. An American equivalent in profession and status might be documentary maker Michael Moore, whose style is more abrasive and combative, while remaining compassionate. Neither filmmaker is polite. They each break social taboos in their own way. And both are trusted with secrets by their interviewees.

If you want to draw secrets out of someone, perhaps you could, somewhat sociopathically, try to mimic or adopt these traits in their presence. Show a rebellious streak, and emphasize disdain for courtesies. Remember: we consider the best people in whom to confide those who *seem* to care (compassionate) and to have the drive to help (assertive), who don't appear to show concern for societal norms (polite) or lack seriousness (enthusiastic). One last thing: people aren't mind-readers. How effective you are in extracting secrets depends on how you *seem*, not how you *are*.

Secrets, I've learned, speak to the essence of what it is to be human. It's important that we understand them. They played a vital role in the development of our social cohesion and the game theory strategies that helped our tribes to thrive. When we've committed transgressions that might get us expelled from our tribes (or cancelled online), secrets protect our reputations. They can be used to enhance status through the lure of mystique. We want to know the secrets of celebrities. We're desperate to possess the clandestine inner lives of the unreachable chosen few.

This was taken advantage of by the paragraph writers in the early gossip magazines of the late 1700s, before the parasocial interaction of talk show hosts led us to today's social media landscape. Just as traditional movie stars sold snippets of their lives to stay relevant, today's influencers sell pieces of their inner selves for clicks and brand dollars. With success comes a downside; being stuck on a hamster wheel of never-ending secrets to satiate the insatiable viewers.

The power of secrets has been understood and exploited by bad actors. It's something we need to watch for. Tyrants, including the Stasi, the Nazis and modern-day China, have used secrets – both those held from civilians and those *about* civilians – to prosper. Cults, such as Scientology and NXIVM, have learned from this blueprint, using secrets to lure unsuspecting members up a ladder to nowhere in the voracious pursuit of status. We use secrets to feel special.

If it was easy to keep secrets, then we'd all be at it, all the time. While we all keep *some* secrets, we're mostly honest. When we do find ourselves the unwitting keepers of secrets (particularly those that involve our identity, provoke shame, and could cause us to be kicked out of our communities if found out), we suffer. The fever model – that feeling when your body acts as though you have a virus to encourage you to reveal your secret – takes hold. It had to be that way; otherwise, we'd all keep secrets from one another, and there's no way that a society could thrive.

Some people are better able to keep secrets. If you want to get the truth out of them, then reading their body language and judging their behaviour can only take you so far. You'll have to be deceptive yourself, by using a device like a Game Boy, or pretending you know more than they do about their lies. Or, like Louis Theroux, just waltz nonchalantly in front of the secret-keeper to assertively flip the power dynamic. They're bound to spill the beans.

Studies find that certain people are told secrets more often than others. Someone who hears about one type of secret is often told about a great range of other ones. If you want to know what someone is hiding, be assertive, be compassionate. Don't be polite or enthusiastic. There's more: confidants who have their own emotional struggles are confided in more often, and people who are generally volatile and inconsistent are not.

My interest in secrets and their revelation was piqued as I received so many from my podcast listeners. Now, I finally understand why: the podcast goes out three times a week. I make a show of its consistency, its dependability. It regularly broadcasts my voice – and those of guests going through their own turmoil – to hundreds of thousands of homes. To empathize with suffering guests, I bring up my own troubles.

This constancy and openness about my own problems might be why listeners confide in me and other podcasters. My style is also in line with the above traits: while I am polite to guests, much of what I say flouts societal norms, whether it be simply swearing or questioning the considered wisdom of the day. I'm rarely enthusiastic (and perhaps a touch nihilistic). Finally, assertiveness: putting out a podcast episode three times a week is an assertive act in itself, as is asking direct questions to guests.

These findings about the attributes that draw revelations explain why listeners get in touch so often to reveal their secrets to me, and I suspect that two-way reciprocated social interaction – years of creating a bond with listeners – adds to that. If I were listening to a podcast, and it touched on an exceptional theme that I had experienced, I'd also feel the urge to get in touch with the host, and reveal my own secrets.

This is especially true if that host has been compassionate and non-judgemental to the interviewee. Listeners know then that the host won't be shocked by their own stories. They feel the shame and burden around the keeping of their secret, and seek closure, advice, honesty and intimacy with a non-judgemental figure in their lives. They want to cure their internal fever of rumination and mind-wandering, and to stop experiencing the shame of in-authenticity.

A podcast or talk show host has no link to the divulger's social circle, so there's little risk the secret will get back to them. Psychologist Sherry Turkle writes: 'This is why people will some-times, often prematurely, tell their "sad stories" to others they hardly know. They hope to be repaid in intimacy', without the risk of it getting back to the people who matter – the people in their immediate social circles.

Being a podcast host is a niche position (well, less and less so). But it is the illusion of compassion and assertiveness in this inter-action with the listener that compels them to spill the beans to the host. 'Illusion' is important to stress. Hosts may not be particu-larly compassionate in real life (see Ellen DeGeneres, James Corden). But good ones are aware that showcasing compassion is part of the journalist's job, as it is that of the influencer, the TV presenter, and the friend who wants to collect secrets from their social circle.

Another simple facet to consider is the sheer size of the audi-ence. We may have grown up in tribes that went from 80 to 150 people, but now podcasters are able to engage in parasocial rela-tionships with tens of thousands of listeners (or millions, in Joe Rogan's case). The larger a podcast grows, the more secrets the host will receive. The larger your social circle, the more salacious gossip you'll hear – just remember not to be too polite.

*

Throughout the writing of this book, I have been keeping a secret – one that has been nagging at me. It's not a whopper, by any means. If it were, I probably wouldn't reveal it. I'd feel a need to protect my status. But it is something that I want to get off my chest. Truth be told, I have experienced some mind-wandering, as well as a sense of burden. It's time to cure the fever.

Here is my confession:

In the introduction to this book, I wrote of my motivating factors for writing it. These included the secrets revealed to me by my guests and listeners. There was the woman who told me how she gouged a man's eyes out in self-defence, killing him in the process, and another story of a young musician teasing cash out of a married woman in her sixties.

These stories are true, and I continue to receive similar ones now. But here's the thing: they are not really what motivated me to write this book. Authors like to have a serendipitous narrative around non-fiction gonzo journalism. It's nice to feel like a book was fated into existence.

I think of my podcast guest, Jon Ronson, who embarked on his book *So You've Been Publicly Shamed* after seeing how a computer scientist who impersonated and harassed him online became the subject of an even greater level of internet harassment himself. Jon also started *The Psychopath Test* after receiving a mysterious package, and being willed by enigmatic forces into the wild encounters and experiences that ensued. I love how Jon was smart and curious enough to pull on these threads and take us along on a journey.

In my case, the truth is not so serendipitous. I enjoy telling stories, and wanted to write about some of the fascinating people I'd encountered in my podcast and TV work, from the exorcist and the Coffin Confessor to the world's first blogger and the female paedophile. But what would that book look like? How would it draw such disparate stories together under one marketable umbrella?

I couldn't make it fit. I was at a bit of a loss, and put the idea for a book on the backburner for a year.

I kept up conversations with my patient and talented literary agent Donald Winchester. When I told him about all the people both burdening and titillating me with their secrets, it was he who had the Eureka moment. The exorcist, the Coffin Confessor, the paedophiles and the first blogger all had something in common with those listeners: each of them was either clinging to – or revealing – a secret. Secrecy would be the theme; and *that* – not fate nor authorial ingenuity – is how the book came to be. I owe Donald the confession.

What are the consequences of revealing my secret? It's fairly low stakes compared to the cases I've written about – but perhaps you'll go away less likely to recommend this book to friends. It might seem less quixotic – less ethereal – now that I'm revealing how the sausage was made. It didn't just 'happen into being'; it came from the mind of a professional literary agent for whom this was a book among many. Rather than one giant journey of discovery, this was in fact the episodic culmination of a journalist's weird career.

Maybe you prefer that. Perhaps that is actually even more authentic and serendipitous than the gonzo journalist journey. But there is a risk that the confession changes how you feel about everything that came before it. It is an admission that I didn't have the smarts to think about how to craft this book myself. You have landed safely at the end of your flight, but have just been told that the pilot had been learning to fly as he went along. You're safe – but would you recommend it? Or do it again? Or fly in other planes under that pilot?

On the other hand, I'm happy I revealed it (the fact that it made the final cut is testament to this). I feel better for having got the burden off my chest, and I think it's important to acknowledge that even though we love the lore of the lone architect, these kinds of projects are typically the products of many minds. The camel may be a horse designed by committee, but it's a damn sight more interesting.

For this book, one thing I have undoubtedly done is delve into the nature of the secret. I've come to understand the revelation of a secret as complex, and dependant on myriad factors. Is the person you're talking to polite and enthusiastic? Or assertive and compassionate? To what degree do you envisage the revelation of the secret will cause you societal ostracism? And how does that compare to the mind-wandering and shame that accompanies the fever of the keeping of the secret?

The consequences of revealing my secret aren't too bad. It's an equation: the penalties are easier to bear than the shame and feelings of inauthenticity that might have arisen by not confessing.

By confessing – like a mobster between murders – I can release the book with a clean conscience, and less of a discrepancy between my inner self and the self I portray to the world. And here's one last secret to go out on, even if you know it already: the secret I've just shared with you isn't big enough to burden you – but it might just increase the intimacy between us.

ACKNOWLEDGEMENTS

I found the shaping and writing of this book challenging but, since little worth doing is easy, it's been a wonderful experience. I first came to my literary agent Donald Winchester at Watson, Little with an idea for a book in which I investigated a very controversial topic. I had sent out emails to several agents, but Donald took a chance. We sent it out to dozens of agents, and many refused to even look at the treatment. I still hope to write it, though.

Donald and I stayed in touch, and he proposed the concept of secrets as the subject that could connect the stories that I wanted to tell. After long having felt uninspired as a writer, and having turned my focus to my YouTube page and podcast, secrets re-invigorated me, and I put together a proposal. I can't stress enough how much this book owes to the determination, optimism and smarts of Donald. Thank you, Donald!

We needed an editor who'd welcome a first-time author. It was with great fortune and relief that Matthew Cole at Pan Macmillan decided to green-light the book. Without his belief in it, this book wouldn't exist. Since I was a newbie, my first draft was muddled. The words and ideas were there – as were the stories of extreme people and subcultures – but they were in the wrong places. Thank you, Matthew, for drawing out a plan for me to follow. From my scattered ramblings, you made a book.

Matthew left his role before I handed in my final draft. His replacement, Ause Abdelhaq, did wonders in taking what we had prepared, and breathing coherence, humour and personality into it. Ause treated the book with care, and gave me the confidence to include more of myself. Thanks, Ause, for your kind words, brilliant suggestions and a very enjoyable lunch – may there be many more.

I'll never forget how excited and relieved I felt when Pan Macmillan first commissioned this. As I received the call from Donald, I was at a spa for my friend Kane's stag. It was the perfect place to celebrate. Then came the very daunting realization that I was going to have to actually write it. And that would involve a *lot* of research. Thank you to Jessica Schulz. We met through a language learning app, when I was living in Berlin. Jess sent me mountains of academic papers about secrets.

After two years and many drafts, I finally put together an almost-complete book. With the camel in mind, I was lucky to get the world's best reviewers on the job. First, my close friend and university lecturer Emma Trott kindly offered to read it and make notes. Her comments were essential to the flow, and she provided countless ideas and corrections that made this a better and more accurate read. She did the same for me while we lived and studied English Literature at university more than a decade ago. I'm grateful she's still at it today. Thank you, Emma, I'm lucky to have a friend like you.

My wife Julieta Finkelstein read the book. She's been by my side, offering advice and even editing my podcast while converting her Argentine law qualifications to British. She has sacrificed so much, moving with me from her home, first to Germany – where we learned the world's scariest language together – and then to the UK. She's claimed some of my dreams as her own, and I hope

I've done the same for her. We're a team. As a lawyer, she was invaluable at spotting mistakes and fallacies in the book. She also made sure I clarified meaning and did justice to the stories she already knew so well.

Juli, at the start of the book, I wrote: 'May we keep each other's secrets, always.' When I wrote it, I wasn't exactly sure what it meant, other than it sounded (to me, at least) vaguely romantic and ethereal. At the end of this journey into the vaults of secrecy, I now think it's about how fortunate we are to be able to share with each other – without judgement – our darkest and grossest thoughts.

Thank you to all of my loving family for your support in everything that I do. If I can be half as supportive of your endeavours in return, then I'll be a great son, stepson, brother, nephew and cousin. Thanks to my loyal YouTube and podcast followers. I'm overwhelmed by your generosity and creativity. You're the most spectacular camel. And thanks to all the fascinating and talented people who agreed to be interviewed or featured in this book.

They say never meet your heroes, but time and time again, they've left me bowled over. Jon Ronson's books enthused me to write (if you haven't already, read *The Psychopath Test*). He took the time to show me around his favourite spots in Central Park, which will always be one of my most cherished memories. I don't know Louis Theroux, outside of a few emails, but without his documentary work, I might not be in this industry. David Baddiel, thanks for taking the time, and for the kind and motivating words.

Richard Dawkins and the late Christopher Hitchens stirred my interest in cults and extreme religions, and motivated me to try to be sceptical of magical thinking and biases. Although I'll sadly never meet the latter, the former took the time to watch my exorcism documentary, and then meet in person for an interview. What a thrill that was – my dad just sent me a photo of me, aged

ACKNOWLEDGEMENTS

eighteen, sunbathing in Spain while reading Dawkins. To former crime boss Shaun Attwood, his YouTube producer Ash Meikle, and podcasters Chris Williamson and Jordan Harbinger: thanks for teaching me to YouTube.

Finally, to the reader: thank you for taking a chance on this book, and for reaching its end. I read somewhere that relatively few readers actually get to the end of non-fiction books, so I'm delighted you've made it this far. I hope you'll also accompany me on future journeys into the darkest and most controversial aspects of humanity. I can't wait for you to read my next book – especially if it's the controversial one that publishers refused to look at. Right now, it's secret, but I hope to share it with you soon.

SOURCE NOTES

I didn't want to inundate you with numbers and parentheses, footnotes and references. This is supposed to be fun; a journalistic adventure with secrets, cults and influencers. So, I decided I'd let the narrative flow, and include my source notes at the end.

Many of the stories in this book were told to me by my podcast guests. Some did so on camera for my podcast and YouTube channel, and you might be able to pick out those moments. Others, such as former NXIVM cult member Kelly Thiel, were told to me in later interviews specifically for this book.

INTRODUCTION

I can't tell you who Melissa is, but she told me her story about the men in the dark alleyway via a WhatsApp message. The stats about the 97 per cent of us who carry secrets, and the kinds of secrets we carry come from the work of Columbia Business School's Associate Professor of Business, Michael L. Slepian. The link between keeping secrets and ulcers, cancer and other physical illnesses came from studies by Larson & Chastain (1990). I read about this in Anita E. Kelly's *The Psychology of Secrets*.

1. SECRETS AND POWER

My knowledge of Scientology comes partly from the countless YouTube interviews I've done with former members. I also used *South Park* and the 'Operating Thetan' texts obtained and published by WikiLeaks. My figures on the decline of Christianity came from the Pew Research Center. Much of my information about Anne Frank came from the museum's official website. Various publications reported on the sums paid by Netflix and Spotify to Prince Harry and Meghan Markle.

2. SECRETS, PRIVACY AND LIES

Madeleine Black told me her story first-hand, and I used her book *Unbroken* for further research. Dr Sissela Bok's description of secrecy as 'intentional concealment' is in her 1983 work *Secrets: On the Ethics of Concealment and Revelation*. Professor James Pennebaker's assertion that secrecy is an 'active inhibition of disclosure' is paraphrased by Anita E. Kelly in *The Psychology of Secrets*. It is from his 1989 work, 'Confession, Inhibition, and Disease' in *Advances in Experimental Social Psychology* vol. 22. Michael L. Slepian's point about the three categories – immoral, relational and aspirational – of secrets came from his 2021 work: 'Identifying the dimensions of secrets to reduce their harms'. Tom Frijns' dissertation 'Keeping Secrets' (2005) helped me understand how privacy protects morally neutral information, whereas secrecy protects morally negative information. My own survey about our secret, private home habits was conducted with Google Forms. For parts on female masturbation, I interviewed Nimko Ali, and included stats from her book: *What We're Told Not to Talk About (But We're Going to Anyway): Women's Voices from East London to Ethiopia* (2019). Sam Harris' 2011 long-form essay *Lying* provided his anecdotes. The stat that 5 per cent of us tell 50 per cent of the lies comes from Professor Timothy R. Levine and Kim B. Serota's 'A Few Prolific Liars' (2014). I learned that we reveal the secrets of those closest to us from V. Christophe and B. Rimé's 'Emotion Elicits the Social Sharing of Emotion: Theory and Empirical Review' (1997). I learned to define secrecy as an act of commission (not omission) from the work of Wegner & Lane that was cited in 'The Experience of Secrecy' (Michael L. Slepian, Jinseook S. Chun and Malia F. Mason, 2017). The explanation of deception as an imposter being unleashed in the place of a secreted truth comes from Bella DePaulo's 'Verbal and Nonverbal Dynamics of Privacy, Secrecy, and Deceit' (2003). DePaulo is also responsible for the 1996 experiment 'Lying in Everyday Life' that found that students lie to 38 per cent of the people in their lives. Leslie Carver, associate professor of psychology and human development at the University of California's San Diego Division of Social Sciences, ran the study to show the different ways parents lie to their kids. I found murderer Edmund Kemper's quote about struggling with confessing his crimes in Anita E. Kelly's *The Psychology of Secrets*.

3. SECRETS, BODY AND MIND

Chris Atkins' story comes from my interview with him, and his book *A Bit of a Stretch: The Diaries of a Prisoner*. Walid A. Afifi and John P. Caughlin's findings about the fever model come from 'A Close Look at Revealing Secrets and Some Consequences That Follow' (2006). The part about mind-wandering – as opposed to the act of hiding a secret – causing anxiety comes from Michael L. Slepian's 'The Experience of Secrecy' (2017). Tom Frijns describes secrecy as a self-inflicted disease in his 2005 dissertation 'Keeping Secrets', and Robin Dunbar writes of language evolving through gossip – with 65 per cent of our conversations involving talking about one another – in 'Gossip in Evolutionary Perspective', *Review of General Psychology* (2004).

4. SECRETS AND DETECTION

The evolutionary theory behind why we're honest comes from Christian L. Hart's *Psychology Today* article 'The Evolution of Honesty' (2020). The dice games in which people are more honest than necessary are from Swiss economist Uri Fischbacher's 'Lies in Disguise – An Experimental Study on Cheating' (2013). Malcolm Gladwell wrote in *Talking to Strangers: What We Should Know about the People We Don't Know* (2019) about his time assessing the dishonesty of participants in videos with Professor Tim R. Levine. I learned about Lena Sisco and her Game Boy tactic in her interview on the Eric Hunley YouTube channel. Much of Amanda Knox's story was in *Talking to Strangers* and the Netflix documentary *Amanda Knox*, while a lot was from her interview on my podcast, *Heretics*. My research into Guantanamo Bay includes *The New York Times*' 'The Guantánamo Docket' (2023) and *The Hill*'s 'US intelligence finds Gitmo prisoners returning to fight' (2015). Scott W. Carmichael, senior counter-intelligence investigator, spoke of being shocked that Ana Montes had betrayed the US in Gladwell's *Talking to Strangers*.

5. SECRETS AND DECEPTION

David C. Raskin and Robert D. Hare wrote about their studies on British Columbia inmates and psychopaths taking polygraph tests in 'Psychopathy and Detection of Deception in a Prison Population'. A great range of studies have polygraph tests as being 70–90% accurate. Forensic psychologist Dr Sophie van der Zee claimed there's no human equivalent to Pinocchio's nose in BBC article 'How credible are lie detector tests?'. Veteran FBI agent Mark Bouton's book *How to Spot Lies Like the FBI* (2010) explained what signs agents look for. The story of an agent discovering a spy by the way he carried flowers is from *Wired*'s YouTube video 'Former FBI Agent Explains How to Read Body Language'. Dr Lieberman's advice about inventing stories to see if the suspect concurs is from episode 773 of *The Jordan Harbinger Show* podcast. Edward T. Hall wrote many times about the concept of high and low context cultures. I got the parts about Lance Armstrong's victory speech and Lacanian analysis of words from psychoanalyst Owen Hewitson's website lacanonline.com. Professor Lera Boroditsky wrote about the tribe in Australia that uses cardinal points rather than left or right in 'Remembrances of Times East: Absolute Spatial Representations of Time in an Australian Aboriginal Community' (2010). The concept of duping delight in psychopaths who inadvertently give themselves away in polygraph tests is explained by psychologist Paul Ekman as 'smug contempt' in *Telling Lies: Clues to Deceit in the Marketplace, Politics, and Marriage* (1992). David Lykken explains that every psychopath he's met enjoys deceiving others in 'A Study of Anxiety in the Sociopathic Personality' (1957). Don Grubin's suggestion of a drawing pin in your shoe to fool the test (though this is extremely difficult and unlikely to work) comes from a *Guardian* article called: '"There is no bomb": what I learned taking a polygraph test'.

6. SECRETS AND TECHNOLOGY

The story of Babis Anagnostopoulos was reported in multiple news publications around the world. The information about the number of Germans nostalgic for the GDR comes from an article called 'Majority of Eastern Germans Feel Life Better under Communism' on *Der Spiegel*. I first found Marvin Chun's work on mind-reading in one of his many videos – including TED Talks – on YouTube. I then interviewed him for my podcast *Heretics*.

7. SECRETS, CULTS AND STATUS

Much of the information from this chapter comes from my own podcast interviews, and my conversations with cult defectors such as Steven Hassan for the book. The story about Arthur Conan Doyle and the fairies – and the Nobel Prize-winner fooled into trafficking cocaine – are from David Robson's *The Intelligence Trap: Revolutionise Your Thinking and Make Wiser Decisions*. The initial article shedding light on Scientology's search for a girlfriend for Tom Cruise came from Maureen Orth in the October 2012 issue of *Vanity Fair* and ex-scientologist Mike Rinder's *A Billion Years: My Escape from a Life in the Highest Ranks of Scientology*. I learned about parts of the Heaven's Gate and Ben Gunn stories – as well as stats about toddlers arguing over possessions, and employees preferring job titles to money – in Will Storr's *The Status Game*. Dr Sissela Bok wrote that we primarily keep secrets out of concern for social consequences in *Secrets: On the Ethics of Concealment and Revelation*, although I read that in Walid A. Afifi and John P. Caughlin's 'A Close Look at Revealing Secrets and Some Consequences That Follow' (2006). I found that 92.8 per cent of reasons for keeping a secret involve the protection of self in Dr Tom Frijn's 'Keeping Secrets: Quantity, Quality and Consequences' (2005). The information about Jeremy Kyle's lie detector possibly being as low as 66 per cent accurate was widely reported, and comes from culture committee chairman Damian Collins, who was investigating the suicide of a participant. The quote from Jason Manning about drop in status leading to suicide is from his book *Suicide: The Social Causes of Self-Destruction*, although I first read it in *The Status Game*.

8. SECRETS AND ESPIONAGE

Research for the passage about Lord Bracken posing as a schoolboy to take a caning came from *Minstrel Heart: A Life in Story* by David Campbell. I learned about the SDS and its secret police who married left-wing activists in my interview with Cara McGoogan and by listening to her podcast *Bed of Lies*. The estimate that Alan Turing saved 14–21 million lives in World War II comes from a couple of sources, including Sir Harry Hinsley, who actually worked at Bletchley Park during the war, and Turing expert Professor Jack Copeland.

9. THE WORST SECRET IN THE WORLD

Much of this chapter is based on the afternoon I spent with Ruby and Sirius in a small town in Germany. The information about 1 per cent of men being paedophiles comes from sexologist Michael C. Seto's interview with the BBC in their 2014 article 'How many men are paedophiles'. I also interviewed Dr Seto. My research into the Kentler Experiment in Berlin came from interviews with Dr Teresa Nentwig, although an article was later published about it by Rachel Aviv in *The New Yorker* entitled 'The German Experiment that Placed Foster Children with Pedophiles' (2021). Mike Freel's stats about adult care workers with attraction to children are in his study 'Child Sexual Abuse and the Male Monopoly: An Empirical Exploration of Gender and a Sexual Interest in Children' (2003).

10. SECRETS AND US

Much of this chapter comes from my interview with Justin Hall. There is also a quite brilliant video he did explaining his rise and sort-of fall on his website, links.net. The fascinating insights from

Crystal Abidin about anchor and filler content, and social media influencers comes from a conversation we had on the phone, and the quotes are from her paper: '#familygoals: Family Influencers, Calibrated Amateurism, and Justifying Young Digital Labor' (2017).

CONCLUSION – JUST ONE MORE THING . . .

The scenes with Louis Theroux are from his documentary *Louis and the Nazis* (2003) and his Jimmy Savile episode from the first series of *When Louis Met . . .* (2000). The part about how swear words change to reflect the norms of a society comes from my podcast interview with John McWhorter (episode 59 of *Heretics*), but I'd also recommend you read his book *Nine Nasty Words: English in the Gutter* (2021). The research into the kinds of people we reveal secrets to (assertive and compassionate rather than polite and enthusiastic) comes from Michael L. Slepian and James N. Kirby's 'To Whom Do We Confide Our Secrets' (2018).